Lessons in Disability

Lessons in Disability

*Essays on Teaching with
Young Adult Literature*

Edited by JACOB STRATMAN

McFarland & Company, Inc., Publishers
Jefferson, North Carolina

LIBRARY OF CONGRESS CATALOGUING-IN-PUBLICATION DATA

Lessons in disability : essays on teaching with young adult literature / edited by Jacob Stratman.

    p.   cm.

    Includes bibliographical references and index.

    ISBN 978-0-7864-9932-8 (softcover : acid free paper) ∞

    ISBN 978-1-4766-2308-5 (ebook)

    1. Children with disabilities in literature.   2. People with disabilities in literature.   3. Young adult literature—History and criticism.   4. Young adult literature—Study and teaching. I. Stratman, Jacob.

PN1009.5.C44L48 2016
809'.933561—dc23   2015035355

BRITISH LIBRARY CATALOGUING DATA ARE AVAILABLE

On the cover: etching entitled *Blue Dress, from the series Topiary: The Art of Improving Nature*, artist, Louise Bourgeois, 1911-2010, publisher, Harlan & Weaver, Julie Sylvester-Cabot and the Whitney Museum of American Art Editions (Yale University Art Gallery Gift of Carol H. and Pierce R. Smith, B.S. 1966)

Printed in the United States of America

McFarland & Company, Inc., Publishers
  Box 611, Jefferson, North Carolina 28640
   www.mcfarlandpub.com

Acknowledgments

It is a blessing to get work as a teacher and an academic, and I cannot do that work without the support of my students, colleagues, and administrators at John Brown University. Special thanks to Samuel Cross-Meredith for his help with copy editing and indexing. Secondly, this book would not be a reality without the scholarly talents of the contributors, and I thank them for their passion for disability studies and the realities of our children. Lastly, I thank my family and friends who show me what is true and beautiful every day.

A portion of all royalties will be given to Ability Tree, a nonprofit that "envisions families impacted by disability being accepted and supported in their local community; we envision individuals and families enjoying healthy relationships in their neighborhoods, schools, workplaces and churches." Learn more at abilitytree.org.

Table of Contents

vii

Introduction: Exploring Disability through Young Adult Literature

Jacob Stratman

As a kid, when I picked up a book, I wanted to read about characters who were just like me. I fell in love with Encyclopedia Brown and any young boy playing sports. However, as I grew up, I often found myself intrigued by characters who were not like me at all: Harper Lee's Scout Finch, Hermann Hesse's Siddartha, and all of the voices in Langston Hughes' poetry. Later, as a teacher, remembering these reading experiences, I took it upon myself to attempt to put the right book in the hands of every kid—a book that would both mirror the reader's experiences and also show him or her a different experience and existence. For the most part, I had very little trouble finding protagonists who mirrored the lives of my students. That is, except for my students who lived with disabilities, be they physical, emotional, or cognitive. During the time I taught in public schools, the only book I used to explore the literature of disability was John Steinbeck's *Of Mice and Men.* While the novel, through the character Lenny, allowed us to discuss how people with disabilities are perceived and treated in American society, I always wished for a variety of characters living with a variety of disabilities that could help my students (and me) resist monolithic (i.e., prejudiced) thinking about disability in general and people with disabilities in particular.

Although there is a growing interest in disability studies in art, literature, film, politics, and religion, there is still a dearth of scholarship that explores the intersection of young adult literature and disability. In the last ten years, according to a routine search using EBSCOhost and MLA databases, I found only a small handful of peer-reviewed articles that explore any issue regarding young adult literature and disability, and most of those articles were in library research journals.[1] What is encouraging, though, is that three of the five articles were published in the last five years. This gap in scholarship among young adult literature scholars and teachers is surprising for three reasons. First, disability is a growing reality in all of our lives. According to a 2012 report by the United States Census Bureau, "About 56.7 million people—19 percent of the population—had a disability in 2010, according to a broad definition of disability, with more than half of them reporting the disability was severe" (2012, par. 1). Second, this reality is influencing our art in the form of film and literature. A simple Google search will provide ample lists of "Best Movies About Disability." There are numerous blogs that review books about teens and disability. Third, in young adult literature, the Schneider Family Book Award, an award that "honors an author or illustrator for a book that embodies an artistic expression of the disability experience for child and adolescent audiences," has been around since 2004. Each year the committee awards a book in each of the following categories: "birth through grade school (age 0–10), middle school (age 11–13) and teens (age 13–18)" (http://www. ala.org/awardsgrants/schneider-family-book-award). This is a fruitful time to continue exploring the intersections of literature written for children and teens and disability studies. Thankfully, as I write this introduction, Patricia A. Dunn has just published *Disabling Characters: Representations of Disability in Young Adult Literature*. She has also begun editing a column for *English Journal* called "Disabling Assumptions." One of my hopes for this book is that it empowers more scholars and practitioners to write about the representation of ability in young adult literature.

My interest in writing about disability and literature and teaching novels that explore disability began after I read the University of Michigan study that concluded empathy is on the decline among college students. This study suggests that, over a 40-year period, the ability to "imagine others' points of view" and feel connections "for the misfortunes of others" among college age students has declined steadily.[2] Thus began a heightened interest in thinking about literature's role in our ability to empathize with others. Although I make it clear in my writing that simply reading a novel cannot, by itself, necessarily change the way we behave toward others, I do believe every reading experience invites readers into an empathic relationship with the characters (and hopefully with those outside of the reading experience). As C.S. Lewis suggests in *An Experiment in Criticism*, "In love we escape from our self into one other. In the moral sphere, every act of justice or charity involves putting ourselves in the other person's place and thus transcending our own competitive particularity" (138). In one way, can an "abled" child, who reads a story about a "disabled" child, be invited into a more just and loving relationship with other children with disabilities? In a more general way, can any reading experience invite us to participate in acts of justice, charity, and empathy? My hope for this book is that it gives teachers the tools and the confidence to introduce young readers to characters with a wide variety of abilities, inviting all involved into more empathic relationships.

This book is separated into two parts: pedagogical strategies and literary theory. The essays in the first part of the book approach disabilities and the literature from a social science background. Most of the writers are housed in university education departments, so the essays use education literature to explore and consider best practices for introducing disability studies and protagonists living with disabilities to young readers. The second part of the book invites literary scholars to analyze representations of fictional characters through a variety of literary and disability theories; most of these writers are housed in English departments.

To begin, in "The Social Construction of Disabilities and Differences: Cultivating Appreciation of Diversity in an Elementary Classroom through Critical Reading, Writing and Reflection," Anne Katz chronicles a year in an elementary class as she "incorporates a critical literacy approach to children's literature. ... [and] focuses on deconstructing children's literature and engaging students in literacy-based activities to examine how these texts portray differences." Although this is the only essay in the book that addresses the needs of elementary readers, I chose to introduce the collection with this essay as an exemplary way for teachers of all age groups to construct a dialogue with students surrounding the literary depictions of difference.

I have included two essays that use literature circles as a pedagogical doorway for students to discuss difference and disability in the literature they read. First, Jeanne Dutton and Jennifer Miller, in "A Little Piece of Evan: Adolescent Literature and the Autism Spectrum," explore how literature circles can be used to encourage students to have more open conversations about the autism spectrum, while also arguing that literature circles can benefit students on the autism spectrum, as they are "given the opportunity to integrate as opposed to learning in isolated or segregated environments." Pedagogically, this essay briefly introduces some of the practical aspects of literature circles. Next, Jeanne Gilliam Fain and Lesley Craig-Unkefer, in "Middle School Adolescents Developing Critical Stances Around Difference in Young Adolescent Literature in Literature Circles," explore "how through the process of literature circles, the teacher can guide the students to possess a greater awareness of exceptionality through common human experiences as well as the social implications of exceptionality." The literature explored here "emphasizes a critical understanding of the various dimensions of exceptionality including general characteristics, self-determination, advocacy, and inclusion" to invite students into critical practices of inquiry and dialogue. Together, these essays suggest that inviting students into social relationships (both with the texts and with each other) can create a positive, empathic environment.

Abbye Meyer and Emily Wender's "Teaching and Reading *Wonder* and *Marcelo in the Real World* with Critical Eyes" helps teachers and readers learn how to read "with" and "against" texts as it "offer[s] current literary and political readings of how Palacio and Stork have represented disabilities in their texts, acknowledging how both texts simultaneously suggest progressive and harmful understandings of disability." Not only do the insights and arguments help readers better understand the complexities of these particular novels, but Wender and Meyer also, through these close readings, provide an accessible framework for any critical reading of a novel that depicts any type of difference.

My own contribution to the collection, "(Re)Defining Disability with the Schneider Family Book Award and Community Engagement," chronicles a year in a first-year college seminar where, as a class, we worked to define, re-define, and un-define disability through reading YA novels that highlight characters with disabilities, exploring a variety of theories located in the world of disability studies, engaging with children with disabilities at a local non-profit organization, and reflecting on all of these experiences through classroom dialogue and academic journaling. As I stated above, reading alone is not enough to invite students into empathic relationships with the other.

The last essay in the pedagogical strategies part recognizes that not all teachers can simply teach whatever young adult novel that they want—school curriculum and common core pressures still privilege the high school canon over contemporary young adult literature. Janine J. Darragh's "Using YA Literature That Portrays Disabilities as Canonical Companions" gives teachers the tools and terminology to connect classroom libraries with required texts. As Darragh argues, "If pairing YA literature with the classics can help students better understand, relate to, and enjoy those works, then the next logical step is finding the perfect companion texts, specifically choosing book pairings that will help students explore, interrogate, and vicariously experience the lives of those who may be different from them, including people with disabilities."

The second part of this book explores young adult literature and disability through particular literary theoretical lenses. My hope is that it will help teachers guide readers through these specific titles (and even genres) to expose them to literature as seen through the eyes of disability studies.

To begin, and as a nice transition from Darragh's work, Darcy Mullen's "*Beowulf* and Aesthetic Nervousness: A Multidimensional Pedagogy" explores the medieval poem often taught in high school classes, as well as many of the modern re-tellings of the narrative, to explore and interrogate issues of monstrosity and difference in the character of Grendel using Ato Quayson's essay "Aesthetic Nervousness" as a theoretical entry point. Alongside *Beowulf,* Mullen analyzes Seamus Heaney's translation of *Beowulf* (1999), Neil Gaiman's "The Monarch of the Glen" (2006), John Gardner's *Grendel* (1971), and Robert Zemeckis' film adaptation of *Beowulf.* Using Quayson's theory of disability representation in literature, she suggests "that conventions of literary aesthetics rely on representations of disability on a fundamental level. In other words, ideas (including stereotypes, fears, and misconceptions) are often subsumed, or even normalized, as a part of the literary landscape."

Marc Napolitano then explores a relatively minor figure in the Harry Potter series to explore the prominence of war and veteran-disability in the book series. "'So tough, so brave, the consummate survivor': War, Trauma and Disability in the *Harry Potter* Series" argues that "Mad-Eye [Moody] is ultimately incapable of reaching the levels of transcendent heroism reserved exclusively for Harry and his closest allies, not because of his physical and mental disabilities, but because of what these disabilities signify. Mad-Eye's physical scars, prostheses, and hypervigilance are presented as indicators of his status as a disabled soldier, and though the series builds toward an epic war between good and evil, that war cannot be won 'on the ground' through the physical and emotional sacrifices of soldiers."

The next essay reminds teachers and students that the genre of science fiction and fantasy continue to be fertile spaces to discuss pressing social issues. By using gender and disability studies as theoretical foundations, Erin Wyble Newcomb's "Deconstructing Disability: The Dragons and Girls in Ursula K. Le Guin's Earthsea and Merrie Haskell's *Handbook for Dragonslayers*" suggests that "neither ability nor disability is necessarily constant, philosophically or personally, and the girls' movement from disenfranchisement and abuse to privilege and domination suggests the instability of bodies as well as the categories we use to define them." Newcombe says, "By examining the false binaries of ability and disability within two fantasy realms, I hope to illuminate the ways that power and (dis)ability reflect and challenge the real world of readers."

The last essay in the book explores the connections between queer theory and disability studies. Angel Daniel Matos' "'Without a word or sign': Enmeshing Deaf and Gay Identity in Young Adult Literature" explores two novels that highlight characters that are deaf and characters that are gay: Brian Sloan's *A Really Nice Prom Mess* (2005) and Andrew Smith's *Stick* (2011). In an effort to connect these two seemingly different theoretical lenses, Matos writes, "Both queer and disability studies thrive in making the normal strange, odd, and unfamiliar. By exemplifying the strangeness that exists in everyday ideologies and practices, these theoretical fields seek to dismantle the power and privilege that people associate with normativity in all of its expressions. Using queer and disability studies as a lens to deconstruct texts that represent both deaf and gay characters illustrates the potentiality of both fields of study, which makes *A Really Nice Prom Mess* and *Stick* ideal novels for this discussion."

Whether read in connection or in isolation, readers will find excellent textual analysis, sound pedagogical advice, numerous textual examples, and a thoughtful introduction into the complex (and sometimes complicated) world of introducing students to people (characters and those in real life) that both reflect and contrast the reader's reality. Ultimately, my hope for this book is that it encourages and empowers teachers to expose students to dynamic characters that may or may not be different from them.

As a final point, any book about disability is really a book about language. In my mind, no one in disability studies is totally happy or content with any words (i.e., categories) we use to define an individual's identity and existence. While I recognize the limitations and barriers of a word like disability, it is the common language available to a wide variety of readers. As editor of this collection, I have asked contributors to be very intentional about the language they use in their essays; moreover, I have given each contributor great freedom to use language that best defines and describes their theories of disability. What you will find, in this one book, is a complex and nuanced conversation regarding books, pedagogy, and disability.

NOTES

1. For an understanding of current scholarship regarding young adult literature and disability, read Wopperer, E. (2011). Inclusive literature in the library and the

classroom: The importance of young adult and children's books that portray characters with disabilities. *Knowledge Quest, 39(3)*, 26–34; Kurtts, S.A., & Gavigan, K.W. (2008). Understanding (dis)abilities through children's Literature. *Education Libraries, 31(1)*, 23–31; Klipper, B. (2011). Great reads, intriguing characters: The Schneider Family Book Award winners. *Young Adult Library Services 9(3)*, 6–7; Prater, M.A. (2003). Learning disabilities in children's and adolescent literature: How are characters portrayed? *Learning Disability Quarterly, 26(1)*, 47; and Gavigan, K.W., & Kurtts, S. (2010). Using children's and young adult literature in teaching acceptance and understanding of individual differences. *Delta Kappa Gamma Bulletin, 77(2)*, 11–16; and Altieri, J.L. (Sept./Oct. 2008). Fictional characters with dyslexia: What are we seeing in oks?" *Teaching Exceptional Children.*

2. Konrath, S., O'Brien, E.H., & Hsing, C. (2011). Changes in dispositional empathy in American college students over time: A meta-analysis." *Personality and Social Psychology Review, 15(2)*, 180–198.

Part 1: Disability, Young Adult Literature and Pedagogical Strategies

The Social Construction of Disabilities and Differences: Cultivating Appreciation of Diversity in an Elementary Classroom through Critical Reading, Writing and Reflection

ANNE KATZ

"Look at her buck teeth!" Kristin proclaimed aloud as she looked over one of the texts contained in the class' newly organized book tubs.

"Ugly," Jason muttered as he peered onto the page.

"She looks funny," Ben stated as he joined in the conversation.

"...and different," Evan interjected.

"I think she's better off without smiling," Carrie chimed in [researcher journal].

This reflection on classroom practice highlights the social construction of disability and differences. I focused on how disability and differences in general are represented in children's literature, and how, through a series of pedagogical interventions, primary grade children arrive at new understandings of "constructed ideas of normative performance" (Ashby, 2012, p. 92). I define "difference" as any trait or characteristic that an individual possesses that causes him/her to stand out in a particular way or impedes his/her ability to perform in a certain way as compared to the majority.

The opening vignette illustrates the classroom context surrounding the intent of this project. The above interaction occurred early in the second week of the school year in a second grade classroom. As students sat in the classroom library (which had recently been organized into genre-based book bins), their discussion turned to the illustrations around the main character in the book *Stand Tall, Molly Lou Melon* (Lovell, 2001). This dialogue alerted me to the importance of teachers bringing students' experiences to the forefront of the classroom, making learning active, interactive, relevant, and engaging (Nieto, Souto-Manning, 2010). Teaching students to develop a sense of open-mindedness and acceptance of individuals who may, in some way, be different from themselves is a powerful real-world message that merits reflection.

In extending this concept to the outside world, students will encounter individuals with a range of abilities and personalities on a daily basis. How can I begin to cultivate increased sensitivity towards others and a constructive approach to differences? Children have an innate perception of "the norm" based upon their life experiences with their peers, family, and media influences. Regardless of whether a person looks, sounds, speaks, or acts differently than what students are accustomed to, all students need to learn that these differences are only superficial. It is important to treat all people with respect and understanding. Ashby (2012) notes that "disability in school emerges through the interaction of the student with the opportunities of the classroom, teacher perspectives, and practices" (p. 92). By deviating from "the norm," Baglieri et al. (2011) describes how "all of these lines, in the end, (are) judgment calls ... premised on our beliefs about what constitutes *normal*, a concept that is itself context-dependent" (p. 271). This includes any trait that an individual possesses which causes him/her to stand out in a particular way or differ as compared to the majority.

I incorporated a critical literacy approach to children's literature around this important topic. Due to my interest in children's literature and my past experiences in witnessing its ability to generate meaningful discussion, I elected to focus on deconstructing children's literature and engaging students in literacy-based activities to examine how these texts portray differences. In describing, interpreting, and explaining the critical literacy learning that occurs over the course of the project as children engage in activities relating to disability, I sought to demonstrate how this message of acceptance and open-mindedness of differences relates to real-world situations.

Merging the two domains of disability and critical literacy is not commonly done—particularly not with second grade children. I set out to explore the trade-offs embedded in implementing a combined critical and accelerative literacy curriculum that focused on the topic of disabilities. Specifically, the research questions that I sought to investigate over the course of my action research study are outlined as follows:

- How does a sample of picture books generally represent disability and differences?
- How do children learn about disability and other differences through the author and illustrator's portrayal of individuals in children's literature?
- How do perceptions of individuals with differences (not exclusively disabilities) change over time with the intervention of critical discussions and writing exercises around children's literature? (If this project is successful in altering students' perceptions regarding disabilities, their newly acquired attitudes will generalize to other differences from the "norm" as they perceive it.)
- How does this framework support and accelerate students as readers and writers? This project took place in an action research framework, a continuous self-reflective process by which educators critically examine one's pedagogy in order to improve student learning.

The research lasted approximately eight weeks. The discussions were audio-taped in order to document student voices and serve as a resource for transcriptions of conversations. The placement of the recorder did not appear to have any impact on the content of class discussions. Field notes were taken directly after each class discussion to serve as archives for me to review. This allowed me to continuously adjust future discussions based upon data garnered from the previous discussion. Student work samples were collected from many of the activities following the whole group and small group discussions and organized in file folders for data collection purposes.

Literature Review

This essay assumes a reconceptualist view of disability which "frame(s) disability as a social construction and, while not denying physiological aspects of impaired function, address disabilities as they gain meaning in social and cultural context" (Baglieri, Valle, Connor, & Gallagher, 2011, p. 267). With this framework in mind, a central goal of this project is to guide students towards an understanding that our society has a tendency to view individuals with disabilities as less competent or able than their non-disabled counterparts, and that steps need to be taken to counteract these invalid and stereotypical stigmas. Mills, O'Keefe, and Jennings (2004) describe how inquiry is an approach that shapes a classroom's teaching and learning. They note that it "respects the individuality and diversities of learning experiences, backgrounds, and abilities in a classroom—it does not impose time constraints or one-size-fits-all standardized ways of teaching" (Souto-Manning, 2013, p. 44). Ashby (2012) further notes that the "separation between general and special education is neither natural nor inevitable. We can envision a way to teach all kids, including those with the most complex needs. We can all assume this responsibility, regardless of training or title" (p. 98). My goal was to invite students to engage in read-alouds, discussion, writing, and research to deconstruct important issues regarding difference.

Together, we would explore picture books and engage in a range of pedagogical strategies in order to view these concepts through a different lens. Picture books convey meaning through the use of two sign systems— written language and visual images (Serafini, 2010). The primary focus with picture books has often concentrated on cultivating skills and strategies that promote an understanding of written text. However, in our increasingly visual world, pedagogical strategies for understanding visual images merit consideration and have only recently begun to be explored in the literature (Anstey & Bull, 2006; Albers, 2008). Clearly, there is value in teaching skills and strategies to enable students to interpret and analyze images.

Picture books can invite readers to view disability and individuals with differences through an alternate lens. As an educator, I believe that it is crucial to create a classroom where every student's resources—his/her individual gifts and talents—are recognized and valued. It is important that students acknowledge differences as an asset rather than a deficiency. Baglieri et al. (2011) note that "considering disability as a social construct does not signify a denial of difference ... it is the meaning we make of those differences that is important" (p. 92). As they enter a new classroom community each academic year, students will encounter diversity in personality, physical characteristics, and varying academic levels among their classmates. It is essential for students to respect and value the unique qualities and characteristics that their peers bring to the classroom "in considering how their own assumptions and actions further reify notions of difference" (Ashby, 2012, p. 92). According to a 2012 report by the United States Census Bureau, "about 56.7 million people—19 percent of the population—had a disability in 2010, according to a broad definition of disability, with more than half of them reporting the disability was severe" (Bernstein, 2012). As children with disabilities are increasingly mainstreamed into classrooms, it is important to facilitate their immersion into a positive setting where all students are equally valued.

Reading and Writing Connections in Practice

An examination of pedagogical strategies and visual literacy approaches will be illustrated through a discussion of picture books which invite readers to view the subject of disabilities and differences through a text-to-self lens. The project commenced with the reading of the text *Stand Tall, Molly Lou Melon* (Lovell, 2001). I decided to begin with picture books that examine the subject of characters who may be different from the students in a more generalized manner before proceeding to books that address more specific issues regarding disability, whether that be physical differences or learning differences. Students examined how a young girl utilized her short stature, buck teeth, a voice that "sounds like a boa constrictor," and the habit of being "fumble fingered" to reflect her unique individuality, adjust to a new school, and make friends. This book served as an introduction to the value of believing in oneself. Students discussed the importance of this view, particularly when others have a distorted perception of you and your place in the world. Since the students' discussion around this children's book inspired the action research, I was eager to learn how facilitation of critical discussion around the picture book might help students' understandings of difference evolve.

The vibrant picture book includes watercolor illustrations in a range of colors with exaggerated animation-type illustrations. I directed the majority of the conversation, posing questions to students such as "What do you notice about Molly Lou Melon from looking at the illustration on the front cover?" and "How would you describe Molly Lou Melon? Is there any evidence from the story that shows you that?" Students commented that "she has a wild hairdo and really big eyes to see the world with." After reading a page in the text which described Molly Lou Melon's voice as "sound[ing] like a bull frog," a student commented that "they're [her peers] looking up at her now when she is singing." Following a page in the text where Molly Lou Melon stacked pennies on her teeth after being called "Bucky Tooth Beaver," a student noted, "I think they are trying to make friends with her now ... because she is different and can do a lot of interesting things." The author's word choice and language selection lent itself to spirited student discussion regarding the main character's sense of individuality.

At the conclusion of the read-aloud, I posed the following question to students: "How would you describe Molly Lou Melon?" A student noted that she was "a little girl who could do all sorts of things ... she can play football really well and make beautiful snowflakes." Another student described her as "a girl who doesn't care that she sings like a duck. She has beaver teeth. And she's a shrimp!" I further inquired as to how Molly Lou Melon helped her peers see that there is more to her than what she looks like—her physical appearance. A student stated, "She just did what she could do. She showed all the people at the school how to do a lot of things a little differently." A final student raised her hand and shared, "I think that she [Molly Lou Melon] can show people that she can be their friend ... even though she doesn't look like them, she is a good person and she can do a lot." These comments indicate that students were internalizing and expressing their evolving understanding of the main character, whom they initially may have judged.

After the discussion, I asked students to retrieve their reading journals from their book baskets in order to respond to the story. Students wrote a letter to the main character in the story, examining how they felt about her approach to "fitting in" with her peers, despite their preconceived notions about her rather unorthodox approaches to everyday life. One student noted, "I am writing to tell you I would treat you nicely. You show them ... do not judge people by what they look like." Another student shared, "I am writing to tell you that you are cool. You do whatever your grandma says. Do you get bullied all the time? I am happy that you made friends at your new school. You showed them that you could play football and make beautiful snowflakes." A third student displayed empathy: "I know how you feel. I know you can have a hard time fitting in a new school ... you believed in yourself." These writing samples demonstrate that students were beginning to "unlearn some of these taken for granted assumptions and recognize that all of these practices reflect choices about what is valued in our culture and what is considered within the range of 'normal'" (Ashby, 2012, p. 95). I was starting to note evidence of text-to-self connections between the main character and some students—a more empathetic reaction towards the text than the chapter's opening vignette illustrates.

The second whole-class discussion proceeded with the book *Different Just Like Me* (Mitchell, 1999), in which a young girl discovers that people have different needs and come in many colors, shapes, and sizes. My rationale in selecting the text was to build upon students' visual literacy skills. I noted that acrylic paints throughout the book highlight only a few of the items and people present in the pen-and-ink illustrations. This visual literacy strategy invites children to take a closer look at the illustrations while reinforcing the text. The story is told from the perspective of a child anticipating a visit to her grandmother's house. Every day as she waits, the girl and her mother go on an errand. On each of these trips, the child discovers someone who is different from her in some way—someone who speaks another language, is of a different race, is older, or has a disability—but is participating in the same activity that she is completing. The picture book gradually highlights that similarities between people are more prevalent and significant than differences. The class constructed a collective chart throughout the book, noting how other individuals completed everyday tasks in an alternate fashion. I introduced three columns on the chart: what the main character did, how other people accomplished the task, and what they both accomplished.

The main character rode the bus into town with her mom and they chatted. The girl across the aisle and her friend used their hands to communicate through sign language. This prompted the realization among students that they both effectively communicated with one another through different modalities. In another part of the text, the main character rode the elevator to her dad's office. A woman on the elevator felt the Braille numbers to locate her floor on the elevator. Students constructed the understanding that they used alternate means to identify the correct floor number while still achieving their goal. As the story continued, the main character saw a range of people who were speaking different languages and encountered a variety of fruits and vegetables at the local farmer's market. Students discussed how a range of people all shopped in the market to purchase their food.

Several students generated text-to-self connections during the read-aloud, continuing upon the thread that I was hoping to establish throughout the initiative. Kristin commented, "I met a person who couldn't see that well." Allison expressed, "I knew someone … my mom's sister has a friend … she can't hear and uses sign language to speak." Audrey reflected on her personal experiences when she stated, "Last year, at my old school, I had a friend … he couldn't hear that well so he had to have a hearing aid." One student expressed a desire to feel the Braille numbers that were presented in the book, and a couple of other students in the class echoed these sentiments. They asked if they could feel the Braille numbers following the read-aloud.

However, I noted that the majority of the students appeared to be uncomfortable during this read-aloud. They fidgeted a great deal on the carpet, avoided eye contact with me, and posed questions regarding what was coming next in the day (field notes). Their comments about disabilities and differences that the main character encountered in the book were rather surface level and did not include detail. Students did not pose questions during the read-aloud or elaborate upon the items that we discussed beyond the observations that I recorded on the chart. It was evident that this was not a topic that students possessed a great deal of knowledge about or felt at ease discussing. Ashby (2012) describes how "educators need to approach teaching as an active and reflective process of altering the environment to make meaningful engagement possible ... [to] help them [students] meet important academic and life goals" (p. 96). I found that students were beginning to arrive at new understandings of representations of disability through this pedagogical exploration and discussions around children's literature.

Later that week, I introduced the book *Susan Laughs* (Willis, 1999) to the class. I advised students that, while this was a rhyming picture book that they could read with a younger sibling with a poem running throughout its pages, it had an important message that I wanted them to reflect upon after the read-aloud. My rationale in selecting this text was to further cultivate students' visual literacy skills as well as the ability to generate text-to-self connections. The picture book details the daily activities of Susan, an energetic redhead who uses a wheelchair; readers learn this fact about Susan from the illustration at the conclusion of the book. Readers discover "that is Susan through and through ... just like me, just like you." The story focuses on the main character's abilities as readers follow Susan through a series of familiar activities. She swims with her father, works hard in school, plays with her friends, and even rides a horse. Lively and colorful illustrations reinforce the text's portrait of a busy, happy little girl with whom children will identify.

I generated a discussion with students following the read-aloud based upon the following questions:

1. What is the genre of this text? How did the author write about Susan? How did the illustrator represent Susan? Why do you think they chose to represent her in that manner?
2. How is Susan similar to you? (inviting students to make text-to-self connections)
3. How is Susan different from you?
4. What did you think after reading the last page of the book? Were you surprised by the illustration? Why or why not?

Following our brief discussion, I invited students to create their own version of the picture book with additional examples of activities that Susan can participate in (such as singing a song and splashing in a pool) as a meaningful extension activity around the text. Having students create their own version of the text prompted discussion and generated additional text-to-self connections. Ware (2003) notes that addressing the concept of disability as curricular material and "infusing disability into existing curricular areas is central to the task of 'imagining disability otherwise'" (Ferguson & Nusbaum, 2012, p. 76). This intervention created a social space for children to explore and discuss these concepts and create new understandings about the world around them.

In light of our class author study on Dr. Seuss, I created "Sneetch Tuesday" to celebrate our reading of Dr. Seuss' *The Sneetches and Other Stories* (1961), a classic story about prejudice based solely on appearance. The book is an effective vehicle to promote discussion surrounding the topic of physical differences. The book describes the conflict between the Plain-Belly Sneetches and the Star-Belly Sneetches due to their mistaken perception about the outward impressions of each other, and their initial inability to get along due to this issue. After another character, Fix-It-Up-Chappie, enters town to "rid the Sneetches" of their problems by offering to add or remove stars (for a fee), the Sneetches eventually come to the realization that "Sneetches are Sneetches.... And no kind of Sneetch is the best on the beaches." The story's strength is that it shows just how arbitrary and constructed these categories are. Features, such as a star, are used to define the Sneetches as either powerful or marginalized.

After listening to the story as a read-aloud and watching a video of the story, I asked students several questions in order to facilitate a discussion about preconceived notions or judgments based on physical appearances. I posed the following questions to the class:

1. Why did the Star-Belly and Plain-Belly Sneetches have trouble getting along at the beginning of the story?
2. Why did the Plain-Belly Sneetches want stars?
3. Why did the Star-Belly Sneetches then want their stars removed?
4. What did the Sneetches learn when Fix-It-Up-Chappie left town?

Students were very engaged, and insightful discussion followed. I then distributed a sheet with a Plain-Belly Sneetch on one side of the page and a Star-Belly Sneetch on the other. Students responded to the following questions on the appropriate Sneetch after I read the directions that had been outlined, facilitating text-to-self connections. Directions for the Sneetch writing project were as follows:

• Plain-Belly Sneetch: How would I feel as a Plain-Belly Sneetch? What did I learn from this story?

- Star-Belly Sneetch: How would I feel as a Star-Belly Sneetch? What did I learn from this story?

Students articulated their thoughts in writing on a worksheet with both a Plain and Star-Belly Sneetch. This activity allowed students to engage in perspective-taking as they "stepped into the shoes" of each respective Sneetch. The writing exercise provided a forum for students to evaluate how they would feel in each character's position. A student noted, "I like how the Plain-Belly Sneetches stood up for themselves. The Star-Belly Sneetches didn't let the Plain-Belly Sneetches play with them." Another student responded by stating, "I think that Sneetches are Sneetches and they don't need to be saying who is better than one another." I was impressed by these insightful responses that illustrated depth.

I proceeded to select picture books that focused on specific disabilities (hearing impairments, visual impairments, and reading disabilities). The discussion continued with the picture book *Moses Goes to a Concert* (Millman, 1998). The book describes a field trip to the symphony, more specifically a "young person's concert," that a boy who is deaf and his classmates attend. This story addresses the ability of hearing-impaired children to pursue any goal that they wish in life with hard work and dedication. Students were very engaged in learning the sign language hand gestures that appeared on each page. Holding balloons that the teacher distributes to help the students "feel the music," Moses and his classmates pick up the vibrations. After the concert, the students visit with the orchestra's percussionist, who is deaf and performs in her stockings to follow the beat.

There was near silence in the class as I read the book. Students made earnest attempts to mimic the sign language gestures on each page, which were precisely illustrated in easy-to-read diagrams. An introductory note explained how to interpret the sign-language diagrams, which are integrated throughout the colorful illustrations. A poster that accompanied the book, which displays hand gestures for all letters in the alphabet, was frequently pointed to as students listened to the reading of the story. At the conclusion of the read-aloud, Ben commented, "That was neat ... how he communicates like that." Jason echoed Ben's sentiments when he said, "I would like to learn how to do that!" Students proceeded to design t-shirt logos on construction paper with the text-to-self message they gleaned from the story. One student's t-shirt read, "Work hard ... don't give up ... believe in yourself." I created a class display of t-shirts several days later—a string with the shirts attached by clothespins—so that the students and other visitors to the classroom could admire their work.

Students focused on the Braille system after reading David Adler's biography of Louis Braille (1997). The local chapter of the Society for the Blind provided each student with individual Braille alphabet and numeral cards, as well as an early chapter book on Helen Keller. Students were very enthusiastic about both the cards and the book. Many expressed a desire to bring the books home to read with their parents, while others wished to place them in their book boxes for independent reading time. Students composed thank-you notes to the outreach coordinator at the Society for the Blind for their gifts.

One student wrote, "Thank you. I liked learning about Braille and Helen Keller. She was a brave person." Another student expressed, "Thank you for my Helen Keller book and thank you for my Braille card. I really like both of them. I think the book you gave me is really interesting." A third student wrote a letter to Helen Keller and said, "On the inside, you are just the same as anybody else. I think it is very good ... to learn different things in different ways ... through Braille and sign language."

Several days later, the class read the book and viewed a video of *Knots on a Counting Rope* (Martin & Archambault, 1987). In the text, the counting rope serves as a metaphor for the passage of time and for the central character's emerging confidence in facing his blindness. The illustrations, executed in watercolors, capture the beauty and strength of the Southwest region of the United States. Together as a class, we created our own "knots on a counting rope" rendition, a yellow string knotted with key events that we summarized in the story.

This activity enabled us to reinforce the events of the story, practice sequencing skills, establish a sense of community, as well as build fluency and confidence in students' reading skills. Students were provided with two circles on different colored construction paper. On one knot, they composed a sentence about how the book made them feel to promote a text-to-self connection; on the other, they wrote about another way that the boy in the story "saw" besides using his vision. These were compiled into a class "counting rope" that served as a variation of Reader's Theater. The "counting rope" was then placed on a table so that students could participate in Reader's Theater as an option during literacy center times. This activity reached kinesthetic learners and served as a valuable perspective-taking exercise.

As autobiographical writing was the next focus of our year-long writing curriculum, I conducted a writing lesson the following week on autobiographical events around Patricia Polacco's book *Thank You, Mr. Falker* (1998). This autobiographical story describes the author's experiences as she struggles to learn to read. I hoped that this lesson would help students develop an understanding of the craft of autobiographical writing and the value it presents to the reader and writer alike. Additionally, I hoped to accelerate students as writers and cultivate text-to-self connections by inviting them to draft their own paragraphs describing a personal challenge, and ways that they ultimately achieved their goals. I introduced the lesson by asking students to consider what it would feel like to be unable to read. I stated, "In this book, the author writes about a little girl who is having some trouble learning how to read, and how she eventually accomplishes this goal with her teacher's support. As I read this story, I would like for you to think about something that was hard for you to do, and what you did to achieve your goal."

I then read the story, pausing along the way for student comments and questions. An excerpt from the class discussion illustrates some of the dialogue that occurred around the text:

> TEACHER: How would you describe Trisha?
> LAURA: A girl who worked hard to learn to read.
> BEN: She learned when the teacher helped her.
> DANIEL: She didn't give up when it was hard for her.
> AUDREY: A good artist ... she drew very well.
> DAVID: I am glad she learned to read.

Students expressed surprise at the conclusion of the story, which reveals that the main character's experiences were actually true and based on the author's life story. We then discussed the term "autobiography," and I read the author blurb on the back cover to confirm to students that this was an autobiographical story relayed by the author. The illustrations in Polacco's signature style, a combination of gouache and pencil compositions, capture the emotional stages of frustration, pain, and celebration throughout the main character's journey.

I proceeded to introduce the writing assignment—students would compose an autobiographical piece describing something that was difficult for them to do, and what they did to accomplish their goal(s). One student in the class who visited the school Resource Room for academic support made a text-to-self connection and wrote about overcoming reading difficulties. "When I was five, I didn't know how to read. I learned the alphabet. I learned the sounds of the alphabet. I practiced reading. Now, I can read." For closure, students shared their autobiographical writing pieces with one another. In addition, I read an excerpt from the author's website that describes her experiences as they relate to the book. I focused on a quote—

"this book was written both to honor Mr. Falker, but also to warn young people that words have a terrible power ... and that they should do all they can to see that teasing stops at their school."

A social studies lesson utilizing *People* (Spier, 1980) as a framework was an additional text. I wanted students to construct an understanding of a global community—the notion that people all over the world have many similarities, despite their differences—to promote further text-to-self connections. My objectives for this lesson were for students to engage in a discussion about cultural universals, and to explain why differences should be respected and valued. Small, detailed illustrations representing a range of languages, communication styles, jobs, religions, foods, homes, and games are colorfully displayed in a museum gallery format throughout the pages of the text. An excerpt from the discussion provided me with assurance that the class was moving towards this understanding:

TEACHER: How would you describe the people in the book?
JAMIE: We are a lot more the same than we are different. This book and its pictures show how we are more similar in all sorts of ways.
BRANDON: People are the same in many ways, like the games kids play.

After the read-aloud, I broke students up into small groups. I modeled the activity that the students were about to participate in and provided each group with a topic (languages people use to read and write, ways people communicate, jobs people have, religions people practice, things people eat, homes people live in, games people play, clothing people wear) as well as an index card detailing the specific information for their topic and a web. For closure, I asked students what they noticed from participating in this activity, and we constructed that the commonalities were cultural universals. I proceeded to ask students, "What are some of the cultural universals that we learned about? Why should these differences be valued? What would the world be like if everyone was the same?" As a result of this lesson, I hoped that the students would acquire a deeper respect for people that differ from them in some way and learn to value the uniqueness of every individual—a central goal.

Small group discussions can be a valuable format to deal with sensitive topics. I selected these texts specifically because I felt that they lent themselves to critical discussion. I met with a small group during reader's workshop to facilitate a discussion around *Through Grandpa's Eyes* (McLachlan, 1983). The group consisted of four students (two males and two females) in the class' mid-level reading group. Each student was provided with a copy of the story, and a round-robin reading followed, with students reading in a circle, alternating turns every few paragraphs. The illustrations are simple, inviting the reader to reflect upon their own interpretation of the text, prompting text-to-self connections.

After we completed the story, students read about the author's background and were receptive to my instructions for the journal. I asked students to respond to the following prompt: "When Grandpa tells John to close his eyes and look through his eyes, what do you think he means?" We discussed how the grandfather is asking his grandson to "see" the world from his perspective or point-of-view. I asked students to write in their journals about several examples from the story in which John "saw" through his grandfather's eyes. Students were asked to consider what John learned from looking at the world in a different way. Then, each student shared a noticing from their journal entry. It appeared that the depth of the conversation around the book was more intense and thorough when compared to whole-class discussions.

Another small group of students read and discussed *Ben Has Something to Say: A Story About Stuttering* (Lears, 2000), the story of a young boy who must confront his trepidation to aid a neglected animal he wants to rescue. This story tells of a child who must confront his fear of speaking (due to his stuttering) in order to help a neglected dog he wants to rescue from a junkyard. I introduced the book by reading some of the resource information at the beginning of the text, which described the communication disorder in greater detail. The background information specified what the disorder is and misconceptions about what it is not. Students then engaged in a round-robin reading of the text and participated in a discussion, responding to the story and their feelings about individuals who stutter. I emphasized to students the importance of focusing on the message (instead of the way in which it is delivered) when speaking to an individual with a communication disorder of any sort. Again, I noted the greater depth in responses that the small group format seemed to elicit.

The following week, I read Meshack Asare's book *Sosu's Call* (2002) to a small group. This book is about Sosu, a young African boy who is unable to walk. He joins his dog Fusa in helping to save their village when a great storm threatens his community. For many years, Sosu saw the world from behind his family's fence. Many villagers thought that he was not capable of achieving very much and that he should remain in the house. However, when the storm approaches, Sosu retrieves a drum so that he can alert his villagers in enough time to save his community members. Sosu becomes a hero, and now he can go to school and be "just one of the boys in the small village, somewhere between the sea and the lagoon." After the reading of the book, students engaged in a discussion regarding how Sosu was represented initially in the book, and how he was represented as the book evolved. A critical discussion ensued.

It was interesting to note how the colors chosen for the illustrations of the text mirrored the character's feelings to further cultivate students' visual literacy skills. Drab hues are evident in the watercolors during the climatic scenes, possibly reflecting Sosu's feelings of deficiency and loneliness. Rainbow colors are utilized when Sosu receives a wheelchair for his heroic deed. This invites a discussion of how the illustrator utilized color selection to correlate with the feelings of the main character in the text.

As a means to document students' learning and reflect upon the project, I created a chart with a list of all of the books that we had read throughout the course of the unit. I also attached a library pocket with small index cards. The quote from Patricia Polacco's website—"to warn young people that mean words have a terrible power ... and that they should do all they can to see that teasing stops at their school"—was displayed along with the chart. I invited students to write words and actions that characters said/did to the main characters in the story on index cards and post them under the appropriate story. This would serve as an audit trail in terms of what we had learned while reading the books—about the harmful impact that words can have on an individual—while providing an additional space for students to generate text-to-self connections. Having a concrete representation of words people uttered or actions characters exerted would hopefully solidify students' commitment to ensuring that such actions do not occur at their own school or in their own communities.

I found that children learn about disability and other differences through authentic discussion about these topics through picture books and other media. Through a critical examination of illustrations as well as word choice, students learn about the social construct of disability and begin to form opinions about the issues at hand. Children also learn by writing down and expressing their thoughts, feelings, questions, and concerns with perspective-taking through literature. I found that students' perceptions of individuals with disabilities and differences generally moved towards acceptance of all individuals as productive and meaningful members of society as the weeks progressed.

A significant implication of critical discussion and other activities surrounding children's literature is that the children, as the year progressed, were increasingly more comfortable discussing issues surrounding disability and differences in the classroom. This affective component of learning is especially important within a critical literacy framework. Pre-study, second grade students generally viewed disabilities as either something the individual is born with or the result of an accident. Some students viewed the individual or character in the text with feelings of fear or uncertainty. Post-study, second grade students generally viewed disabilities as "special" and "unique" characteristics of individuals that make valuable contributions to the world.

After participating in this unit, I interviewed several students. One student, Audrey, commented, "I think it's special for people to be different because if people weren't different, the world wouldn't be fun and interesting. Every person has something to contribute." She admitted that, "before [the project], I was kind of afraid.... I saw a lady who couldn't walk well at the grocery store and I was afraid. Now [after the project], I think people shouldn't make fun of her and [should] not be afraid. They can still play games and the same things we can do ... if they are in a wheelchair, you can still play with them ... or if they can't see or hear, you can still play. They may be different in what they can do with some things ... but on the inside they are still the same. I would tell [other kids] it's OK and be open to other people ... they can teach you something and you can teach them too."

A Conversation with a Guest Speaker

A guest speaker can facilitate an authentic exchange about disabilities and other critical matters. It also allows students to learn to focus on individuals' "regular traits" first, rather than exclusively upon their disability. Ashby (2012) noted that her College of Education colleagues "want teachers to feel empowered to be a part of a change process with students and to teach with an eye on constant improvement and striving toward more just and inclusive school communities" (p. 97). A woman in the community with cerebral palsy visited the second grade, speaking about her condition with great candor. She discussed the errors of judging an individual purely based purely upon appearance or pre-conceived notions of what they can and cannot do. Before the guest speaker addressed the students, she invited them to watch her exit her van with specialized equipment. The guest speaker also demonstrated how she navigates the world with the assistance of a wheelchair.

The speaker introduced herself and explained that the students should ask her to repeat anything that they did not understand, as "I speak a little differently." She spoke about her condition with great candor and humor: her experiences as a child and as an adult with other peers and individuals, the importance of valuing the abilities of individuals with disabilities, and the significance of being kind to others. Valle and Connor (2011) note that conversations about disability have the potential to "dispel discomfort and shift the perspective about disability from deficit or disorder to part of natural, human variation and the foundation of a truly inclusive school community" (Ferguson & Nusbaum, 2012, p. 77). The guest speaker went on to explain that some people become uncomfortable when they hear people who do not sound like everyone else. She proceeded to explain that one should not fear people who look, speak, or sound differently than others.

She then posed the following question to students: "If you have a disability, can you also have ability? Do I have ability?" A student responded with an enthusiastic affirmation: "Yes! You have many abilities. You are smart and have a lot to teach us." Other students nodded in agreement. The speaker asked students what the phrase "You cannot tell a book by its cover" meant. A student explained that it implied that "what is on the inside of the book may not be what is on the outside. You can't always tell." Another student explained that "you should get to know the person on the inside and not judge someone by what they look like."

She proceeded to ask students to brainstorm some ideas that they could employ to assist an individual with reading difficulties. Student responses included "Showing them the pictures.... Taking them on a picture walk.... Read to them." The guest speaker relayed her initial challenges with learning to read, and how difficult it can be to persevere, especially when you are trying your hardest. Her final message of treating all people with kindness was greeted by a round of applause by the attentive audience.

These findings have provided me with some basis for providing recommendations in terms of pedagogical implications for future projects. I have been impressed with the capacity of well-selected children's literature to stimulate discussion and prompt meaningful conversation. This project has reinforced my belief in the rich opportunities that children's literature presents for students and teachers alike in the classroom to instigate powerful discussions about challenging topics. Over the course of this initiative, I learned that there is no "one-size-fits-all" approach to how primary grade children learn to conceptualize how individuals with disabilities and other differences are represented. Rather, each individual student approached the project with personal experiences, feelings, and background knowledge. Their participation and entry into the discussions occurred as a comfort level with the material was established.

I have learned that the benefits of an intervention such as this project in a classroom setting are two-fold. Through observations, I have noted that students without disabilities have a newfound sense of acceptance and appreciation for individuals with disabilities after their participation in the project. These students are generally eager to assist their peers, creating a more welcoming learning environment for all. In addition, I have found that children with special needs can enhance both their social and behavioral skills when they feel good about themselves. I have noted that there is less of a stigma attached to the students who attend the school's resource room, reading specialist, speech and language therapist, and/or occupational therapist to gain additional targeted support for a variety of difficulties. Whereas prior to the project, these students tended to be teased among their peers for requiring additional targeted support, it is hoped that students would be more conscious of the harm that such behavior could inflict and be more sensitive to their peers after the intervention. This project validated all students. I believe it resulted in more positive self-perceptions for students throughout the class.

Concluding with a Service-Learning Connection

Concluding the project with a service-learning initiative is a valuable means for students to apply and share their learning. Oyler (2011) describes the importance of students utilizing their knowledge to bring about social action. In this case, students decided to create literature boxes for the younger students in the school, with recorded copies of the books that they had read for the project. In addition, the students recorded fairytales and created felt puppets for students who utilize the school's resource room. Vasquez (2004) emphasized that spaces need to be constructed in the classroom where social justice issues can be raised and a critical curriculum can be constructed with children.

The box for the first grade classrooms was an effort to educate their younger peers about individuals with disabilities and differences. Students were asked to select among several books that I had read to them over the course of the project, and design an activity around a few of the books for the first graders to enjoy. Students also recorded these books for their younger peers to listen to as a literacy center. This served as a meaningful forum for the second grade students to practice their reading skills. The class composed a letter to accompany the box, delineating what they had been learning about. In this way, the second grade students are taking steps towards educating their younger peers about ways to make the world a more tolerant place for all.

The box for the school's resource room consisted of several recorded fairytales as well as decorated masks and puppets to accompany the story. Prior to recording the tales, students engaged in Reader's Theater, practicing performing the story in order to ensure that it was their best work. This also served as a means to accelerate students as readers, as it provided them with an authentic opportunity for them to reinforce their reading skills. This box was donated to the resource room for students to enjoy. It was intended that students could listen to the story with a partner, and perhaps re-enact it with the puppets and masks. The class composed a letter to accompany the box, explaining its purpose. Invite students to share their knowledge and educate others about what they have learned over the course of the project.

Schneider Family Book Award Text Selections

Although I did not use these texts during the project time, these award-winning picture books invite readers to view disability in a different light and encourage meaningful conversation on the subject. The Schneider Family Book Award "honors an author or illustrator for a book that embodies an artistic expression of the disability experience for child and adolescent audiences" (Schneider Family Book Award Manual, p. 2, 2004). Dr. Katherine Schneider and her family endowed this American Library Association Award in 2003. Three awards are given annually to recognize and honor books for their distinguished portrayal of people living with a disabling condition—younger children, ages 0 to 8; middle grades, ages 9 to 13; and teens, ages 14 to 18. Dr. Schneider has intentionally allowed for a broad interpretation by her wording, the book "must portray some aspect of living with a disability, whether the disability is physical, mental, or emotional." This allows each committee to decide on the qualifications of particular titles. An examination of how some of these award-winning books could be incorporated into such a project will be included in this section in order to introduce readers to recent titles in this genre.

A Splash of Red: The Life and Art of Horace Pippin (Bryant, 2013) was a 2014 winner of the Schneider Family Book Award. This vibrant children's biography recounts the life of Horace Pippin, who was born in Pennsylvania in 1888. He loved to draw and paint as a child. When he was in eighth grade, his father left the family. Horace left school and worked to support them. After being wounded as a soldier in World War I, he never regained full use of his right arm. Pippin returned home and began painting again, using his left arm to guide his right. His painting subjects are drawn mainly from observation, memory, family stories, and the Bible. In time, this self-taught African American artist was eventually discovered and recognized by the art community. Major museums throughout the United States display his works.

Students could write journal entries from Horace's perspective at different points in time throughout the story in regards to overcoming challenges to achieve one's goal. In addition, they can reflect upon the range of illustrations and quotes that are present throughout the book. Students can review and analyze these quotations and their meanings, describing what they interpret in terms of the context of Mr. Pippin's life story. Furthermore, students can read and reflect upon the Historical Note, Author's Note, and Illustrator's Note at the conclusion of the text in order to gain additional insight into Horace Pippin's story. There are also websites posted at the conclusion of the book to guide supplementary research that students can explore in order to gain additional background knowledge of this celebrated artist and remarkable man.

Back to Front and Upside Down! (Alexander, 2012) was the recipient of the Schneider Family Book Award in 2013. While the rest of the class is busy writing cards for the principal's birthday, Stan becomes frustrated when his letters appear a bit jumbled. Stan is afraid to ask for guidance until a friend assures him that "we all have to ask for help sometimes." With a great deal of practice, Stan's letters come out the "right way round and the right way up." This book deals with a common childhood frustration and will remind students that practice often yields rewards. This story could be used as a social skills lesson that reflects how tenacity can be instrumental in overcoming challenges.

The Pirate of Kindergarten (Lyon, 2010) was the recipient of the Schneider Family Book Award for Young Children in 2011. The author dedicates the story to "everyone who sees the world differently." The book describes the experiences of Ginny, who is having a difficult time in her kindergarten class, where she sees two of everything. This handicap makes it hard for her to find a seat for reading group, causes difficulty reading words in a book, and makes it very challenging to cut bunny ears out of construction paper. Ginny does not realize that this is not how the world appears to everyone else. After taking an eye exam at school, Ginny's condition is diagnosed and she is given an eye patch to wear, transforming her into the "Pirate of Kindergarten."

The picture book presents students with opportunities to practice their visual literacy skills. The vibrant illustrations (chalk, pencil, and acrylic) help "paint a picture" in the reader's head regarding how double vision might appear to a young child. Students can reflect upon how Ginny experienced the world before she acquired her eye patch. Furthermore, readers can consider Ginny's courage in adapting to her new eye patch.

In keeping with the thesis, I found the majority of the literature to represent the "difference" in a positive light, emphasizing the abilities, rather than disabilities, of these individuals. While some texts "talked around" the issue, the majority of the children's literature that I utilized portrayed the disability or "difference" in a fairly straightforward and upfront manner, as an asset as opposed to a deficit. Disability is rarely a curriculum focus in the elementary school classroom. This intervention created a social space for children to explore and discuss these concepts and create new understandings about the world around them.

Reflections and Pedagogical Implications

Utilizing targeted children's literature can have powerful implications for young people and is a format that can be a vehicle to launch discussions of critical issues. The participation structure shifted over the course of the project from teacher-directed to more student-directed. In reviewing the transcriptions, I noted more student-initiated comments and questions as the project progressed. For example, in *Stand Tall, Molly Lou Melon* (Lovell, 2001), I directed the majority of the conversation, asking students questions such as "What do you notice about Molly Lou Melon from looking at the illustration on the front cover?" and "How would you describe Molly Lou Melon? Is there any evidence from the story that shows you that?" and "Why do you think people focus on how people look?" Discussions became increasingly student-centered as I altered the format, inviting students to fill in a chart around *Different Just Like Me*, considering the author's struggle with reading in *Thank You, Mr. Falker*, discussing Louis Braille and Helen Keller's struggles, and navigating the issues that the Sneetches faced, among other topics that emerged throughout the course of the project within the picture books that we were reading.

I found this framework to offer great potential in terms of the support and acceleration of students as both readers and writers. Students were provided with authentic opportunities for re-reading of previous texts that were presented as whole class read-alouds, as well as other books related to the topics as they perused the back table during independent work time. Writing was interwoven throughout many read-alouds. Students also were provided with many occasions for writing through activities and journals available on the back table during independent work time. Incorporating authentic literacy instruction via tools, strategies, and approaches such as those detailed in this chapter can provide a valuable mechanism to create a positive experience for all students in the classroom.

My intent was to interrupt the often negative and stereotypical assumptions that society often imposes upon individuals with disabilities and other differences. Through a series of pedagogical interventions, I sought to raise awareness of how primary grade children learn to conceptualize differences among individuals in the world around them, and view their unique qualities as assets and positive contributions to the world as opposed to deficits. Although this intervention took place with a limited sample size, I believe that many of the ideas would be translatable to other educational settings, and can provide a meaningful framework for educators addressing the topic of social justice. Throughout the semester, I noted increased social cohesion among the group. The educational and social implications of this intervention cannot be overemphasized, as reflected in the chronicles of this essay.

REFERENCES

Albers, P. (2008). Theorizing visual representation in child's literature. *Journal of Literacy Research, 40(2)*, 163–200.

Anstey, M., & Bull, G. (2006). *Teaching and Learning Multiliteracies: Changing Times, Changing Literacies.* Newark: International Reading Association.

Ashby, C. (2012). Disability studies and inclusive teacher preparation: A socially just path for teacher education. *Research & Practice for Persons with Severe Disabilities, 37(2)*, 89–99.

Baglieri, S., Valle, J.W., Connor, D.J., & Gallagher, D.J. (2011). Disability studies in education: The need for a plurality of perspectives on disability. *Remedial and Special Education, 32(4)*, 267–278.

Bernstein, R. (2012). Nearly 1 in 5 people have a disability in the U.S. Census Bureau Reports: Report released to coincide with 22nd anniversary of the ADA. Retrieved from https://www.census.gov/newsroom/releases/archives/miscellaneous/cb12–134.html.

Ferguson, P.M., & Nusbaum, E. (2012). Disability studies: What is it and what difference does it make? *Research and Practice for Persons with Severe Disabilities, 37(2)*, 70–80.

Mills, H., O'Keefe, T., & Jennings, L. (2004). *Looking Closely and Listening Carefully: Learning Literacy through Inquiry.* Urbana: National Council of Teachers of English.

Nieto, S. (2010). *Language, Culture, and Teaching: Critical Perspectives,* 2d ed. New York: Routledge.

Oyler, C. (2011). *Actions Speak Louder Than Words: Community Activism as Curriculum.* New York: Routledge.

Schneider, K. (2004). Schneider Family Book Award Manual. Retrieved from http://www.ala.org/aboutala/sites/ala.org.aboutala/files/content/schneideraward manual-2–2.pdf.

Serafini, F. (2010). Reading multimodal texts: Perceptual, structural, and ideological perspectives. *Children's Literature in Education, 41,* 85–104.

Souto-Manning, M. (2013). *Multicultural Teaching in the Early Childhood Classroom: Approaches, Strategies, and Tools, Preschool–2nd grade.* New York: Teachers College Press.

Souto-Manning, M. (2010). *Freire, Teaching, and Learning: Culture Circles Across Contexts.* New York: Peter Lang.

Valle, J.W., & Connor, D.J. (2011). *Rethinking Disability: A Disability Studies Approach to Inclusive Practices.* New York: McGraw Hill.

Vasquez, V. (2004). *Negotiating Critical Literacies with Young Children.* Mahwah, NJ: Lawrence Erlbaum Associates.

Ware, L. (2003). Working past pity: What we make of disability in schools. In J. Allan (ed.), *Inclusion, Participation, and Democracy: What is the Purpose?* (117–137). Boston: Kluwer Academic.

CHILDREN'S BOOK REFERENCES

Adler, D. (1997). *A Picture Book of Louis Braille.* New York: Holiday House.

Alexander, C. (2012). *Back to Front and Upside Down!* London: Eerdmans Books for Young Readers.

Asare, M. (2002). *Sosu's Call.* California: Kane-Miller EDC.

Bryant, J. (2013). *A Splash of Red: The Life and Art of Horace Pippins.* New York: Alfred A. Knopf.

Lears, L. (2000). *Ben Has Something to Say: A Story About Stuttering.* Morton Grove, IL: Albert Whitman.

Lovell, P. (2001). *Stand Tall, Molly Lou Melon.* New York: G.G. Putnam's Son.

Lyon, G.E. (2010). *The Pirate of Kindergarten.* New York: Atheneum Books for Young Readers.

MacLachlan, P. (1983). *Through Grandpa's Eyes.* New York: HarperCollins.

Martin, B., & Archambault, J. (1987). *Knots on a Counting Rope.* New York: Henry Holt.

Millman, I. (1998). *Moses Goes to a Concert.* New York: Farrar, Straus and Giroux.

Mitchell, L. (1999). *Different Just Like Me.* Watertown: Charlesbridge.

Polacco, P. (1998). *Thank You, Mr. Falker.* New York: Philomel Books.

Seuss, Dr. (1961). *The Sneetches and Other Stories.* New York: Random House, 1961.

Spier, P. (1980). *People.* New York: Doubleday Books for Young Readers.

Willis, J. (1999). *Susan Laughs.* New York: Henry Holt.

A Little Piece of Evan:
Adolescent Literature and
the Autism Spectrum

JEANNE DUTTON *and* JENNIFER MILLER

A number of young adult and middle-grade appropriate novels, including Gennifer Choldenko's *Al Capone Does My Shirts* (2006), Cynthia Lord's *Rules* (2008), Francisco X. Stork's *Marcello in the Real World* (2011), and Kathryn Erskine's *mockingbird* (2011), tell important stories of autism. Either they have neurotypical[1] main characters with some proximity to a person on the autism spectrum like an older sister or brother or a close friend, or a narrator with autism-like traits relates his or her experience coping with neurological differences using a language that belongs uniquely to his or her identity. Stories about autism reinforce the idea that the condition is one of many diverse ways of experiencing the world. They reveal that teens with autism[2]—like their neurotypical peers—are on an important path to adulthood, one that may have a slightly different internal landscape than the journey of neurotypical teens, but which is driven by similar passions and challenged by similar emotional struggles.

In order to teach these books well, educators should think of them as tools of inclusion and a means to discuss how teens come of age in neuro-diverse ways. They should consider classroom approaches that enhance a universal educational experience, one that provides a valuable service to all students regardless of their place on the spectrum. Literature circles are a pedagogical practice designed to engage readers in the response and discussion of literary texts. They rely on small, temporary, student-centered groups formed around a shared book choice (Daniels, 2002). Literature circles require face-to-face interaction between participants and encourage the routine practice of social skills. They also provide an intimate space and fewer environmental distractions for teens to engage in interpersonal communication. Teachers using literature circles in their classrooms should familiarize themselves with the difficulties teens with autism face in the pursuit of public education and in mainstreaming alongside their neurotypical peers. They should develop perspectives about young adult novels and the information about autism they might share, as well as the stereotypes a text might promote or dissemble. Finally, they should develop teaching methods that bring students together rather than letting their natural anxiety about one another drive them apart. This essay explores each of these aspects of teaching novels about young adults with autism in the hope of building respectful learning environments that are open to all.

Autism and School Environments

Consider the obstacles facing Evan,[3] a fifteen-year-old with Asperger's Syndrome[4] as he attempts to explain his autism to his neurotypical peers. Evan has difficulty focusing, the result of many sensory distractions. Streamlined, logic-based thinking suits him better, and he disperses facts about himself rather than employing the nuanced emotional information more likely to evoke friendly responses. Evan needs time and space to "read" the reactions of his listeners, and he occasionally misconstrues the conversational intentions of people he is speaking with which increases his feelings of anxiety. Although his efforts to educate the neurotypical world make it possible for him to be more comfortable in some school related situations, the exhaustion of attempting to "sell himself" and the unpredictable reactions he receives interferes with his progress. Teens like Evan often struggle during their adolescence as isolated entities overwhelmed by crowded hallways and bright fluorescently lit classrooms, or—worse—as the victims of bullying. Many teens on the autism spectrum participate in rigorous therapies to adapt to school settings. Evan has learned ways to simulate the social protocols of the neurotypical world like greeting others or making eye contact using "safe" facial points, but these actions do not come naturally. Saying hello and looking someone in the eye can cause him feelings of sensory overload.

Temple Grandin, in addition to being a doctor of animal sciences, has written several autobiographical works that elucidate the emotional experiences of being a person with autism. She is quick to point out that hers was a segment of the population that once suffered institutionaliza-tion for outward differences, and that adolescence represented the most fraught period of her maturity because of its social demands. Grandin describes the difficulties of her teen years this way:

> I got teased by the kids who tended to be more social kids, those whose idea of a good time was just hanging around and talking. It had nothing to do with intelligence—many of the highly social kids were smart, too. It was just a different developmental path we seemed to be on. It's like we were all walk-ing the same road through elementary school (even though we tended to walk in different groups) and then in adolescence we came to an intersection. Some of us turned left—the project-type people whose interest was more on things and facts—while the majority of kids turned right, onto the Avenue of Social Connection [Grandin & Barron, 2005, p. 20].

Grandin's insights about a developmental divide between the social needs of neurotypical teens and teens with autism suggests that beyond autism lies a dynamic all teens must learn to negotiate as they interact with one another. The ways in which the struggles of adolescence increase the discomfort neurotypical teens and teens with autism feel in each other's presence means there is more than one autism story taking place within a blended classroom and that teens with autism, like Evan, should not have to bear the burden of supplying all the advocacy or promoting all the awareness. Autism, with its facile "pattern" thinking has advantages over neurotypical thinking in various kinds of problem solving situations.

Children and adults with autism often "specialize" or develop focused interests that can introduce high levels of knowledge to certain fields. "Persons with AS truly enjoy their special interest. In a world that can be wildly unpredictable, the special interest is an oasis of predictability, calm, and control" (Bashe & Kirby, 2005, p. 41). A special interest can also draw a child or teen with autism further into a neurotypical community (Gabriels & Hill, 2007). Neurotypical teens with similar interests may hap-pily join an autistic teen in the pursuit of a shared passion like Pokemon or Minecraft. A teen on the spectrum with an interest in history may do as much reading about World War II as a college professor and thus expand discussions in his or her classroom beyond the routine level pre-sented in textbooks. Special interests, however, can also become obstacles that prevent a teen with autism from reading the social cues others.

> The dynamic nature of the process of competent social interaction creates complexity for teaching social skills. In kids with ASD, it is not just a lack of a particular behavior or friendship skill, or knowledge of when the behavior

should be applied, but also the absence of a rich narrative history of social experience and successful social interactions on which to draw when confronting a social situation. The challenge this presents to a person with ASD cannot be overemphasized [Koenig, 2012, p. 110].

Students on the autism spectrum have a need for pragmatic practice in social interaction with their peers to help them accumulate patterns for relating to a world with a neurotypical majority. Some of these methods can be taught in classrooms, instead of by those specialists who only have a limited access to a general population of students.

Public schools have education plans that include periods of time in which teens with autism are routinely separated from their peers. This time away from the general population of students may help teens with autism release tension, or soothe their nervous systems and recalibrate, but it can also impede some aspects of social education, especially when segregation becomes the norm. Due to a greater societal understanding of autism spectrum disorders, there is no question that for the Evans of the world, life might not be as grim as it once was. Still, the media often miscasts autism as a form of mental illness instead of a variation in how the brain processes neurological information. This means that the neurotypical peers of teens with autism often still react under the influence of pervasive stereotypes. Some of these stereotypes include the idea that teens with autism are without empathy, or that they are mentally deficient, or, incongruently, super-geniuses only interested in math and science. An inability to understand autism beyond a taxonomy of scientific terms or preconceived stereotypes prevents neurotypical teens from bringing down their walls of exclusion. A lack of proximity to teens with autism and an absence of reading materials about autism makes it easier for stereotypes or misunderstandings to persist.

Some narrowness in the ways neurotypical people view autism become culturally pervasive because of society's tendency to bias toward a medical model of disability. A medical model of disability is "one that focuses on an individual and their impairment" as opposed to a social model which seeks to encourage a view of autism that is "a form of naturally occurring neurodiversity" (Conn, 2014, pp. 24–25). A medical model of disability identifies traits of autism like poor coordination or language deficits as symptoms in need of a cure, and reinforces the impression that students on the spectrum engage in therapies to reach a "healthier" state of neurotypical behavior. Instead, good autism therapies help autistic individuals discover ways to advocate for and integrate their autistic identity into a world with a neurotypical majority (Eyal, Hart, Emine, Oren, & Rossi,

2010). Since autism is not a condition that can be cured in the medical sense, the development of coping skills along with the re-education of parents, families, and peers, is the best means by which the experience of living with autism can be improved.

A social model of disability recognizes autism as one cognitive processing type belonging to society of diverse thinking and perceiving styles. It promotes a better understanding of the individual nature of the disorder and assists in mediating its underlying neurological triggers. Some current examples of changes schools have made to improve social models of autism include the use of sensory rooms, which are places for students with autism to adjust their reactions to overstimulation so that they can more comfortably return to and persist in crowded, loud, or brightly lit classrooms. Adaptive educational methods can also help students with autism use their strengths and generalize their understanding of social behavior. Educators should guide neurotypical students in autism awareness through routine methods like books on the subject, which illuminate the experience of autism in neutral, academic ways. Autism has historically existed in the back corridors of schools, but it is time to acknowledge openly both the interior experience of living on the spectrum and the social tensions experienced by a neurotypical peer group who are relatively new at negotiating difference. In this way, the Evans in in our classrooms might thrive.

Young Adult Novels and the Stories of Autism

When given the opportunity to integrate as opposed to learning in isolated or segregated environments, children on the autism spectrum have a greater likelihood to achieve important breakthroughs in thought and imagination. Neurotypical teens who share classrooms with students on the spectrum also tend to be more open and less wary of the condition than those who have no close contact. English/Language Arts classes and the texts taught in them are uniquely suited to teach the differences of the autistic culture and may help stand in for or enhance first-hand knowledge when autism is not present. They may also mediate tensions when it is. Novels like *Al Capone Does My Shirts* (2006), Cynthia Lord's *Rules* (2008), Francisco X. Stork's *Marcello in the Real World* (2011), and Kathryn Erskine's *mockingbird* (2011) introduce teens to autistic characters from multiple perspectives, providing a broad view that leads to a greater awareness of the complexities of autism.

The stories of autism do not just play a role in helping neurotypical teens relate to the experience of being on the spectrum. When taught in interactive ways, they also enable teens with autism to enter into a conversation about themselves. All stories of autism promote understanding, but particular examples do it in distinctly useful ways. Novels that describe autism from the outside through third-person or neurotypical perspectives potentially normalize the discomforts of "difference awareness" experienced by neurotypical readers. They teach neurotypical teens that feeling strange in the presence of a person with autism is a response they can control and reflect on. Because young adult novels attract teen readers with engaging plots and likeable characters, they make this process of social transformation seem adventurous, heroic, and connected to a plot arc leading to an enviable or likeable form of maturity. Young adult novels that provide a glimpse of autism in the first person, as opposed to stories from the point of view of siblings, parents, or close friends, attempt to remove the barrier of otherness all together by inviting a reader inside the head of a person with autism so that readers can feel what autism is like through vicarious experiences. Autistic narrators often illuminate the internal complexity and potential parallels between themselves and their neurotypical peers and autistic adolescent emotional struggles.

In thinking about choosing texts for classroom use, educators should consider how well a novel depicts its neurotypical and autistic characters, and about how autism threads into the plot, but mostly they should consider how a novel reinforces or undermines pervasive thinking about autism. They should be aware that novels in general are approximations of true experiences and that Marcelo of *Marcelo in the Real World* (2013), for example, might resemble someone on the spectrum that a neurotypical teen knows, or he might not, since not all people with autism are autistic in the same way. There are degrees of artificiality to the first-person autistic point of view because the writers who create these perspectives are not autistic themselves in the way that Temple Grandin or Sean Barron, authors who have told their own stories, are. Novels with autistic narrators sometimes rely on voices that use unfamiliar language patterns meant to mimic autistic thinking. This means readers sometimes have to readjust their preconceived ideas about narrative and language, a shifting in stance that can cause them to readjust their assessments of personhood both positively and, sometimes, negatively. Autobiographical works by autistic authors do not disrupt language and to read these works is to understand the slight-of-hand novelists use to recreate identity. One potential negative aspect of the fictional means of telling the story of autism is that narrations can lapse into oversimplification, stereotyping, or a complex form of wishful-thinking that connects with some aspects of the autism, but ignores others.

A goal of reading novels about autism should be to examine the verisimilitude of characterizations in each text. If a novel successfully reveals that teens with autism grow and evolve, have distinct personalities, and dream and endeavor on their way to adulthood, then despite its voice it is probably doing a valuable service for a community of readers who are seeking to learn in a lived way. Voice, after all, is an important aspect of adolescent identity, a means of expressing uniqueness of self through language. The best of these novels about autism use voice carefully. They grapple with complex and less relatable traits of living on the spectrum, such as perseveration or maladaptive expressions of anger, in ways that make the behavior relatable, forgivable, and human to readers on both ends of the spectrum. These novels may or may not validate the lives of the autistic reader, depending on a person with autism's own personality and experience, but their inclusion in reading courses are a recognition and approval of the culture of autism as a world worth entering and exploring.

In addition to relying on voice, authors of some young adult novels about autism never use the words Asperger's or Autism in their rendering of autistic characters. Their rationale for exclusion of these terms is likely to avoid the impression that a single depiction stands for all autistic people. Thus, authors infer rather include explicit medical language. This practice employed by the writers of *The Big Bang Theory* (a popular television show about a group of super-bright young scientists) allowed them to create an autistic-like character whose true diagnosis is never revealed in any of its episodes. The choice to exclude overt mention of autism as a diagnosis embraces the idea that medical-labels can be damaging, and that character is a more important aspect of identity than scientific terminology. The autistic community, however, sometimes perceives the omission of the descriptive autism as a form of sweeping a very personal human experience under the rug, a practice that can deny a person with autism access to a cultural feeling of pride. Arguments within the autistic community rage with respect to ownership and usage of the term autism as a self-defining expression. To be autistic to some people is akin to being identifiably part of a culture, the way being male or female or Irish or French is. Some teens live openly with their autistic identity, and others prefer to avoid discussing it as a means of avoiding stigmatization. This relationship to language is a small piece of the story of autism that these novels engage in. Young Adult novels about autism illuminate the experience of autism and the language that currently shapes its cultural character.

Ten Renderings

An example of a novel that tells the story of autism through the lens of a neurotypical narrator is *Rules* (2008) by Cynthia Lord. The main character Catherine has a severely autistic brother, David. David's needs consume Catherine's parents, causing them to be unreceptive to Catherine when she approaches them for emotional support and validation of her talent as an artist. Catherine begins to resent the drain autism puts on her family, and she expresses her frustrations as David ages and develops increasingly challenging autistic characteristics. Though she loves her brother, Catherine wants him to be more like other children his age so that her family life does not seem different or unusual from the outside. Her eventual realization that David's condition is immutable ultimately deepens and matures her. She learns how to advocate for herself and for a healthier family-balance, which improves David's situation as well, because he is no longer the focus of so much family strife. The novel's plot arc dismantles the idea that families need to bear the struggles of autism in isolation, though many do.

The role autism plays in Catherine's family is symbolic of the way outsider-ness might appear in high school or middle school settings. Catherine's desire to fit in induces empathy in readers, but also reveals the work she must do as a sister with an unbreakable connection to a brother. Her struggle to make things normal and the anxiety she feels about David echoes the discomfort both neurotypical and adolescents with autism endure in their efforts to approve of and be approved by their peers. Teens and middle-grade students reading this novel may begin to recognize their own patterns of inclusion or exclusion. The text acknowledges the particular frustrations teens who have relatives on the spectrum encounter, and reinforces the idea that autism is not a medical condition experienced by a single individual but rather a social event that influences others, sometimes negatively, but only when the lens for looking at it is too narrow.

In a second novel that describes sibling relationships, *Al Capone Does My Shirts* (2006) by Gennifer Choldenko, the teen narrator Moose describes life with his older sister Natalie. Natalie's autism prevents her from speaking or articulating her own needs, and her welfare has become such a matter of importance to Moose's parents that the family relocates to the island of Alcatraz so that she can attend a special school to improve her condition. The novel is set at a time in which neighbors mistake Natalie's autism for schizophrenia. In order to shield her daughter from concerned neighbors who think she should be institutionalized, Moose's mother lies about Natalie's age and dresses her like a much younger girl. Moose spends his days taking care of her and one afternoon, he notices her talking to one of the inmates.

Al Capone Does My Shirts (2006) departs from stereotypical perceptions of autism as an emotionless state of being. When Moose witnesses Natalie talking to the inmate, he recognizes that Natalie is driven by adolescent yearnings which none of the other characters suspects she has. Moose begins to understand the importance of her social education and the degree of vulnerability she faces without it. He schemes to get her the schooling that will enable her to function better in the outside world. Moose resolves his conflicts with strategies that embolden him to rise above the tensions of peer acceptance and peer pressure. Moose's small group of island friends rethink their perceptions of Natalie and follow his lead as he strives to unlock her from the prison that the social experience of being autistic at this time in history has locked her in.

These two examples of novels with neurotypical narrators interacting with siblings with autism teach lessons of acceptance and ways of seeing that alleviate the tension to judge or discriminate. The novel *mockingbird* (2011) by Kathryn Erskine is about a fifth grader named Caitlin. *Mockingbird* (2011) explores the interior world of autism in a way that lets autism tell its own story. Caitlin's struggles do not include difficulties in speech or communication, but she is isolated by her literal and excessively fact-driven thinking and expression. Caitlin has recently lost an older brother to a school shooting, and her grief-stricken father cannot assist her in unraveling her emotional confusion because his own suffering is so overwhelming. Caitlin's school days increase in difficulty until a counselor steps in and encourages her to make strides in social awareness in a way that appeals to her logic-based way of interacting. She embarks on a quest to bring closure to her father's suffering, a term she understands pragmatically. His neurotypical misapprehension of her earnestness has a cruelty to it that readers can perceive. Caitlin is young enough that her way of viewing her dilemma makes sense to readers who will not see her as backward or lesser because of her confusion, instead, ideally, they will be moved to empathy.

Another novel with an autistic narrator is *Anything But Typical* by Nora Raleigh Baskin (2009) which tells the story of Jason Blake, a twelve-year-old with autism who does his best to be "untypical" as he navigates a "typical" world. On page one, we hear from Jason in his own voice telling readers that he will convey his story in the first person, even though that is not his usual style of referencing himself. He is aware that he is communicating to a neurotypical audience and if the audience is to understand his message, he must speak in a way that is comfortable. Jason is a writer at heart and interacts with the outside world through a website called Storyboard. On Storyboard he is a member of the community, just like anyone else. No one there knows if he is typical or not. He does not have to make eye contact or try to read facial expressions or body language. He posts his stories, reads those of others, and sends messages back and forth. In this realm, he feels safe until he begins to correspond with Phoenixbird, a girl who likes Jason's stories and seems to like him. The opportunity arises for Jason to travel to Dallas to attend a Storyboard convention, but he must sacrifice his anonymity in the process. He fears immediate rejection, especially from Phoenixbird, once people discover that he is autistic.

The strength of Jason's voice provides readers an opportunity to have the lived-through experience of knowing his struggles and fears. Jason tells the reader how lights, sounds, or smells overload his senses. He tells the reader how he likes it when his dad hugs him because his dad knows how to leave him room to breathe and not bend him backwards making him feel off balance. When he breaks a piece of equipment in the art room, he is not misbehaving. His sensory overload and anger are too great for him to control. His explanation of these experiences alerts readers to what happens in his mind and body and the frustrations teens with autism face when they have to negotiate or make complicated social decisions, ones with forking paths or no clear right or wrong. Jason gets into a fight with his cousin on a visit. His cousin is not one to compromise or show compassion for Jason or his younger brother, Jeremy. When his cousin is cruel, Jason finds himself reacting in a negative way. One minute Seth is being mean, and the next he is falling to the floor knocking down CDs and other objects, and Jason is being pulled into the hallway. Frustration and over-stimulation lead to an outburst that he cannot self-regulate, an autistic meltdown, which if only ever viewed from the outside may seem without logic or sense. Jason's voice explains the after effects in an emotional language meant to reveal the truth of that experience. The novel glosses over Jason's feelings in the moment in an attempt to simulate the interior experience of losing control. His actions occur in an out of body way, leaving a blank that readers fill with their own versions of why. The mutual search for an explanation has potentially binding implications, as the novel attempts to recreate the splitting apart and piecing together teens with autism may experience in the wake of these moments.

Though novels about autism induce empathy, they occasionally fall into patterns that can build on a reader's sense of stereotypes. The first person voice of Edison (Eddy) Thomas in Jacqueline Houtman's *The Reinvention of Edison Thomas* (2010) engages readers with its likeable character named Eddy. Eddy is a wordsmith who concentrates on words and letters as a calming strategy and an arena where he can feel success. For Eddy, that arena is science. To calm himself, he recites facts from what he calls his "random access memory." He and his father collect broken appliances and gadgets that Eddy uses for parts to build new inventions. Eddy enters the school science fair with a device he builds that uses electric current and magnetic fields to launch a copper ring into the air. When the school fires their crossing guard, Eddy turns his attention and his invention skills to monitor the crosswalk without a guard, building a traffic camera to collect data and evidence in hopes of proving that children are not safe at this crossing without human intervention.

Houtman alludes to the famous inventor Thomas Edison who purportedly also had autistic traits. She follows in the wake of other authors and filmmakers who have also created autistic characters with scientific qualities of genius. The critic Anthony D. Baker notes that sometimes people with autism seem to "only come in a limited variety of flavors" (Baker, 2008) in media representations. Young adult novels on any topic rely on main characters who exhibit high levels of intelligence or exceptionality, characters who use magic, who suffer in unusual ways, or find themselves at the center of important historical or political events. The fact that Eddy is also exceptional is not usual, but the way in which his remarkableness expresses itself can limit readers in their thinking about what autism is. Alone, the portrayal of Eddy as math/science geek is a good thing, but repetition of this trope on television and in young adult literature creates the impression that super-science skills are the only kind of exceptionality an autistic person might possess.

A second novel which falls into this same pattern is *Mindblind* (2013) by Jennifer Roy about a boy-genius who grapples with his emotional distance from his father as he also pursues a long-term neurotypical love interest. The main character pursues cool-seeming activities like playing in a rock band, but he experiences an autistic breakdown over a difficult math problem. Throughout the novel, Nathanial does not become as obsessive about music as he does about math, though music is one of many specialized interests of autistic people and successful musicians on the autism spectrum abound. This secondary side of Nathanial's personality isn't colored by the same kind of autistic thinking and processing as his math interests. Teens want emotional payoffs from the novels they read, and they want to be flattered by portrayals of themselves, but Nathanial's behavior might be more appealing because of a neurotypical bias about what cool or likeable should look like. The novel humanizes the adolescent experiences of autism in ways that may inadvertently neuro-typify them. Roy's construct of autism is one that acknowledges important aspects of autism, but may ignore others as means of wooing readers, and this ultimately weakens the work the book might do toward autism awareness. Nathanial's story is entertaining, but a portrayal that may veer on incongruity.

In the novel *Marcelo in The Real World* (2011), by Francisco X. Stork, the seventeen-year-old narrator Marcelo describes himself as having a cognitive make up similar to Asperger's Syndrome, though in his case, a medical diagnoses is never defined. His casualness and self-confidence in describing his personality reveals that he sees his social-neurological differences more as a matter of uniqueness in character than a hindrance. He attends a school for children with disabilities that shelters him from the challenges of being atypical in a world that values normalcy until the summer his father requires him to take a job as an intern at his law practice. Marcelo begins to react to the politics, deception, and ambition present in his new setting, behavior that feels illogical to him and causes him to doubt the friendliness and basic goodness of the people around him. He awkwardly befriends a coworker named Jasmine, and, as his feelings for her deepen, so does his awareness that he is off in the eyes of others, even people as close to him as his father. Marcelo's story becomes a struggle for the right to be himself and to live in the manner he chooses, despite the recognition that this choice makes his father uncomfortable. His journey to manhood resonates as a coming of age story because of the intensity of the challenges Marcelo faces in his journey toward independence, self-awareness, and self-reliance.

At the beginning of the novel, Marcelo's areas of interest include religion, spirituality, and ponies. He possesses heightened intelligence, but is often childlike in reactions to the world, a combination that makes him seem at once wise and overtly naive. His romantic relationship to Jasmine lends sweetness to the story, and the unfolding of his personality, his movement from child to adult includes some lessons he learns pragmatically and some he begins to sense more intuitively. The fact that Marcelo never mentions autism in his narrative makes his story seem detached and fairy-tale like, as if Marcelo is a metaphor for a way of being, rather than being itself. Brief discussions of spirituality and use of poetic language enhance the symbolic quality of Marcelo's experience, and elevate the novel's themes.

The novel *A Curious Incident of a Dog in the Night-Time* (2004) by Mark Haddon also relies on an artful voice whose self-expression can seem overly simplified, innocent, and occasionally digressive, but which nonetheless engages the reader in an interesting version of a mystery. Christopher Moore has a passion for math, though instead of being regarded as a genius, he suffers isolation in a school for academically backward kids. His level of autism impairs his ability to communicate with or relate well with others. He discovers a murdered dog in his back yard, disturbing evidence that something in his neighborhood is amiss. He begins a quest to solve the crime, but his autistic perspective limits his ability to see all the facts of the case and to understand the ways in which his complicated behavior has driven a wedge between his parents and caused their marriage to fray. His engagement in the world around him requires him to view all things as a mystery and as a result, readers lean in, search with him, and make sense of the seeming nonsensical barrage of stimuli that confuse and overwhelm his perspective. The reader invests in Christopher's quest and must beat their way forward with the clues they have been given, a disorienting process, but one that makes a reader be the stranger in a strange land as they experience some of Christopher's sensitivity to sound, light or touch.

Critics have argued that Christopher's idiot/savant voice evolves from an outdated perception of autism, one that once found purchase in films like *Rain Man* (Molen, McGiffert, Mutrux, Peters, Johnson, & Levinson, 1988), which portray people with autism as mostly simple with surprising bursts of genius. These kinds of portrayals may inadvertently justify a diminished respect for the intelligence and independence of people on the spectrum (Baker, 2008). At times, it seems Christopher is incapable of functioning in any other environment but his school, and that he is unrealistically dependent on people who understand and translate for him. The publication and acclaim of *Curious Incident of a Dog in the Night-Time*, precedes the publication of *Marcelo in the Real World* or *Rules*, and some critics have argued that as an artifact it represents a breakthrough in the ways in which autism is viewed according to a social model, one that for the first time sees autism as a character trait rather than a plot problem. Christopher struggles in his attempts to understand his fighting parents. He suffers in his socioeconomic status (Berger, 2008) and he uses his autism to solve his problems. The story invests in the centralization as opposed to the marginalization of an autistic experience, and may bear the hallmarks of a society in transition.

Two other novels that include themes of autism have plots that include characters on the spectrum, but whose intention is less to explore the autistic personality than it is to weave autism into the fabric of an expected and anticipated plotline. *Harmonic Feedback* (2011) by Tara Kelly and *House Rules* by Jodi Picoult (2010) engage readers, in a romance about a lonely girl with Asperger's, and a mystery with multiple narrators and a wrongly accused teen with autism whose innocence must be proven. These novels tug autism into familiar literary territory and normalize the disorder through their inclusion. Autistic characters fill the roles of previously occupied by neurotypical characters, and solve the case or fall in love the way their counterparts might.

Authors of plot driven novels about autism might vary in how much they adhere to and detract from the portrait of spectrum disorders in order to create a desired outcome. In *Harmonic Feedback* (2011), true love saves the main character Jasmine from the crushing isolation many autistic people feel in their social settings. This form of ending provides an emotional escape for teen readers from the pain of loneliness associated with the condition since Jasmine's love story is satisfyingly hopeful. Prince charming swoops in and saves the day without much need for her to engage in difficult social transformation. The storyline is gratifying to readers who desire a happily-ever after reading experience, but less useful in developing an understanding of autism as a culture.

House Rules (2010) by Jodi Picoult is a novel with multiple perspectives that presents some of the external social debates and conflicts surrounding autism's portrayal in the media. Jacob Hunt is a teen with autism accused of murdering a family friend. His special interest in forensics leads police to suspect his guilt, though his mother Emma rushes to defend him and eventually persuades the lead investigator to take Jacob's autism into consideration as he unravels the crime. Picoult is careful in how she provides an internal and external view of autism and the painful sibling dynamics that can occur in some families, but the extremes of the plot require her to over-characterize Jacob's personality as suspicious. Critic Stuart Murray points out in regard to film depictions of autism, "it is the terms of such usage that warrant investigation, as they point to the *desire* of commercial contemporary culture both to be fascinated by the appeal of autism and fit it into generic, pre-existing narrative concerns" (Murray, 2008). Picoult's characterization reads as if she were thumbing a textbook of taxonomic symptoms. Reading *House Rules* (2010) is a page-turning experience, but Picoult's pat symptomology flattens Jacob as a character in favor of creating narrative tension in the neurotypical characters around him. How much books like *House Rules* (2010) and *Harmonic Feedback* (2011) overly sweeten or overly exaggerate the portrait of autism is something young readers can explore for themselves once they have become familiar with how autism is portrayed in other texts.

English and language arts classrooms and the readings taught in them expand personal perspectives on human experience. Teachers should encourage the reading of texts that explore themes of neurodiversity the same way they might teach texts that illuminate racial or cultural diversity. Readers on both ends of the spectrum can use these texts to palpate feelings of similarities and difference in order to shape new definitions of what it means to be human. The reading of young adult novels about autism allow students to argue, debate, resolve their misapprehensions, tensions, or connectedness to autism, and work more interdependently as a social community.

Literature Circles

No discussion of texts for young adults should exclude a universal means to teach them, since access to discussions of these reading experiences is just as important as reading itself. Literature circles represent a neuro-diverse means of introducing teens to novels about autism. The approach is grounded in a transactional theory of reading and closely aligned to many of the reading standards outlined in the Common Core State Standards (National Governors Association Center for Best Practices & Council of Chief State School Officers, 2010). For literature circles to be successful, teachers need to engage students in mentored-practice, teach strategies for response, and model the level and depth of discussion necessary so that each group or circle is successful in accomplishing curricular goals.

Early on, literature circles were defined by role sheets, which were worksheets created to help students prepare for discussions. Roles included things like a discussion director, connection contributor, travel tracer, and vocabulary master. Role sheets directed students to write discussion questions, focus on text-to-text, text-to-world, and text-to-self connections, investigate the various settings in the story, and define unfamiliar words. Their role was the focus of their contribution to the shared discussion. Open-ended questions that spark discussion, making various types of connections between X and Y, and examining unknown words are all important parts of a rich book discussion; however, many teachers and students found role sheets restrictive and perfunctory exercises that got in the way of meaningful conversations. Current conceptions for using role sheets have evolved to focus student response more on connections, especially text-to-self, and on supporting opinions and observations with support from the text. Discussion preparation does not need to follow a prescribed pattern. Once students have practiced literature circle discussions through teacher-led modeling, discussion preparation can take many forms. Students can jot ideas on sticky notes marking passages that are important to their interpretation and response. This practice aligns with standards for citing textual evidence that support analysis and making inferences as outlined in the Common Core State Standards (National Governors Association Center for Best Practices & Council of Chief State School Officers, 2010). Another method of preparation might be to write or draw. Students may keep notes in a response journal and that journal may include text and sketches or drawings to capture thoughts and reactions during the reading.

The best model for successful literature circles begins with student self-selection of the text. Variations are possible, but student choice is an essential component. Providing students choices within the theme of autism will allow readers to choose the point of view from which they want to approach the topic based on story elements or reading level. They also get to opt whether they prefer an inside or outside view, whether they want to understand the ways characters relate to autistic siblings or friends, or how a character with autism negotiates his or her own experience. Teachers may facilitate choices in multiple ways. If there is a range of reading abilities in the classroom, teachers should group two or three texts at a particular reading level and allow students to choose from that group. Another method for choosing texts is a book pass. Teachers can pass books around the room for students to examine. Students scan each book and then rank their top three choices. Groups are formed based on similar choices. A third option is for teachers to use book talks to introduce each title and then ask students to choose. To make their selection, students list and rank titles, move to a designated spot in the classroom for each book, or place chips or cards in a box designated for each title.

Once students have selected a novel, literature circles progress through a pattern of reading sections of the novel and holding small group discussions. When dealing with a mix of neurotypical students and autistic students, this process teaches social and collaborative skills in addition to promoting useful reading and discussion. All students must be able choose freely. Students need to learn to communicate with each other not only to discuss the story, but also to negotiate and agree upon the amount of text to read in each section.

Literature circles are grounded in reader-response and transactional theories of reading. Louise Rosenblatt defines this transaction as a reading event that is different with each combination of reader text, and moment in time (Rosenblatt, 2005). She writes, "every reading act is an event, or a transaction involving a particular reader and a particular pattern of signs, a text, and occurring at a particular time in a particular context" (Rosenblatt, 2005, p. 7). Literature circles connect the text the students select with the group that will share this reading event in the classroom at a given time. Within this reading event, teachers need to ensure that students are "given the opportunity and the courage to approach literature personally, to let it mean something to him directly. The classroom situation and the relationship with the teacher should create a feeling of security. He should be made to feel that his own response to books, even though it may not resemble the standard critical comments, is worth expressing" (Rosenblatt, 1995, p. 63). To approach literature personally, students must experience a range of texts with a range of characters to allow for personal connection and identification. Including texts with main characters or secondary characters on the autism spectrum creates an environment that not only presents dimensional portraits of autism to neurotypical students but also may provide students with autism a sense of security and belonging in the classroom and in the discussion.

The need to see oneself reflected in the text is essential to fostering an aesthetic response to literature. Rosenblatt's theory is based on a continuum of responses between the efferent and the aesthetic. Efferent responses are more public in nature, rooted in information that the readers take from the text as information or shared meanings that are intended to be retained, recalled, or analyzed after the reading event. Aesthetic responses are more private in nature, rooted in the lived through experience that takes place during the reading, the thoughts, feelings, and attitudes that are evoked in the transaction between reader and text (Rosenblatt, 2005). Literature circle discussions fluctuate between efferent and aesthetic responses, with the general goal of increasing aesthetic responses.

It is important to note that a student with autism may initially rely on efferent readings. A ten year old on the Autism spectrum[5] might relate to the perceived humor in James Patterson's middle grade novel *I Funny* (2013) and experiment by using jokes in the book in his interactions with peers. Modeling behavior in pragmatic ways is important to some autism therapies and fuels the thinking behind social stories and other simple narratives that walk children with autism through potentially difficult situations like dealing with a bully, or recovering from disappointment. Texts, charts, and lists can be more useful learning tools in developing mental patterns that lead to generalized behavior (Koenig, 2012). The purpose of shared discussions is to begin to engage aesthetic responses, times when the reader is immersed in the "lived through current of ideas, sensations, images, tensions" that during the shared discussion "will be recall of the experience, remembering of, and reflection on, the evocation and the reactions" (Rosenblatt, 2005, p. 45). In autism therapies, this transition to aesthetic understanding is called generalization.

The need to build community and collaboration in literature circles extends into small group book discussions. Book discussions generally take place all at once with multiple groups in one classroom all discussing different books at the same time. Teachers must help students be able to maintain respectful, independent discussions without an adult present to guide or direct them, clearly articulating the rules and patterns of discussion and allowing for modeling and practice. Teens with autism might begin this process with neurotypical partners with whom they already have a bond in order to limit social challenges and so that the discussion of the texts can absorb their focus. Matching students with autism with peers with whom they already have a connection provides a venue for positive reinforcement when the exchange of ideas take place. Students with autism need to know when they have achieved success in a social situation in order to improve, expand upon and generalize the behavior (Koenig, 2012). Not all teens with autism will need guidance as they interact with their peer groups. Not all teens with autism will read efferently as opposed to aesthetically, since autism is a nuanced way of thinking and processing with a wide variety of skill sets, but teachers should be prepared to meet the social needs of the group as well as the academic ones. The guidance provided to peer-groups should remain flexible, adaptive, and focused on building awareness of both sides of the spectrum.

The purpose of choosing books with autism as part of the story, whether in the life of the main character or a secondary character, is to allow students with autism and those without, to respond to the story and make text-to-self connections. Rosenblatt writes,

> The teacher, realistically concerned with helping his students develop a vital sense of literature cannot, then, keep his eyes focused only on the literary materials he is seeking to make available. He must understand the personalities who are to experience this literature. He must be ready to face the fact that the students' reactions will inevitably be in terms of their own temperament and backgrounds [2005, p. 50].

Teachers need to be aware of students in their classes who are on the autism spectrum or if someone in their family has autism, and they need to be aware of how neurotypical students respond to their peers who are not typical. Addressing autism as a culture with varying characteristics will lead to more sophisticated literary definitions of humanity.

Conclusion

Using literature with autistic characters allows students with autism to see themselves in the literature, to discuss the story, and respond to the character making text-to-self connections in ways that they may not able to do when reading books with neurotypical main characters. Seeing oneself reflected in the literary experience creates connection between reader and text, between student and teacher when the teacher facilitates the students' entry into the text, and between students of varying backgrounds and abilities as they share insights and experiences during small group discussion. Stories about autism allow a student with autism to see themselves reflected in a work and through aesthetic response and discussion, to validate the story as similar to his lived through experience or to refute it as unrelated to their life experience. For neurotypical students, reading about a character with autism allows them to explore through the vicarious experience what life might be like for their autistic peers. As they read, they hear the voice of Christopher in *The Curious Incident of the Dog in the Night-time* (2004) describe to the reader why he does not like to be touched or how hard it is for him to decipher body language to interpret emotions. Understanding that many students with autism have difficulty interpreting body language and facial expressions, an issue which leads to difficulty in social interaction and communication skills, can lead to discussions of many ways of perceiving and coping with the challenges of the world around us. Eddy, the main character in *The Reinvention of Edison*

Thomas (2010), works with a therapist named Tiffany using a variety of techniques including analyzing video clips and cards with pictures of faces on them, asking Eddy to tell a story based on the facial expressions. By itself, this can be a powerful reading experience, but combined with a small group discussion and potentially a small group discussion that includes a peer for whom autism is a reality and not a vicarious experience, all students have the potential not only to improve their reading skills, but also their ability to become part of an equal, collaborative and diverse society.

Notes

1. The term neurotypical describes people whose neuro-processing patterns resemble a majority.

2. The term "people with Autism" forwards the idea of "person" first description, suggesting that a person's humanity comes before a condition like Autism, but this choice of phrasing may ignore how significant Autism can be to a sense of self and identity. Some Autism advocates prefer "Autistic people," or "Aspies," since "neurotypical people" is the approved term for "people with typical neurobiology." Either way, it is our authorial intent to be respectful.

3. Evan is not a real person but a composite portrait.

4. In 2013, the American Psychiatric Association listed in DSM V Asperger's Syndrome/disorder under the umbrella diagnosis of Autism Spectrum Disorder.

5. My son has similarly learned to list and generalize.

References

Baker, A.D. (2008). Recognizing Jake: Contending with formulaic and spectacualarized representations of autism in film. In M. Osteen (ed.), *Autism and Representation* (229–243). New York: Routledge.

Bashe, P.R., & Kirby, B.L. (2005). *The Oasis Guide to Asperger Syndrome: Advice, Support, Insight, and Inspiration.* New York: Crown.

Berger, J. (2008). Alterity and autism. In M.H. Spectrum (ed.), *Autism and Representation* (271–302). New York: Routledge.

Conn, C. (2014). *Autism and the Social World of Childhood: A Sociocultural Perspective on the Theory and Practice.* New York: Routledge.

Eyal, G., Hart, B., Emine, O., Oren, N., & Rossi, N. (2010). *The Autism Matrix.* Malden, MA: Polity Press.

Gabriels, R.L., & Hill, E.D. (2007). *Growing Up with Autism: Working with School Age Children and Adolescents.* New York: The Guilford Press.

Grandin, T., & Barron, S. (2005). *Unwritten Rules of Social Relationships.* Arlington, TX: Future Horizons.

Koenig, K. (2012). *Practical Social Skills for Autism Spectrum Disorders: Designing Child-Specific Interventions.* New York: W.W. Norton.

Murray, S. (2008). Hollywood and the fascination of autism. In M. Osteen (ed.), *Autism and Representation* (245–255). New York: Routledge.

Rosenblatt, L. (1995). *Literature as Exploration.* New York: Modern Language Associates.

_____. (2005). *Making Meaning with Texts.* Portsmouth, NH: Heinemann.

NOVELS

Baskin, N.R. (2009). *Anything But Typical.* New York: Simon & Schuster for Young Readers.

Choldenko, G. (2006). *Al Capone Does My Shirts.* New York: Puffin.

Erskine, K. (2010). *mockingbird.* New York: Puffin.

Haddon, M. (2003). *The Curious Incident of the Dog in the Night-Time.* New York: Random House.

Houtman, J. (2010). *The Reinvention of Edison Thomas.* Honesdale, PA: Boyds Mills Press.

Kelly. T (2010). *Harmonic Feedback.* New York: Henry Holt.

Lord, C. (2006). *Rules.* New York: Scholastic.

Picoult, J. (2010). *House Rules.* New York: Atria.

Roy, J. (2010). *Mindblind.* Las Vegas: Amazon.

Stork, F.X. (2009). *Marcello in the real world.* New York: Scholastic.

Middle School Adolescents Developing Critical Stances Around Difference in Young Adolescent Literature in Literature Circles

JEANNE GILLIAM FAIN *and*
LESLEY CRAIG-UNKEFER

Understanding how to critically analyze literature is a skill that is developed over time using a range of instructional strategies. Skills such as asking questions, seeking answers and establishing validity of claims are common practices associated with this skill (Young, 2011). The focus of this chapter is to promote skills of exploring content, with a specific emphasis on various aspects of exceptionality. Through the use of literature circles, teachers will facilitate discussions that will lead to an understanding of a range of issues that introduce and inform aspects of exceptionality. These issues include self-determination, advocacy, general characteristics of various types of exceptionalities, and promotion and understanding of differences. Of interest in this chapter is the role that students and teachers jointly play in focusing upon "critical analysis of texts" within literacy instruction (Beers & Probst, 2012, Lehman & Roberts, 2013) that includes a range of young adolescent literature with a focus on exceptionality for middle school readers.

In addition, we show how students with diverse knowledge can try on these texts as readers with knowledge and power as they make these texts their own and develop critical stances from the literature. Critical literacy research informs our understanding of building intentional space for critical connections with texts (Vasquez, Tate, & Harste; 2013). Curricular decisions were grounded in social and cultural perspectives on literacy (Bloome & Egan-Robertson, 1993; Gee, 1999; Street, 2005) that highlight the cultural basis for reading and writing. While examining various responses to texts, the authors paid attention to texts and contexts that were culturally authentic and relevant to the contemporary and diverse audiences of learners in today's times (Street, 2005). In order to develop a critical literacy stance, learners need authentic literacy experiences. These experiences, in the form of literature circles, facilitate multiple ways of knowing and create an opportunity to collaboratively examine analytical texts that invite students to see critical connections. Critical stances within literature circles are the means by which the reader can develop a more informed perspective about exceptionality and meet the challenge of change and acceptance by exploring "whose voices are missing, and who gains and who loses" and how asking and answering these questions leads students to develops a critical stance (McLaughlin & DeVoogd, 2004, p. 2).

Key to the process of literature circles is asking and answering questions. Three questions (Ware, 2001, p. 114) that can assist teachers and students as they explore exceptionality across the four themes are: (1) What can I understand about the identity of others who appear different than myself? (2) What can I learn about my own identity through understanding the identities of others? and (3) How can I expand my critical stance on exceptionality, and how can I expand my understanding of exceptionality through various lenses?

Exploring Difference in Middle and Young Adolescent Literature

The literature highlighted in this essay emphasizes a critical understanding of the various dimensions of exceptionality including general characteristics, self-determination, advocacy, and inclusion. As we think about using books that promote critical perspectives about exceptionality in the middle school classroom, we have developed a criteria that guides our book selection that includes the following: the main character or a central character has an exceptionality, and there is realism in the story with complex characters that highlight layers of difference or exceptionality which allows the reader to ponder and question the actions in the story.

The rationale for book selection was based on the need for realism to provide middle school students with texts that they can relate to and that force them to grapple with true events that they may have experienced in their own lives or through the lives of their peers or family members with exceptionalities. Complex characters refer to the real differences across exceptionalities in humans. Through purposeful selection of texts, middle school students cannot only identify but also relate to the strengths and weaknesses of characters. Beyond exceptionality, the characters in these books have layers of complexity, and students working together to make meaning from the texts create shared meaning about these characters (Rogoff, 1990). Characters from the literature really struggle and triumph with the differences that they have as they move forward in life. In exploring these differences, adolescents can construct their thoughts and questions, and, in doing so, they are able to reflect critically upon the events and realities in the book as they think about the role difference plays in our lives. We considered multiple information sources and reviews for book selection including the Worlds of Words organization, International Board on Books for Young People, United States Board on Books for Young People, Newbery Award, Hans Christian Andersen Award, Pura Belpre, *Bookbird*, *Horn Book*, American Library Association, *Language Arts*, and Amazon. We intentionally attended to exceptionality first and then considered gender, culture, identity, and language in the book selection process. Our goal was to select literature written between 2010 and 2015 that reflect the range of exceptionality by disability category and provide teachers with material that will yield rich opportunities for critical discussion around multiple perspectives.

Developing Critical Stances About Exceptionality

Critical stances through literature circles should provide students with meaningful opportunities to "unravel" the layers of complexity in novels as students jointly explore how they can "read the world" and simultaneously bring changes in thinking about exceptionality to their world (Freire, 1970). Research supports critical dialogue about issues of complexity within texts in the classroom (Foss, 2002; Martinez-Roldan, 2003; Fain, 2008). Dialogue is transformational as power is shared within literature discussion and participants gain additional insights into themselves. Critical thinking is considered as essential within genuine dialogue.

Dialogue also includes the careful construction of identity that is crafted to influence the perceptions of others and includes conscious speech, non-verbal communication, and actions of individuals (Goffman, 1959). Critical stances are created when students critically examine their positioning or their stances within their world and evaluate the realities of the world. Lewison, Flint, and Van Sluys (2002) condense 30 years of critical literacy research into four dimensions: disrupting commonplace, interrogating multiple viewpoints, focusing on sociopolitical issues, and taking action and promoting social justice. These four dimensions are woven throughout the literature examples. These dimensions are highlighted within the literature examples with an emphasis on four themes that emphasize aspects of exceptionality.

- Disrupting the commonplace: challenges learners to closely examine the familiar through new lenses and considers new ways of looking at old ideas. Students closely read and rethink the familiar within the text.
- Interrogating multiple viewpoints: requires us to put ourselves into positions and perspectives of others. Adolescents think about developing an empathetic stance to the literature.
- Focusing on sociopolitical issues: challenges us to explore institutional systems and the power relationships and language embedded within these systems. Students examine rules and how the impact that they might have.
- Taking action and promoting social justice: take an "informed" stand against oppression or promoting social justices. For purposes of this chapter, this dimension of critical literacy will include advocacy.

Critical literacy allows learners to step back, reflect, and take action (Freire, 1970). Students learn to consider multiple points of views and settle into their perspectives after taking risks within the dialogue (Foss, 2002). Teachers act as facilitators, encouraging students to consider multiple historical perspectives and simultaneously communicating to the students that their sharing is valuable. Students need space in the curriculum to talk about literature within a community of readers as they learn to read to learn and think (Short & Pierce, 1998). Critical stances through literature circles provide students with intentional space to engage in critical dialogue by finding textual evidence with the literature through active participation. Literature circles are an integral part of classroom inquiry that draws upon the strengths of learners within intermediate and middle school classrooms.

Critical dialogue about the literature is transformational as power is shared within the talk among the students and teacher as participants gain a deepening knowledge of themselves and the texts (Freire, 1970). Literature circles can be set up in small group discussions and peer-led or large group discussions facilitated by the teacher. Students are ultimately in charge of their turn talking through the dialogue, and the teacher often moves to the position of a group member. Students assume the speaker and listener roles within the literature circles and informally structure the interactions around their connections and responses around the textual evidence from the literature. This structure leads student to develop a critical approach to understanding the literature about exceptionalities.

Themes That Promote Understanding of Exceptionality

The critical focus of the literature circles that promote discussion and understanding of exceptionality are based on four themes: aspects of exceptionality, inclusion, self-determination, and advocacy. Each theme has distinct characteristics but there are overlapping concepts and constructs that will assist the teacher in identifying appropriate texts that will allow for critical analysis of one or more of the themes.

These themes have an extensive base of evidence (Hornby, 2014; Zigmond, N., Kloo, A., & Lemons, C.J, 2011; Wehmeyer, 2002). The descriptions provide teachers with a general overview of each theme. Next, literature considerations specific to the young adult population that best illustrate the theme are identified with a more detailed discussion of how to explore the theme in a literature circle with one or more of the four dimensions of developing a critical stance with questions specific to the text example.

Areas of Exceptionality

The Individuals with Disability Education Act (U.S. Department of Education, 2010) is a legislative mandate that identifies the characteristics of fourteen distinct exceptionality categories. Each category has specified criteria for students that experience difficulty in learning or students with enhanced abilities. In either situation, supports are developed and implemented to ensure that students with exceptionality have the same rights and privileges of their typically developing peers. The fourteen categories of exceptionality are learning disabilities, speech or language impairment, other health impairment, intellectual disability, emotional disturbance, autism, multiple disabilities, developmental delay, hearing impairment, orthopedic impairment, visual impairment, traumatic brain injury, deaf-blindness, and gifted and talented.

Students that qualify for services under IDEA may need special education services throughout their preschool to high school career. The evaluation and eligibility process includes assessments and input from the student's family members, teachers and school administration, and support services. These individuals work as a team to identify supports or modifications as part of a program planning. IDEA mandates ongoing progress monitoring, annual review, and evaluation of those plans.

Identifying literature that either introduces or expands understanding of a specific exceptionality should align with the characteristics per IDEA. Although a tenet of Special Education is individualized planning and support, general knowledge of the unique aspects of each exceptionality category is an essential element in identifying literature.

Literature Examples with a Focus on Aspects of Exceptionality

Rain Reign (Martin, 2014) is a novel that provides the reader with an in depth description of Rose, an individual with Autism Spectrum Disorder. It also addresses two dimensions in the development of a critical stance: disrupting the commonplace and rules of institutional systems. Rose Howard, a fifth grader at Hatford Elementary, finds comfort and intrigue with homonyms. For Rose, she is obsessed with finding homonyms in her world. Her dad is not pleased that Rose spends considerable time obsessing on homonyms. He desires for Rose just to be normal and control her tendencies to obsess about homonyms. Rose has an assistant in school, Mrs. Leibler, who continually attempts to convince Rose that she should use conversation starters in her talk with her peers.

The book begins telling the reader that Rose has been placed on a serious behavior plan and that notes are continually sent home to her father because Rose struggles with conformity in school. Her dad repeatedly asks Rose why she chooses not to follow her behavior plan. As a result of her nonconformity, Rose is banned from riding the bus, and her Uncle

Weldon has to drive her to school and pick her up regularly. According to Rose, she has "high functioning autism." Rose's acute hearing causes her difficulty in focusing within the classroom. She struggles to communicate in appropriate ways within the classroom.

In terms of the critical literacy dimension of disrupting the commonplace, middle school students can think and discuss by exploring textual evidence within a literature circle about the role of homonyms in Rose's life. It may seem as if Rose is just trying to annoy others as she points out information that doesn't fit within a particular context. Rose states, "The purpose of most of my rules is to limit homonyms to words that are pure and also that are English" (p. 17). Rose is all about the rules and struggles with understanding the complexity of when rules in English and in other contexts aren't followed.

What role does tolerance play for middle school students as they socially interact with their peers that may display difference within their talk across a school day? Upon thinking about multiple viewpoints, how would it feel to constantly hear buzzing sounds and not be able to focus upon the learning in the classroom? How could a middle school student support another student that works at communicating and conveying thoughts clearly in school? What type of listening might be required of that student? Middle school students could try to empathize with Rose's plight as an outsider that is trying too hard in most cases to fit into a world of difference.

Institutional systems have rules. Many of the rules make sense and have a real purpose in providing safety for everyone. In the case of educational systems, schools construct rules developed by administrators and educators. In this novel, Rose is kicked off the bus, and her parent has to find her a new mode of transportation in order for her to attend school. Middle school students could discuss the equity of this decision. In addition, what role should rules play in schools? Who should make the rules and why should they matter? Are rules always fair? If the rules aren't fair, what can middle school students do the change them? These types of questions lead students to critically discuss the text while they provide evidence of the text to back up their different perspectives.

Rose discovers that her dad found Rain, and the dog ultimately doesn't belong to her. Rose learns to advocate for herself and make a tough decision on her own without parental support. Across the novel, Rose learns to use her verbal skills to effectively communicate with her dad, uncle, teachers, and her peers. She learns to be patient with others as she expresses her thoughts and opinions. Her dad ultimately gives Rose up as

Uncle Weldon accepts guardianship over Rose. He seeks to understand Rose on her own terms.

As a middle school student, how would you handle making a decision that was in contrary to your parent's decision-making? If you were in Rose's position would you be able to return a dog to an original owner if you truly loved the dog? How can you support students that are learning to effectively communicate in another language or verbally in your class? Do you take a supportive stance or are you mean? These questions can assist adolescents as they think about exceptionality and the role difference plays within their middle school world.

Inclusion

The context of how inclusion is implemented influences how it is defined. In a school or classroom context, inclusion means educating students with exceptionalities in the classroom of their typical peers (Heward, 2013). The benefits and challenges of inclusion have been extensively investigated (Kaufman & Badar, 2014; Jones, 2013) with critical analyses of the benefits and challenges for students with and without exceptionalities. Inclusion promotes the development of a community where diversity is the norm rather than the exception (Skrtic, 1994).

The promotion of an inclusive environment occurs when students with and without exceptionalities participate in shared educational experiences with the individual supports outlined per IDEA (Giangreco, 2011). Exposure and participation in an inclusive environment can result in gains in academic and social skills as well as preparation for living in community (Karagiannis, Stainback, & Stainback, 1996). Given the board scope of inclusion, literature selection could focus on themes of both inclusion and exclusion. By identifying the characteristics of what is exclusive in a given environment, the aspects of inclusion may become more evident which is the creation of an environment that is adaptive to and supportive of everyone.

Literature Examples with a Focus on Aspects of Inclusion

Out of my mind (Draper, 2010) is an example of a novel that provides the reader with an in-depth description of the challenges and benefits of inclusion. Melody has cerebral palsy, and her complexities are written about with realism as the reader is exposed to the strengths and weaknesses of inclusion and exclusion. It also addresses all four of the dimensions in the development of a critical stance.

Eleven-year-old Melody is very intelligent, but she certainly struggles in showing what she knows as she has no way of communicating her knowledge verbally. Melody states, "When I try to talk, the words are exploding in my brain, but all that comes out are meaningless sounds and squeaks" (p. 87). She is frequently frustrated when teachers move in and out of her self-contained special education classroom and continually use lower-level instructional strategies that one would use with preschool students. Many of the teachers frequently make incorrect assumptions about what Melody knows. In the beginning of the novel, Melody rarely ventures out of her self-contained classroom. It feels as if the room is a prison to Melody, as she is not exposed to fifth grade learning material and her peers. The room is viewed as a safe-haven when Melody is mainstreamed into fifth grade and she cannot control her physical mobility and she needs a reprieve from concentrating so hard on fitting in physically with her peers.

In order for middle school students to critically examine this text, we promote that they examine the four dimensions of critical literacy (Lewison, Flint, & Van Sluys, 2002). Middle school students can use this book within a literature circle discussion to closely examine Melody's plight of being placed into a special education room and moving into the fifth grade room with her peers. Students should be challenged to think about Melody and the reactions of the fifth graders who befriend her and humiliate her. Using another dimension, interrogating multiple viewpoints could assist middle school students in discussing the position of Melody. How would it feel to have so many important things to say and contribute and yet know that no one could understand you? Or, how would it feel to not be able to eat socially with your peers because you could not eat without the assistance of a support person? In the case of Melody, she is able to use her medi-talker to communicate and participate in the official competition but she is locked out of going to Washington, D.C., because no one stood up for her or ultimately wanted to viewed as the team with the "special girl." Melody is excluded in many smaller incidents within the story.

Middle school students could also discuss the importance of institutional systems and how they support and exclude students with differences. In the case of the educational system and school, how does school offer support and resources for students that need assistance? In the case of Melody, how did the school fail her as a learner, and how did the school use their resources to support her as a learner? In the case of the substitute, who taught Melody skills that she already learned, in what ways could schools rethink these types of occurrences? In the critical literacy dimension of taking action and promoting advocacy, how did Melody learn to advocate herself? Why was it important for her to analyze her action and stand up for herself to her teachers, peers, and family members? Melody's mom took several action steps with the school as she actively advocated for equity for Melody in terms of Melody achieving success within the classroom. In addition, Melody's neighbor held Melody to high standards and taught Melody to use her intelligence in school and not get caught up in some of the inequities she experienced in the social interactions with her peers. Adolescents then should consider how they can take critical stances to advocate for peers with differences and how it might feel to overcome learning with differences.

Self-Determination

Self-determination has historical roots in political science and philosophy. There are various dimensions that define self-determination and it is associated with empowerment and self-governance. For the purposes of its application to individuals with disabilities, a functional definition is to provide individuals with the support needed to allow them to achieve their desired goals and enhance their quality of life (Wehmeyer, 2002).

Self-determination evolves over an individual's lifespan. Individuals become self-determined. The introduction to self-determination and ongoing use of the various elements of self-determination are based on purposeful and intentional instructional programming and is aligned with the learning experiences. There are multiple elements to self-determination and individuals attain or demonstrate self-determined behavior through the use of elements such as choice making, decision making, problem solving, goal-setting, and self-awareness and self-knowledge Wehmeyer, Agran, & Hughes (2000).

Of the various elements of self-determination, there are three key aspects of the elements that have a cumulative effect and can be incorporated at multiple stages of an individual's life: choice making, decision-making, and goal setting. With the opportunity to make choices at a young age, the individual experiences and recognizes the same constraints and options of a given choice as experienced by all people. With age, decision-making skills are incorporated in choices, and a child experiences the complexities associated with making a decision while promoting the understanding of consequences. Finally, those choices and decisions impact selection and pursuit of individual goals. Supporting an individual in making short and long term goals and creating plans with the opportunity to reevaluate and refine individual plans further promotes self-determination.

In considering how to introduce or promote self-determination through literature, it is important to reinforce the key aspects. Consider literature choices that have characters that make both simple and complex choices. The types of choices may be based on the age of the character or the individual abilities or challenges that the character is presented with in a given situation.

Literature Examples with Self-Determination

In *Fish in a Tree* (Hunt, 2015), Ally is positioned as the dumb student that cannot read. Her peers are very aware about this fact about her, and two mean girls take every moment to remind her that she is stupid and cannot comprehend texts effectively. Ally uses her intelligence to effectively maneuver out of literacy tasks and instead frequently misbehaves to miss having to tackle reading or writing tasks. Ally states, "I can't think of anything worse than having to describe myself. I'd rather write about something more positive. Like throwing up at your own birthday party" (p. 2). A new teacher, Mr. Daniels, enters the classroom and sees the possibilities in every student. He discovers that Ally has dyslexia and advocates for her to receive support from several reading teachers. He slowly works to show Ally that she can answer questions, use her art creatively in class, solve complex math problems, and think critically in problem-solving exercises. It takes time for Ally to trust him and herself as she slowly learns to read and control her impulsivity.

Reading and writing are skills that we take for granted. For many of us, we do not even remember how we learned to read and write. For Ally, she knows that she cannot do it and is reminded every day, as she has to creatively think about how she can save face as she conquers her constant anxiety regarding literacy. Middle school students can discuss how they learned to read and write. Questions these groups could consider are, How would you cope with a learning difference? What would you do if you learned differently? How would you cope with ridicule from your peers? Would you tolerate the ridicule or fight back? As part of examining multiple viewpoints, middle school students can contemplate what similar experiences they may have with reading and writing or different content areas.

Sociopolitical issues could include exploring the institution of school and how could schooling allow a sixth grader with dyslexia to fall through the cracks as a learner? Why did so many teachers miss Ally's plight as a learner? Why was the blame for learning placed on her parents and ultimately Ally? In this case, Mr. Daniels took the time to research and observe Ally over time. He wasn't fooled by her identity as a troublemaker. He took the time to reflect upon her as a learner. He consistently advocated for Ally and repositioned her in the classroom as someone with knowledge. He didn't always make the correct decisions on her behalf, but he cared enough to take the correct steps to help Ally see herself as a reader and writer. Adolescents can think about how they can look beyond themselves and support others that may have learning differences. They can work at developing an empathetic stance toward others.

Advocacy

Advocacy has multiple definitions and applications. Advocacy is essential support that is either provided by another (e.g., parent, peer, teacher) or self-support, self-advocacy. Areas where advocacy concentrates on the needs of exceptional populations include the implementation and oversight of official policy and mandates, and equal protection of rights. An essential tenet of advocacy is participation.

The role or position of advocacy can be based on the needs or supports of an individual or a whole group or community. Advocacy is embedded within the other themes as it prompts for engagement and exploration of the "difficult questions" about the nature of exceptionality per the IDEA categories, the support and inclusion of individuals with exceptionality in educational settings in the workplace and in the community, and providing options for individuals with exceptionality to enhance their quality of life (Ferguson & Nusbaum, 2012).

Identifying literature that draws on situations where either advocacy has been demonstrated or is needed include relationship development, finding commonalities, situations that require compromise, or the need for expertise and communication (Whitby, Marx, McIntire, & Wienke, 2013). In any of these scenarios or situations, the literature selection should provide the reader with choices that be explored to bring about social change.

Literature Example with Advocacy

In *Navigating Early* (Vanderpool, 2013), Jack quickly becomes friends with Early Auden. Early Auden has isolated himself from the other boys within the boarding school. Early is easily angered and frustrated with the structure of school and learning. He frequently finds himself on the outside and is challenged socially with understanding the expressive components of communication. Early doesn't have a genuine desire to get along with others. In addition, Jack quickly positions himself in the school as another odd character, which ultimately sits on the edge of the outside. He wants to belong, yet his grief from losing his mom consumes him at odd times as he grapples with getting along with his peers.

Auden reaches out to Jack by teaching him how to steer and navigate a boat. Both boys are strange, and it is their strangeness that brings them together as they set out on an adventure during their spring break on Auden's boat. Jack thinks, "Still, the question remained. Was he straight-jacket strange or just go-off-by-yourself-at recess-and put-bugs-in-your-nose strange" (p. 28). Their relationship has twists and turns, showing them the benefits of advocating for each other. Jack tries to show Auden how to fit in with his peers. In turn, Auden pushes Jack outside of his comfort zone.

In terms of critical literacy, taking a stand is the dimension that fits this book the best. Both boys take turns advocating for each other. They push each other to take action as they stand up to the peer pressure and the events in the story. Critical stances within literature circles could facilitate conversations around taking a stand within relationships with people that may be outside of your peer group. Adolescents could use textual evidence to discuss the importance of advocating for a friend that has an exceptionality.

Inclusive Classroom to Inclusive Communities: Implementation Considerations

Because of the range of options of implementation and focus, literature circles can provide teachers the opportunity not only to introduce, but also explore exceptionality in depth and encourage students to move toward developing critical stances. There is a range of literature to understand the four themes discussed: aspects of exceptionality, inclusion, self-determination, and advocacy. The themes are unique, but there is a commonality to them that allows the teacher to identify a literature selection and make a determination of how one or more of the themes applies to the selection.

The effect of exploring exceptionality using this strategy promotes the development of a critical stance that can have both short and long term impact on the reader. Each dimension of critical literacy (Lewison, Flint, & Van Sluys, 2012) either challenges or encourages the reader to take action on a topic that addresses exceptionality through the core concepts of disability studies (Ferguson & Nusbaum, 2012). One of these core concepts includes the development of the foundational aspects of exceptionality. The literature identified in the aspects of exceptionality can be means to build this foundation. Through literature circles, a teacher can progress through the four identified themes. The understanding of a specific disability category can lead to a better understanding of the barriers and benefits of inclusion, which furthers the process of self-determination and advocacy.

These themes discussed through the four dimensions of critical literacy promote the infusion of exceptionality across content areas, particularly science, social studies, history and art. By expanding the discussion of exceptionality, exploration can occur in multidimensional, interdisciplinary, personal and critical ways (Brantlinger, 2006). But only through questioning and discussion can exploration and understanding occur and ultimately lead student to develop critical stances that creates a wider view of exceptionalities.

Appendix

* *Absolutely Almost* (Graff, 2014)
  Area of Exceptionality: Learning Disabilities
  Critical Dimension: Disrupting the commonplace; Interrogating multiple viewpoints

* *Blue Fish* (Schmatz, 2013)
  Area of Exceptionality: Learning Disabilities
  Critical Dimension: Disrupting the commonplace; Interrogating multiple viewpoints

- *Fish in a Tree* (Hunt, 2015)
  Area of Exceptionality: Learning Disabilities
  Critical Dimension: Interrogating multiple viewpoints; Focusing of sociopolitical issues

- *Handbook of Dragonslayers* (Haskell, 2013)
  Area of Exceptionality: Other Health Impairment
  Critical Dimension: Disrupting the commonplace; Interrogating multiple viewpoints

- *The Meaning of Maggie* (Sovern, 2014)
  Area of Exceptionality: Learning Disability; Other Health Impairment
  Critical Dimension: Disrupting the commonplace; Interrogating multiple viewpoints

- *mockingbird* (Erskine, 2010)
  Area of Exceptionality: Autism/Asperger's
  Critical Dimension: Disrupting the commonplace; Interrogating multiple viewpoints

- *Navigating Early* (2013)
  Area of Exceptionality: Autism
  Critical Dimension: Taking action and promoting social justice

- *Nest* (2014)
  Area of Exceptionality: Other Health Impairment
  Critical Dimension: Disrupting the commonplace; Interrogating multiple viewpoints

- *Out of My Mind* (Draper, 2010)
  Area of Exceptionality: Other Health Impairment; Inclusion
  Critical Dimension: Disrupting the commonplace; Focusing of sociopolitical issues; Interrogating multiple viewpoints; Taking action and promoting social justice

- *Paperboy* (Vawter, 2013)
  Area of Exceptionality: Speech Impairment
  Critical Dimension: Disrupting the commonplace; Interrogating multiple viewpoints; Focusing of sociopolitical issues

- *Rain Reign* (Martin, 2014)
  Area of Exceptionality: Autism
  Critical Dimension: Disrupting the commonplace; Focusing of sociopolitical issues

- *The Running Dream* (Van Draanen, 2011)
  Area of Exceptionality: Other Health Impairment

Critical Dimension: Disrupting the commonplace; Interrogating multiple viewpoints

* *The Wild Book* (Engle, 2014)
  Area of Exceptionality: Learning Disabilities
  Critical Dimension: Focusing of sociopolitical issues; Taking action and promoting social justice

* *Wonder* (Palacio, 2012)
  Area of Exceptionality: Other Health Impairment
  Critical Dimension: Disrupting the commonplace; Interrogating multiple viewpoints; Taking action and promoting social justice

* *Wonderstruck* (Selznick, 2011)
  Area of Exceptionality: Hearing Impairment
  Critical Dimension: Disrupting the commonplace; Interrogating multiple viewpoints

REFERENCES

Beers, K., & Probst, R. (2012). *Notice and Note-Taking: Strategies for Close Reading.* Portsmouth, NH: Heinemann.

Bloome, D., Carter, S.P., Christian, B.M., Otto, S., & Shuart-Faris, N. (2005). *Discourse Analysis and the Study of Classroom Language and Literacy Events: A Microethnographic Perspective.* Mahwah, NJ: Lawrence Erlbaum.

Bloome, D., & Egan-Robertson, A. (1993). The social construction of intertextuality in classroom reading and writing lessons. *Reading Research Quarterly, 28(4)*, 304–333.

Brantlinger, E.A. (ed.). (2006). *Who Benefits from Special Education? Remediating (Fixing) Other People's Children.* Mahwah, NJ: Lawrence Erlbaum.

Campbell-Whatley, G. (2006). Why am I in special education and what can I do about it? Helping students develop self-determination. *Teaching Exceptional Children Plus, 3(2).* Retrieved May 2015 from http://escholarship.bc.edu/education/tecplus/vol3/iss2/art4.

Fain, J.G. (2008). "Um, they weren't thinking about their thinking": Children's talk about issues of oppression. *Multicultural Perspectives, 10(4)*, 201–208.

Ferguson, P., & Nusbaum, E. (2012). "Disability studies? What is it and what difference does it make?" *Research and Practice for Persons with Severe Handicaps, 37(2)*, 70–80.

Foss, A. (2002). Peeling the onion: Teaching critical literacy with students of privilege. *Language Arts, 79(5)*, 393–403.

Freire, P. (1970). *Pedagogy of the Oppressed.* New York: Continuum International.

Gee, J. (1999). *An Introduction to Discourse Analysis.* New York: Routledge.

_____. (2002). A sociocultural perspective on early literacy development. In D. Dickinson & S. Newman (eds.), *Handbook of Early Literacy Research* (30–42). New York: The Guilford Press.

Giangreco, M.F. (2011). Educating students with severe disabilities: Foundational concepts and practices. In M.E. Snell & F. Brown (eds.), *Instruction of Students with Severe Disabilities* (7th ed., p. 4). Upper Saddle River, NJ: Pearson.

Goffman, E. (1959). *The Presentation of Self in Everyday Life.* New York: Doubleday.

Heward, W. (2013). The purpose and promise of special education. In W. Heward (ed.), *Exceptional Children: An Introduction to Special Education* (17–32). Boston: Pearson.

Hornby, G. (2014). From inclusion and special education to inclusive special education. In *Inclusive Special Education* (19–40). New York: Springer.

Jones, P. (ed). (2013). *Bringing Insider Perspectives into Inclusive Teacher Learning: Potentials and Challenges for Educational Professionals.* New York: Routledge.

Karagiannis, A., Stainback, S., & Stainback, W. (1996). Historical overview of Inclusion. In S. Stainback & W. Stainback (eds.), *Inclusion: A Guide for Educators* (17–28). Baltimore: Brookes.

Kauffman, J., & Badar, J. (2014) Instruction, not inclusion, should be the central issue in special education: An alternative view from the USA. *Journal of International Special Needs Education 17(1),* 13–20.

Leake, D., & Skouge, J. (2014). Introduction to the special issue: "Self-determination" as a social construct: Cross-cultural considerations. *The Review of Disability Studies: An International Journal, 8(1).*

Lehman, C., & Roberts, K. (2013). *Falling in Love with Close Reading: Lessons for Analyzing Texts—and Life.* Portsmouth, NH: Heinemann.

Lewison, M., Flint, A., & Van Sluys, K. (2002). Taking on critical literacy: The journey of newcomers and novices. *Language Arts, 79(5),* 382–392.

Martinez-Roldan, C.M. (2003). Building worlds and identities: Case study of the role of narratives in bilingual literature discussions. *Research in the Teaching of English 37(4),* 491–526.

McLaughlin, M., & DeVoogd, G. (2004). *Critical Literacy: Enhancing Students' Comprehension of Text.* New York: Scholastic.

Office of Special Education Programs, Data Accountability Center. http://tadnet.pub lic.tadnet.org/pages/712. Accessed 21 July 2014.

Pazey, B.L., & Cole, H.A. (2013). The role of special education training in the development of socially just leaders building an equity consciousness in educational leadership programs. *Educational Administration Quarterly, 49(2),* 243–271.

Rogoff, B. (1990). *Apprenticeship in Thinking: Cognitive Development in Social Context.* New York: Oxford University Press.

Short, K.G., & Pierce, M.K. (1998). *Talking About Books: Creating Literate* Communities, 2d ed. Portsmouth, NH: Heinemann.

Simmons, T.J., Luft, P., & Baer, R.M. (2013). *Transition Planning for Secondary Students with Disabilities.* Boston: Pearson.

Skrtic, T.M., Sailor, W., & Gee, K. (1996). Voice, collaboration, and inclusion democratic themes in educational and social reform initiatives. *Remedial and Special Education, 17(3),* 142–157.

Society for Disability Studies (n.d.). *SDS mission.* Retrieved from http://disstudies. org/about/mission-and-history.

Street, B. (2005). Literacy, technology, and multimodality: Implications for pedagogy and curriculum. Paper presented at the 55th Annual Meeting of the National Reading Conference, Miami, FL.

U.S. Department of Education. U.S. Office of Special Education and Rehabilitative Services (2010). Thirty five years of progress in educating children with disabilities through IDEA. Washington, D.C., 2010.

Vasquez, V., Tate, S., & Harste, J.C. (2013). *Negotiating Critical Literacies with Pre Service and In-Service Teachers.* New York: Routledge Press.

Wehmeyer, M.L., Agran, M., & Hughes, C. (2000). A national survey of teacher's promotion of self-determination and student-directed learning. *The Journal of Special Education, 34(2),* 58–68.

_____. (2002). *Providing Access to General Curriculum: Teaching Students with Mental Retardation.* Baltimore: Paul Brookes.

_____. (2015). Framing the future self-determination. *Remedial and Special Education, 36(1),* 20–23.

_____. (2015, February 11). Michael Wehmeyer: History of the disability movement in the United States [video file]. Retrieved from https://www.youtube.com/watch?v=v9k66lWb0-w.

Weiss, N. (n.d.). Recommended books about the disability experience. Retrieved from http://www.nlcdd.org/resources-books-movies-disability.html.

Young, C. (2011). Taking a critical stance in the classroom. Retrieved from http://www.thebestclass.org/crit.html.

Zigmond, N., Kloo, A., & Lemons, C.J. (2011). IEP Team decision-making for more inclusive assessments: Policies, percentages, and personal decisions. In S. Elliott, R. Kettler, P. Beddow, & A. Kirz (eds.), *Handbook of accessible achievement tests for all students* (69–82). New York: Springer.

Zigmond, N. (2003). Where should students with disabilities receive special education services? Is one place better than another. *The Journal of Special Education, 37,* 193–199.

LITERATURE FOCUSED ON DIFFERENCE FOR MIDDLE SCHOOL ADOLESCENTS

Draper, Sharon. (2011). *Out of My Mind.* New York: Atheneum Books for Young Readers.

Engle, M. (2014). *The Wild Book.* New York: HMH Books for Young Readers.

Erskine, K. (2010). *mockingbird.* New York: Penguin Young Readers Group.

Esther, E. (2014). *Nest.* New York: Wendy Lamb Books.

Graff, Lisa. (2014). *Absolutely Almost.* New York: Philomel Books.

Haskell, Merrie. (2013). *Handbook for Dragon Slayers.* New York: HarperCollins Children's Books.

Hunt, Lynda M. (2015). *Fish in a Tree.* New York: Penguin Group.

Martin, Ann. M. (2014). *Rain Reign.* New York: Feiwel and Friends, an Imprint of Macmillan.

Palacio, R.J. (2012). *Wonder.* New York: Alfred A. Knopf.

Schmatz, Pat. (2013). *Bluefish.* Somerville, MA: Candlewick Press.

Selznick, Brian. (2011). *Wonderstruck.* New York: Scholastic Press.

Sovern, Megan Jean. (2014). *The Meaning of Maggie.* San Francisco: Chronicle Books.

Vanderpool, C. (2013). *Navigating Early.* New York: Delacorte Press.

Van Draanen, W. (2011). *The Running Dream.* New York: Ember.

Vawter, V. (2013). *Paperboy.* New York: Delacorte Press.

Teaching and Reading Wonder and Marcelo in the Real World with Critical Eyes

Abbye Meyer *and* Emily Wender

Popular young adult novels, R.J. Palacio's *Wonder* (2012) and Francisco X. Stork's *Marcelo in the Real World* (2009) are emerging as classroom favorites and as praised examples of texts about disability. *Wonder* is already being used by educators to teach kindness and acceptance, and the novel's website consequently features a section for teachers; in January 2015, *Time* included *Wonder* in the top twenty-five of its list of "100 Best Young-Adult Books" of "all-TIME" ("Our All-Time Favorite," 2015, p. 61). Also well received, *Marcelo* received a Schneider Family Book Award, given to "honor an author or illustrator for a book that embodies an artistic expression of the disability experience for child and adolescent audiences," in 2010 and has become a staple in classrooms ("Schneider," 2015). Though reviewers have noted that *Marcelo* is one of an emerging category of novels with protagonists with spectrum disorders, *Marcelo* has been celebrated for its complexity.

Both novels approach disability and adolescence in engaging ways, presenting middle- and high-school teachers with opportunities to explore literary concepts while simultaneously challenging students to think creatively and critically about disability. Because understandings of disability are continuing to grow and change—disability studies itself is still an emerging academic field, and the disability rights movement, as noted by Davis (2006), "is at best a first- or second-wave enterprise" (p. 231)— teaching these novels can be difficult.

Quite noticeably, both novels present their protagonists' conditions in medicalized language, and both novels begin by immediately throwing their protagonists in normative, mainstream environments after they have been living otherwise ignorant of popular opinions, perceptions, and treatments of disability and difference. This change in environments forces readers to encounter common socialized behaviors and treatments of people living with disabilities. Understood through a disability-studies lens, both texts position their protagonists primarily as traditional, common literary "freaks"—characters marked by difference who ultimately serve to inspire others or teach others about acceptance. Neither text, however, feels entirely comfortable relegating its protagonist to such a demeaning, sidelined role; the ways in which the novels play with the traditional role of literary freak are discussed in this article and may provoke critically important classroom discussion.

The novels are far from perfect in regard to political messages, but they should not be ignored in response; rather, exploring how disability is treated in the texts allows teachers to introduce students to critical theories and to the important notion that literary texts do more than entertain. In this chapter, we offer current literary and political readings of how Palacio and Stork have represented disabilities in their texts, acknowledging how both texts simultaneously suggest progressive and harmful understandings of disability. Part of this both/and approach emerges partly from our knowledge of teaching middle and high school, partly from our appreciation that these texts include voices of adolescents with disabilities, and partly from our belief that these texts are being and could be read in damaging ways. We worry that readers might walk away from these texts with simplistic and even dangerous ideas about disability without purposeful maneuvers by a teacher. Ultimately, we argue that middle, high school, and even college students will be challenged by these novels if teachers push them to read both with and against their various and sometimes contradictory messages of disability.

How We See Freak Characters in (Young Adult) Literature

In Western literature, including young adult literature, the freak is perhaps the most common and consistent representation of a disabled character: marked as non-normative, usually supporting and underdeveloped, and functioning to help other characters develop. Garland-Thomson (1997) chronicles this shallow use of "corporeal otherness" in literature that forces biologically different characters simply to "operate as spectacles, eliciting responses from other characters" (p. 10, p. 9). Particularly in regard to child and adolescent characters with disabilities, the freak character often emerges either as a kind of monster or as a kind of innocent, special child. Indeed, Garland-Thomson (1996) explains that those who are "visually different" have been "known since antiquity as 'monsters' and more recently as 'freaks'" (p. 1), and Carey (2009) characterizes a similar "special child role," most typically a child with an intellectual disability, who is "exceptionally moral," "viewed as unfailingly loyal, innocent, and selfless," and who illustrates goodness (p. 7). Both monsters and special children, with their marked identities (either bodies or explicitly marked personalities), provoke moral growth, pity, sympathy, and kindness among other characters and readers; too often, they are portrayed too shallowly and simply depicted to receive empathy. These freak characters allow nondisabled peers and readers to indulge in curiosity and horror, as well as to find self-definition in seeing what they (presumably) are not. Those who stare may in fact be growing as individuals and reconsidering ideas of what constitutes personhood, but perhaps without regard to the personhood of their stares' objects.

In *Wonder*, we meet the freak character as a "monster." *Wonder* tells the tale of Auggie, a fifth-grader with "'single nucleotide deletion mutations' that made a war on his face" and other genetic differences that are "just incredibly bad luck" and cause very noticeable physical deformities (Palacio, 2012, p. 104, p. 105). In the text, Auggie prepares to and then attends his first year in school, a private school in Manhattan, where he ultimately teaches others about acceptance, tolerance, and kindness. With his severely deformed face and body, Auggie is a "monster" who both attracts stares and repels encounters (p. 22).

Similarly, with his overwhelmingly "childlike" and innocent demeanor, that which "makes …[him] who … [he is]," Marcelo—a seventeen-year-old with a spectrum disorder in *Marcelo in the Real World*—is characterized as a simple child who puzzles others and receives patronizing treatment (Stork, 2009, p. 29). Narrated entirely by Marcelo, the novel begins in the summertime, when his father dictates that he will work at his father's law firm in order to "be in a normal environment"; until the book's opening, Marcelo has had a home at Paterson, the private school for students with disabilities (Stork, 2009, p. 20). At the end of summer, if Marcelo has satisfied his father's command to follow "the rules of the real world," he will be allowed to choose whether to return to Paterson or enter a mainstream public school; if Marcelo does not succeed, he will be forced to attend the public school. Thus, the plot is set up to ask whether or not Marcelo can rise above his role as a "special child."

While almost all freak characters are necessarily secondary characters and rendered simplistically in order to provoke emotional reactions, a number of contemporary young adult novels—including both *Wonder* and *Marcelo*—are beginning to push the bounds by which freaks, like all disabled characters, have been restricted.[1] A politically powerful genre, young adult literature rarely shies away from societal and personal struggles and problems, particularly in regard to human rights; illustrated by the American Library Association's creation of the Schneider Family Book Award in 2004, these first years of the twenty-first century have seen young adult novels flock to address disability, both as a personal identity and as a larger civil rights movement. For instance, one of the strongest young adult texts focused on disability, Harriet McBryde Johnson's *Accidents of Nature* (2006) argues unabashedly for societal changes, civil rights, and progressive politics. Johnson's semi-autobiographical text about a camp for disabled teenagers specifically calls for disability to be accepted and celebrated, rather than ignored or changed; for people with disabilities to resist patronizing treatment, such as being expected to "show spirit in just being alive; persistence in not curling up and dying; determination in doing ordinary things; courage in showing [their] faces in public"; and for unity and inclusivity within the disabled community, "The Crip Nation," in order to create a strong, cohesive-though-heterogeneous group to fight for civil rights and reject "the views of our oppressors" (p. 207, p. 82, p. 111).

Neither *Wonder* or *Marcelo* is as politically conscious as McBryde's novel. However, even though both Auggie and Marcelo clearly fit the classic definitions of a freak character, both are also the protagonists of their stories, and both freak characters narrate—Auggie only at times—their stories; such positioning challenges longstanding literary traditions and portrayals of monsters and special children. Thus, while neither overtly political or closely aligned with disability-rights movements, both *Wonder* and *Marcelo* challenge popular perceptions of disabilities, as well as challenge their protagonists' positions as freak characters.

How We Approach Reading with Critical Eyes

Literary theory, as used in our analyses, is not new to the high-school classroom, or even many middle school classrooms. Appleman (2009) demonstrates how literary theory can fuel students' critical thinking about their own worlds, making the case that literary theories enable student readers to "sharpen [their] vision" (p. 4). Perhaps most important to our purposes in this chapter, Appleman argues that theoretical approaches "recontextualize the familiar and comfortable, making us reappraise them"; at the same time, "they make the strange seem oddly familiar" (p. 4). Reading novels through a disability-studies framework—a kind of literary theory based heavily in feminism, queer theories, and Marxist theories—we must "recontextualize the familiar and comfortable" by considering and questioning what we consider "normal" and "best." At its most fundamental, a disability-studies approach forces us to recognize and question ideologies that are so deeply ingrained in our perceptions of the world that we need help rendering them explicit and visible. We are referring to our binary constructions of being normal or different, of being able or unable, of being independent or dependent, of living a worthwhile life or a life we cannot help but pity.

To do this work as readers, we embrace the types of questions literary theorists have been using for decades. For example, when describing her feminist lens, Paul (1998) captures how her reading has had to shift: "As a teacher and critic I am learning, slowly, to take notice of texts and ideas I couldn't see or didn't notice before; to question the approaches to analysis I used to accept as 'natural.' The questions I employ are changing too" (p. 16). Many of Paul's questions are echoed in our own readings in this chapter, such as "Whose story is this?"; "Who speaks? And who is silenced?"; "Who acts? And who is acted upon?"; "Who looks? And who is observed?" (p. 16). The questions we apply to these novels specifically emerge from a disability studies perspective: How does the text destabilize normality, and how does it not? How does it approach disability as a category? (Is it inclusive? Is it rooted in the body? Does it acknowledge and appreciate difference?) How does it give voice to the complex experiences of adolescents with disabilities? These questions support our shared belief that literary representations can shape, as well as expose, readers' perceptions of the world (p. 16). As teachers, we have an ethical responsibility to pay attention to the messages those representations send to our students.

When we discuss reading "with" the world of the text, we are specifically attuned to the progressive and useful messages being delivered about disability. What civil rights issues might the text be asking us to consider? How is the author confronting problematic stereotypes? How is the author rewriting traditional characterizations of disability? How is the disabled community positioned as inclusive and deserving of humanity and rights?

Ultimately, what can we learn from and celebrate through this author's representations of disability?

At the same time, we model and invite readers to "read against the grain, to read critically, to turn back, … to ask questions [the author] believe[s] might come as a surprise, to look for the limits of [the author's] vision" (Bartholomae, Petrosky, & Waite, 2014, p. 10). We provide both ideas and tools to enable this kind of "dialogue" with the text (p. 10), and we ultimately suggest that students' awareness of the world—how they see "normal" challenged every day, for example—can aid them in this speaking back and even disagreeing.

Ultimately, as Thein, Sulzer, and Schmidt have argued (2013), "if we want to engage students in democratic reading, thinking, and discussion about their own lives and those of others, we must become critical consumers of YA literature and encourage students to do the same" (p. 58). As teachers, we must allow ourselves to read both with and against the texts we teach, and we must work to empower our students to do the same. The following literary analyses are meant to assist with such work, and they provide the background needed for teaching the lesson plans and discussion questions that conclude the chapter.

How We Teach and Read *Wonder* with Critical Eyes

Reading with Wonder

Though Auggie's character in Palacio's *Wonder* quite clearly inhabits the role of freak—a monster who is "probably worse" looking than his readers suspect (Palacio, 2012, p. 3)—*Wonder* offers a few progressive messages about understanding and living with disabilities. The text begins to blur lines between primary and secondary characters by allowing Auggie occasional first-person narration, the text emphatically teaches its characters and readers to exhibit kindness, and the text begins to question social definitions and treatments of disability.

Even though Auggie does not narrate the entire novel, he does speak for himself for a full three-eighths of it ("Part One: August"[p. 1], "Part Six: August" [p. 205], and "Part Eight: August" [p. 249]). As the only narrator to receive three parts, including the first and last, one could argue that Auggie is indeed the principal character, and all others secondary; it is not only a story *about* Auggie, but in three sections, it is Auggie's story, and he begins where it matters most: "I know I'm not an ordinary ten-year-old kid" (p. 3). However, because so many pages are focused almost exclusively on how other narrators perceive Auggie and are defined or changed by Auggie, he may function as "the Sun" in others' solar systems, but the reader—in five of the eight sections—reads with those "asteroids and comets" (p. 82). In that way, Auggie ultimately functions to illustrate the emotional and moral lives of every other character.

Palacio's narrative strategy ultimately takes control of the story away from Auggie, and we are forced to consider whether *Wonder*'s "appeal relies not on the individual strivings of the main character but on a vision of a community transforming itself" (Wheeler, 2013, p. 338). While Wheeler (2013) argues that this is representative of "social change," she fails to consider that this text's "main character" deserves a story of his "individual strivings" (p. 338); "*Wonder* shows how the public presence of people with disabilities benefits a whole society" (p. 335), but we must question why it is Auggie's responsibility to serve as a public presence for the benefit of others. Such a reading of the text, which is supported by Auggie's presence within five characters' narratives, only reinforces traditional uses of freak characters, functioning to benefit nondisabled characters and readers and to improve the moral compasses of communities.

One of the reasons that *Wonder* has been so successfully and enthusiastically received by educators and readers is its emphasis on kindness; indeed, the novel—through its plot and through English teacher Mr. Browne's prominent use of "precepts," or "RULES ABOUT REALLY IMPORTANT THINGS!" especially about "WHO WE ARE!" (Palacio, 2012, pp. 46, 47)—explicitly urges its readers to "choose kind[ness]" above all else (p. 48). In addition to this important and strongly delivered message, which of course applies to all students and all people, including those with disabilities, *Wonder* also uses its plotline so that Auggie begins to question what it means to be different or to be disabled.

While Auggie's narrative voice exhibits very little pride in his identity as someone with a disability, *Wonder* places Auggie in the position to begin to question his role as a marginalized character who allows others to grow. Auggie makes clear to us that he understands, at least in part, his problematic role at school and in his family—and consequently in his text. He listens to his principal describe the Henry Ward Beecher Medal, and of course, the medal goes to Auggie, the "student whose quiet strength has carried up the most hearts," and who is able to encompass "something like greatness" (p. 304). In response, Auggie almost articulates the problem with using him to carry up others' hearts and to improve the school community, before cutting himself off and simply accepting his role:

> I wasn't even sure why I was getting this medal, really.
>
> No, that's not true. I know why.
>
> It's like people you see sometimes, and you can't imagine what it would be like to be that person, whether it's somebody in a wheelchair or somebody who can't talk. Only, I know that I'm that person to other people, maybe to every single person in that whole auditorium.
>
> To me, though, I'm just me. An ordinary kid.
>
> But hey, if they want to give me a medal for being me, that's okay. I'll take it. I didn't destroy the Death Star or anything like that, but I did just get through the fifth grade. And that's not easy, even if you're not me [p. 306].

Though Auggie and *Wonder* finally decide the award is "okay," the simple articulation that the award ought to be questioned does signal an attempt at challenging problematic traditions (p. 306). However, as discussed in greater depth below, we are concerned that the text fails to alert its readers, both teachers and young students, to those problematic traditions.

Reading Against **Wonder**

Notably and consistently throughout *Wonder*, Auggie uses demeaning and self-deprecating jokes as social lubricant. Even though he knows the names people call him—"Rat boy. Freak. Monster. Freddy Krueger. E.T. Gross-out. Lizard face. Mutant" (p. 79)—Auggie faces and expresses enormous hurt when he hears one of his two real friends, Jack, say about him: "If I looked like him, seriously, I think that I'd kill myself" (p. 77). Auggie takes some control of his situation by earning friends through humor, as when he calls himself the inspiration for "Uglydolls," allowing others to laugh both with and at him (p. 209). While Auggie's jokes may indeed dispel tension, they also position Auggie as someone at whom it is acceptable to laugh. When he and Jack laugh about another student's reaction to Auggie, prompting Jack to ask if Auggie is "always going to look this way," and whether he "can't get plastic surgery or something," Auggie "smile[s] and point[s] to [his] face. 'Hello? This *is* after plastic surgery!'" (p. 64). Both laugh so hard that they are reprimanded by a teacher; on the surface, Auggie is having fun, but again, he is positioning himself as not fully human— or at least not one worthy of respect.

Auggie even dismisses his mother with self-deprecating jokes, telling her, "We're kind of like Beauty and the Beast," when she comments that his friend Summer is "very pretty" (p. 56). But such jokes, of course, disguise very real feelings and insecurities that Auggie only occasionally reveals:

> "Why do I have to be so ugly, Mommy?" I whispered.
> "No, baby, you're not..."
> "I know I am."
> She kissed me all over my face. She kissed my eyes that came down too far. She kissed my cheeks that looked punched in. She kissed my tortoise mouth.
> She said soft words that I know were meant to help me, but words can't change my face [p. 60].

His face remains a problem for him throughout the novel, whether accepted or not, and we must wonder if there *are* words—words that suggest pride and acceptance rather than sympathy and denial—that could change his (perception of his) face. As a narrator, Auggie lacks the self-awareness needed to find pride and to suggest more useful words and ways of understanding himself.

Returning to Auggie's presentation with the Henry Ward Beecher medal, we want to emphasize that Auggie must be read as beginning to question his role as an adolescent with a disability, but then stopping. By allowing Auggie to become an actual spectacle, "smiling a big fat happy smile for all the different cameras clicking away," in the aftermath of the award ceremony, the novel again reinforces Auggie's role as a freak, used primarily to serve others (p. 307). As he receives his award, Auggie does consider his role in the school community, but as discussed above, he does not push himself or anyone else to reject or change that role. He does not recognize patronizing or condescending overtones in the principal's praising of him as that "student whose quiet strength has carried up the most hearts," even though he knows that this award traditionally has "acknowledg[ed] volunteerism or service to the school," which Auggie has not done (pp. 303, 304). Further, when he begins to tell us and himself that the award exemplifies his presence at school and in the auditorium as a way for others to "imagine what it would be like to be ... somebody in a wheelchair or somebody who can't talk," nothing in the text prompts readers to want Auggie to continue to push (p. 306). Nothing reminds us how Auggie is being publicly recognized for making his peers question themselves in the very way freak characters have traditionally asked readers to "make sense of ourselves and our world" (Garland-Thomson, 1996, p. 1). Auggie stops himself—as the text stops philosophically with him—and he thinks,

"But hey, if they want to give me a medal for being me, that's okay" (Palacio, 2012, p. 306). As readers, we need to keep pushing and assert that such treatment is *not* okay.

When Auggie takes to the stage, he notes that his receiving the award has made "everyone kind of teary-eyed and wet-cheeked" and that "[e]veryone started taking pictures of" him (p. 307). Eerily, we readers must note further that Auggie, placed on a stage in front of cameras, calls to mind a very familiar and problematic image. Garland-Thomson's description of P.T. Barnum's famous American "freak shows" of the nineteenth and twentieth centuries, which "challenged audiences not only to classify and explain what they saw, but to relate the performance to themselves, to American individual and collective identity" (Garland-Thomson, 1997, p. 58), captures quite accurately Auggie's award presentation: "The freak show is a spectacle, a cultural performance that gives primacy to visual apprehension in creating symbolic codes and institutionalizes the relationship between the spectacle and the spectators. In freak shows, the exhibited body became a text written in boldface to be deciphered according to the needs and desires of onlookers" (p. 60). As much as we may feel moved and pleased that Auggie "wasn't even thinking about [his] face" (Palacio, 2012, p. 307), we must not lose sight of the context of his smile and the spectacle that celebrates the growth of others, while ignoring the lack of growth and agency awarded to Auggie.

Simply, the novel shies away from acceptance and celebration. As the others who populate the text of *Wonder* illustrate their growth and acceptance, their kindness too often turns into pity, sympathy, or simply tolerance. Even as Auggie begins to feel a sense of belonging with his peers, especially after they have defeated older bullies at a campsite, Auggie himself tells us that, as the small and deformed member of the group, his role in the bully story is one of the only things that "always stay[s] the same," "no matter who was telling it" (p. 282): "I got picked on because of my face and Jack defended me, and those guys—Amos, Henry, and Miles—protected me" (p. 282). Whether or not he realizes it, Auggie's only place in the cut-throat social world of fifth grade is that of the "little dude" who attracts sympathy and requires protection and defense (p. 282). The language in *Wonder*, certainly, encourages little more than tolerance. Even Auggie's best friend Jack never grows to love or to celebrate Auggie as a friend who is different; rather, Jack—like the others, we're left to assume—simply "get[s] used to his face" (p. 142). As a visibly different character, Auggie is tolerated in *Wonder*.

In *Wonder*, a text that works tirelessly to humanize its disabled character through kindness and sympathy, disability is explicitly denied, rather than embraced; in no way are we encouraged to see disability as an identity worthy of pride. Throughout the text, characters refer to Auggie with different names, and he never identifies himself as "disabled." Just as Auggie's mother tells him he's not ugly, his principal Mr. Tushman reassures parents in an email that the school "is not an inclusion school" (Palacio, 2012, pp. 60, 162): "As for your other concerns regarding our new student August, please note that he does not have special needs. He is neither disabled, handicapped, nor developmentally delayed in any way, so there was no reason to assume anyone would take issue with his admittance to Beecher Prep—whether it is an inclusion school or not" (p. 163). While Auggie's mother and principal may be attempting to explain to both Auggie and his community that he is not "wrong" or "bad," they do so by denying his disability, rather than by accepting it as a current and important part of his identity. In a quite inclusive definition, Garland-Thomson (1997) defines disability as "an overarching and in some ways artificial category" that certainly includes Auggie's deformities, as "physical differences … chronic and acute illnesses, fatal and progressive diseases, temporary and permanent injuries, and a wide range of bodily characteristics considered disfiguring" (p. 13). The characters in *Wonder*, as well as the text itself, ignore the heterogeneity of Auggie's identity category, and they do not accept the identity as one that can lead to pride and confidence. Rather, people with disabilities are further stigmatized; while we may love Auggie, we are not allowed to love him as someone with a disability. Such an inaccurate and troubling denial of Auggie's obvious differences and disabilities removes all political energy from the text, and it most likely leaves us wondering how to respond to the novel. This wondering, then, must inform our class lessons and discussions; we must encourage younger readers to ask the questions we ask of the text and to consider how Auggie—as a character with a disability—could be more appropriately represented.

How We Teach and Read *Marcelo* with Critical Eyes

Reading with Marcelo

Marcelo in the Real World both explicitly and implicitly offers a number of suggestions about adolescents who live with disabilities. Most progressive and in line with disability rights movements, *Marcelo* questions normality and presents identity as malleable and complex, allows Marcelo to express pride in his difference, and attempts—though somewhat imperfectly—to show that people with disabilities can live full lives with love and sexuality.

Not only are few disabled characters allowed to narrate their own stories, literature "tends to objectify disabled characters by denying them any opportunity for subjectivity or agency" (Garland-Thomson, 1997, p. 11). One of the most powerful attributes of *Marcelo in the Real World*, and indeed one of the biggest reasons to teach it, is that Marcelo, our narrator and protagonist, is disabled. Marcelo's subjectivity as someone with an Autism Spectrum disorder—or as he says, something close to Asperger's Syndrome, though he does not "have many of the characteristics" (Stork, 2009, p. 55)—is compelling and believable. His words guide us to understand, appreciate, and celebrate his experiences of the world. Marcelo tells us early on that he embraces being different but doesn't characterize his difference as abnormal or wrong. When asked about his "cognitive disorder" on his first day of work in his father's office, he reflects to himself on his experiences at Paterson, the school he has attended for students with disabilities:

> Explanations about my condition are based on the assumption that there is something wrong with the way I am, and at Paterson I have learned through the years that it is not helpful to view myself or the other kids there that way. I view myself as different in the way I think, talk, and act, but not as someone who is abnormal or ill. But how do I explain the difference to people? [p. 55].

As Marcelo confides in the reader, he embraces being different, but he doesn't characterize that difference as a problem, a burden, or something deserving of pity. Marcelo, in other words, does not wish to be someone else, in particular a someone who lacks a disability. Given that we live in a culture that "assumes in advance that we all agree: able-bodied identities, able-bodied perspectives are preferable and what we all, collectively, are aiming for," it is significant that though Marcelo does aim to please authorities in his life (his father and his boss, Jasmine, for example), he never confides in the reader a desire to be other than what he is (McRuer, 2002, p. 93). As McRuer explains, our society "demands that people with disabilities embody for others an affirmative answer to the unspoken question, 'Yes, but in the end, wouldn't you rather be like me?'" (p. 93). It is precisely through Marcelo's first person narration that we see Marcelo's rejection of this assumption.

Marcelo's narrative voice also invites readers into how he experiences interactions with others. Frequently, "disabled people must learn to manage relationships from the beginning" in order to "relieve nondisabled people of their discomfort" (Garland-Thomson, 1997, p. 13). With Marcelo— a character who had to "stud[y] small talk" in order to ease others' reactions to his often unusual speech patterns—positioned as our narrator, we experience vividly his awareness of others' judgments of his difference (p. 74). Often assuaging his father Arturo's reactions to his disability, for example, Marcelo is adept at steering the focus away from his disability. At the novel's beginning, when Marcelo returns home from a CT scan, performed by a doctor interested in his "mental music" or "internal music" (IM), Arturo immediately questions him about the session (p. 5). As he answers, Marcelo narrates his constant management of his father: "Talking about the IM, I have learned, makes Arturo nervous. I attempt to change the subject" (p. 18).

Garland would characterize Marcelo's social maneuvers in this scene as an example of how "disabled people must use charm, intimidation, ardor, defense, humor, or entertainment to relieve nondisabled people of their discomfort" (p. 13). She goes on to characterize this performing and/or sidestepping as the acts that force people with disabilities to act as "supplicants and minstrels, striving to create valued representations of ourselves in our relations with the nondisabled community" (p. 13). Though Marcelo does not express a desire to be other than who he is, he continually manages the feelings of others in order to ease the difficulty or nuisance that he senses his presence causes. We appreciate the reality of these moments that Stork offers, and we hope that in watching Marcelo try to turn the gaze away from his disability in order to alleviate others, readers are arrested and disturbed by his efforts. Ultimately, Stork draws our attention to Marcelo's attempts to create a "valued representation" of himself in the eyes of nondisabled others, such as his father.

As evidenced above, Arturo's source of unease is a dilemma for Marcelo and for readers. On the one hand, he seems to reject the notion that Marcelo has a disability, espousing the perspective that with work and the right environment Marcelo can be like everyone else, yet on the other hand, he prepares others to meet Marcelo by explaining that he has a cognitive disorder. Thus, for Arturo, Marcelo's summer experiment is less about trying out the world of grown-ups and more about getting him away from Paterson, the school where Marcelo trains Haflinger ponies and belongs to an inclusive community of teachers, therapists, and "kids with all kinds of disabilities," including visual and hearing impairments, autism, cerebral palsy, multiple sclerosis, spina bifida, Down Syndrome, and attention deficit disorder (p. 10). While Marcelo feels comfortable at Paterson, Arturo places more value in his son experiencing and becoming a part of the "life out there that is healthy and *normal*" (p. 23; emphasis added).

However, even in the cutthroat capitalist environment of Arturo's office, Marcelo encounters other kinds of difference, all of which call into question Arturo's insistence that a normal "real world" exists—separately from Marcelo's Paterson world, which Arturo sheepishly calls "not ... normal" (p. 20). In fact, a number of the book's major characters, all a part of the "real world," are othered in some way: by socioeconomic backgrounds, non-white racial and ethnic identities, and disabilities. Jasmine, for instance, comes from a working-class background, has lost her brother and mother, and—as a young adult herself—is responsible for the care of her father, who is "half gone with dementia" and, consequently, another disabled character (p. 222). Furthermore, Arturo is Mexican-American, and when Marcelo grows embroiled in a legal case at the firm, racial and ethnic identities become more prominent. As readers come to identify the racist, classist, and sexist reality of the "real world" Arturo's law office represents, it seems as if fewer and fewer people fit the remarkably narrow definition of "normal."

Thus, normality, the book suggests, is impossible, an idea theorized by McRuer (2002): "Everyone is virtually disabled, both in the sense that able-bodied norms are intrinsically impossible to embody fully and in the sense that able-bodied status is always temporary, disability being the one identity category that all people will embody if they live long enough" (p. 96). Though McRuer is speaking of the degeneration of the body here, his sentiment that no one can fully represent the abled ideal is a powerful concept within Stork's fictional world. There is no one who perfectly embodies "normal"; in the novel, those who have power and are least othered (wealthy white men) function as the least developed and most archetypal characters, the villains. And as it turns out, their power is not nearly as extensive as it seemed (Marcelo can shatter it quite easily, in fact). Ultimately, Marcelo's disability is simply one way—one way of many—that identity is shaped.

In addition to complicating understandings of identity and difference, the novel positively suggests that there are unique satisfactions in living with a disability. Throughout the novel, we see how Marcelo's special interests, religion and music, stimulate his thinking and help him sort through complicated personal situations. With passionate descriptions of conversations with Rabbi Heschel about religion and spirituality, including enjoyable "questions, especially the hard ones," and his emotional descriptions of the connection he feels between "deep prayer," "playing the piano," and "remembering" (pp. 115, 145), Marcelo echoes Harriet McBryde Johnson (2005), who explains, "We [people with disabilities] enjoy pleasures other people enjoy, and pleasures particularly our own. We have something the world needs" (p. 208). Marcelo's internal music or "remembering" (IM) best captures McBryde's expression of a "pleasure particularly our own"; it causes the most confusion to non-disabled others, yet it is most consistently part of Marcelo's descriptions of enjoyment.

Massumi and Manning's (2014) concept of "neurodiversity" can help readers appreciate Stork's inclusion of the IM as well as Marcelo's defense of it. Through their interviews with individuals on the autism spectrum, Manning and Massumi explain that a widened perception of life's "textures" is one way individuals with autism challenge both the dominance of neurotypical thinking and, they argue, our assumptions that to be human is to be "neurotypical." Though Marcelo is not autistic, his descriptions of "remembering" summon Manning and Massumi's explanations of the increased textures life can present to those on the autism spectrum. "'It is a big watermelon … when the internal music is there, Marcelo is one of the *seeds*,'" Marcelo explains early on in the novel, eager to "expand on the image" that has just occurred to him (p. 3). Such a description may seem odd to some readers and characters in the novel, but it is clear Marcelo finds the IM enriching. Manning and Massumi would point to the feeling of being a watermelon seed as part of his expanded sense of life's textures:

> Texture is patterned, full of contrast and movement, gradients and transitions. It is complex and differentiated. To attend to everything "the same way" is not an inattention to life. It is to pay equal attention to the full range of life's texturing complexity, with an entranced and unhierarchized commitment to the way in which the organic and the inorganic, color, sound smell, and rhythm, perception and emotion, intensely interweave into the "aroundness" of a textured world, alive with difference. It is to experience the fullness of a dance of attention. For all the challenges of autism, this is not without joy [p. 4].

The simple idea that "joy" could be found through perceiving the world without a neurotypical lens is quite revolutionary, as Manning and Massumi explicate. One of the features of this novel that we applaud, then, is Stork's efforts to capture the privileges of the texture Marcelo experiences because of his disability. Some readers may even envy Marcelo's ability to "remember" ("It is actually a very neat sensation," he confides in the reader early on [p. 3]). Stork's novel does not deny that there is joy to be found in Marcelo's perception of the world.

Finally, *Marcelo in the Real World* begins to show that people with disabilities can, in fact, live full lives with love and sexuality. Such a notion is rare in literary portrayals of disabled characters; Anna Mollow and Robert McRuer (2012) assert in their introduction to *Sex and Disability* that "rarely are disabled people regarded as desiring subjects or objects of desire" (p. 1). Though very much a literary freak, always depicted as close to animals and regarded as childlike and innocent, Marcelo is allowed to experience the beginnings of a potentially romantic—though not sexual—relationship. Late in the novel, while on a camping trip with Jasmine, Marcelo begins to question his and others' assumption that he is not yet a man, and still only a child. "Maybe Jasmine doesn't see Marcelo as a man," he suggests, when she pulls her sleeping bag next to his (p. 260). As his relationship with Jasmine develops, it seems as if Jasmine might think of Marcelo as a man, capable of attraction and romantic love. Marcelo, too, begins to see himself this way. The book ends with Marcelo recognizing a new look from Jasmine, a "serious and tender look" that he "has never seen before" (p. 312). In this turn in the plot, the novel begins to challenge the traditional and popular assumption that a disabled person cannot desire or be desired.

Reading Against Marcelo

While *Marcelo* certainly begins to push us to reconsider stereotypes and ideas of normality, it also continues to rely on some longtime messages about disability that work against current disability-rights movements and ideas. The novel emphasizes growth and change in Marcelo's character, themes that come close to suggesting that disabilities are conditions worthy of cures or remedies; separates Marcelo from other people with disabilities, which complicates the otherwise progressive themes and prevents a message of true acceptance and inclusivity; and ultimately stops just short of freeing Marcelo from his literary role as a special child or freak. Ultimately, we worry that readers will read Marcelo as a character who simply needed new challenges in order to "get over" his disability, a message that undercuts any of the book's pioneering themes regarding disability and identity. We believe teachers can help students identify how this novel progresses beyond simplistic notions of disability while also pushing them to recognize where it might work against inclusivity or even encourage uncomplicated views of living and with a disability.

Our primary concern is that *Marcelo in the Real World* works to separate its narrator from other people with disabilities in addition to reaffirming the belief that disabilities are unwanted conditions that ought to be overcome or remedied. Perhaps this occurs because Marcelo either never had a disability or was able to rid himself of his disability (both readings that deny the book's progressive messages regarding disability), or perhaps this occurs in the text simply as a way to allow assumed-to-be nondisabled readers to connect with their narrator, a character who is disabled but really is more like them and able to pass as normal in the real world. Moments of exposition regarding disability (i.e., Marcelo's explanations of his disability and disability in general) not only suggest that the novel's implied reader (and Marcelo's addressee) is not disabled—a feature typical of most young adult novels that feature a disabled character, but they also contribute to the novel's overall distancing of Marcelo from the disability community. For example, as Marcelo continues to explain to Jasmine how to understand his condition, he quickly announces he has an unclear diagnosis (yet he still relies on the medical language he has received): "From a medical perspective, the closest description of my condition is Asperger's Syndrome. But I don't have many of the characteristics that other people with Asperger's Syndrome have, so that term is not exactly accurate" (p. 55). He reflects on this separation for us, asserting his difference from others with disabilities: "I feel dishonest when I say I have AS because the negative effects of my differences on my life are so slight compare to other kids who have AS or other forms of autism and truly suffer" (p. 55). At other points in the novel, Marcelo also characterizes others with disabilities as "suffering" in ways he does not. In all of these instances of division, others with disabilities seem to be excluded from the story, including the implied reader, who the text seems to hope is not someone with a clear diagnosis who truly "suffers."

Several implications arise from this crafted boundary between Marcelo and the implied reader and those who have clear diagnoses, all of them problematic messages to draw from the book: most prominently that others with disabilities suffer, and they deserve our pity—and Marcelo's. Whether or not Marcelo does function so much more ably than actual or other people with disabilities is unclear for readers; we only receive our narrator's explanations, and we fail to see the other students from Paterson as actual characters. Indeed, "disabled literary characters usually remain on the margins of fiction as uncomplicated figures or exotic aliens" (Garland-Thomson, 1997, p. 9), and we have celebrated how *Marcelo* overturns that literary tradition simply because Marcelo is our narrator. Yet, with Marcelo treated differently from the "other people [with disabilities] who truly need help," those other disabled characters are non-existent (Stork, 2009, p. 6).

Specifically, Marcelo's reliance on the word "suffer" in describing others with disabilities is problematic. McBryde Johnson (2003) has challenged the conception that disabled people are "worse off" (and thus deserving of pity), a conception captured in the word "suffer": "Are we worse off?" she wonders. "I don't think so. Not in a meaningful sense. There are too many variables. For those of us with congenital conditions, disability shapes all that we are. Those disabled later in life adapt. We take constraints that no one would choose and build rich and satisfying lives within them" (p. 5). Notice McBryde Johnson's use of "we," an inclusive pronoun that bespeaks a disability community, albeit a diverse one (including those with congenital conditions and those who find themselves disabled later in life). Though McBryde-Johnson's perspective echoes that of Marcelo's when considering himself (he would not consider himself "worse off," for example) because his understanding of disability (and subsequently the novel's) is not inclusive, the "worse off" mentality is sustained throughout the book and even encouraged by Marcelo.

Through this division and avoidance of diagnosis, we cannot help but read the book's ultimate answer to McRuer's question ("Yes, but in the end, wouldn't you rather be like me?") to be "yes." Real readers have the opportunity here, though, to push back. For example, there are moments of inclusivity in the novel that challenge the separation Marcelo seeks to draw (e.g., Marcelo's references to how Paterson's community has made him feel confident and comfortable, for example, or his immediate and interesting connection with Ixtal—a character who suffers a temporary disability). We can also consider how we can read Marcelo as a narrator shaped by society's values. Despite the many inclusive messages he has received at Paterson, he is also very much aware of how mainstream society reacts to his mannerisms and speech patterns and thus might react to other peers with disabilities at Paterson. It takes an incredibly strong perspective to push against the ingrained belief that living without a disability is always better than living with one, and even Marcelo is not up to the task.

A related concern is that the novel could suggest to readers that people with intellectual disabilities simply need to work hard to overcome them. Because Arturo looms as such a dominating authority figure who works rationally and logically, readers may very well read with and in agreement with Arturo's position that Marcelo must "overcome" his challenges in order to accept that he is "*not* disabled" (pp. 29, 40; emphasis added). Arturo spends much of the novel refusing to accept Marcelo's disability or difference, arguing that all he needs to become normal is the "real world." In many ways, Arturo is right. Marcelo grows immensely over the summer: he takes dramatic steps to exercise his own moral conscience, he begins to acknowledge sexual attraction, he confronts his father in more than one conflict, and he manages previously disorienting situations with growing confidence.

Marcelo's changes, provoked by Arturo's orders, move dangerously close to operating as a cure; such a reading of the text offers us an important way to critique the novel. Most notably, the part of Marcelo's disability that most pleases Marcelo and most troubles Arturo—the internal music (IM)—disappears. At times, Marcelo searches for it, "trying to recollect" it and wanting it to help him calm down or navigate a situation, but it first grows "different," "disjointed, jagged, with unexpected flashes," and by the midpoint of the novel, he simply "can't find it" (pp. 93, 36, 159). Eventually, Marcelo and his readers learn that the internal music is being replaced with "real" sounds and emotions, rendering the IM a kind of metaphor for intense concentration and spirituality that Arturo—and perhaps many readers—would probably find far more understandable. Illustrating this change, Marcelo tells Jasmine that, rather than finding the IM, he finds "the memory of the music I used to hear, and then even this went away and I listened to all the sounds the lake makes. And also the sound of Jasmine trying to fish" (p. 255). This description of attentive listening is far more understandable to most readers (and to Arturo and Jasmine, we can assume) than his early description of being a watermelon seed surrounded by the IM. Ultimately, as the novel progresses, Marcelo's descriptions of the IM are no longer so imaginative or unfamiliar. They are less "strange," less indicate indicative of a true disability. Again, these descriptive changes highlight a troubling shift in Marcelo's perspective that suggests he has erased or moved beyond his disability.

Further complicating Marcelo's identity as disabled or different and suggesting a need for cures, Stork echoes Arturo and uses the problematic language of "overcoming" in his "Author's Note" (2009): "I want to dedicate this book to my nephew Nicholas, who I know will one day read this book with pride in his ability to overcome the negative aspects of autism" (p. 313). He also problematically praises his experiences working with "the 'mentally handicapped'" and "persons with developmental disabilities" for "the gift of love … [he] received from them" (p. 313); in doing so, Stork exemplifies the problems with using disabled people and characters as

freaks positioned to catalyze moral growth among nondisabled protagonists. However well-intentioned Stork's note and novel—positioned as
"acknowledge[ing] the gifts of these young people" with disabilities (p.
313)—may be, they still rely on problematic tropes and on trivializing,
condescending language.

Clearly, parts of Stork's novel urge us to believe that Marcelo is more
than just any young person with a disability, yet Marcelo does continue
to occupy the role of special child, or freak, until his story's end; he may
speak in his own voice as an active narrator-protagonist, and he may act
confidently, but Marcelo remains asexualized, as well as linked with innocence and the natural world. While aware and capable of a kind of romantic love, Marcelo is introduced to us as someone who "think[s] like a child"
and has "a knack" for communicating with animals, remains innocent,
childlike, and "harmless" (pp. 32, 11, 123). He is desexualized as a non-
normative, disabled character. On the same trip to Vermont that prompts
Jasmine to reveal her attraction to Marcelo, Marcelo himself talks to his
dog and to Jasmine's horse, who smiles at him—and he "know[s] a horse's
smile from working with the ponies at Paterson" (p. 237). Meanwhile, his
physical relationship with Jasmine never moves beyond a kiss on the
cheek. If Stork had crafted a more recognizably romantic relationship
between Marcelo and Jasmine, it would have done much to overturn the
freak character Marcelo continues to embody at the end of the novel.

Of course, in some ways we wish Stork had written this novel to
emphasize its messages of inclusivity, pride, and neurodiversity while eras-
ing those components that undercut them. That said, we still believe this
novel is well worth reading and teaching. In fact, we think its ambiguities
and contradictions offer readers a great deal of freedom in making inter-
pretive decisions. The more readers are aware of what a disability-studies
lens offers when reading *Marcelo in the Real World*, the more purposeful
they can be in identifying and navigating those decisions.

Conclusion

Ultimately, we present a reading with/reading against approach in
order to help readers recognize the complexity that emerges when these
novels are read through a disability-studies lens. With this lens, we hope
that new textual moments become important, new problems arise, and
new decisions become relevant; we offer these analyses as examples of how
to isolate these textual moments, consider their impact, and identify inter-

pretive decisions. The pedagogical material below is designed to help teachers begin to apply the approach we model in our analyses. For example, the discussion questions can be used to invite students to see the novels primarily as texts that represent disabled adolescents and to open up both ways of reading with the novels and ways of reading against them. Similarly, each lesson plan is designed to help students complicate their interpretations of the novels in relation to particular concerns we offer in our analyses. For *Wonder*, we offer this lesson plan as one way to help students acknowledge and intervene in the problematic awards scene. For *Marcelo in the Real World*, we offer this plan as one way to begin complicating the idea that the "real world" is a single, stable entity that Marcelo needed in order to overcome his disability. Each lesson can deepen students' consideration of the novels' characters, open up possibilities for themes, and push them to consider progressive ways of thinking about disability.

There is significant pedagogical worth in teaching novels that leave important political interpretations open to ambiguity, but the teacher's guidance of students through such novels becomes crucial. For example, we would hesitate to recommend *Wonder* if we knew middle school students would simply walk away from their reading feeling sorry for students with disabilities; similarly, we would steer clear of *Marcelo in the Real World* if we knew that high school students would end the novel convinced that students with intellectual disabilities would finally "get better" if they were just pushed to be normal. Unfortunately, though, we believe that there are students reading these books and finishing them with exactly those mindsets. Therefore, though we do not argue that there is a single way to read either novel, we do argue that it is irresponsible to teach these novels without addressing the detrimental notions of disability presented by them. In our own classrooms, we hope to lead readers to recognize how these novels attempt to make genuine strides against stereotypical understandings of disability yet how they also fall short, leaving both Marcelo and Auggie still functioning as freaks and separated from a proud and inclusive disability community.

Resources for Teaching *Wonder*

Lesson Plan: A New Awards Presentation

Objective

Identify the problematic messages delivered during the awards presentation through close reading (most importantly, the scene positions Auggie as a freak character on a stage who inspires pity and allows audience members to reaffirm their own identities as normative). Create alternative plotlines for this scene, create alternative awards, and consider the scene's messages.

CCSS Standards

Key Ideas and Details
CCSS.ELA-Literacy.RL.6-8.1
CCSS.ELA-Literacy.RL.6-8.2
CCSS.ELA-Literacy.RL.6-8.3

Text Type and Purposes: Narrative
CCSS.ELA-Literacy.W.6-W.8.3a-e

Rationale

The awards scene is a culminating scene in the novel, and it is also one of its most problematic moments. One of *Wonder*'s strengths is its use of Auggie's narrative voice during this scene, because he begins to question his role at school. Narration plays a pivotal role in helping students think about how this scene addresses disability, and it also gives students a good opportunity for close reading. Students must recognize the root of Auggie's confusion about the award, as we do not want students to take away the message that people with disabilities deserve awards simply for being themselves. Auggie wants to deserve this award, and he isn't sure that he does.

Resources

- Books for students
- Tool for recording classroom brainstorm (doc cam, white board, chalk board, poster)

Lesson

- Read through important parts of the awards scene aloud. Share with students that when a character realizes something, it is an important moment for readers to pay attention to and worthy of close reading; the character and the text may both change because of the moment. At the end of the awards presentation, Auggie realizes how others see him. We're going to reread this scene closely and then use it to recognize other ways we could write this scene.
- Depending on your goals, ask students to work on the questions below on their own, with others, or in the whole group. Feel free to do all three groupings in order to scaffold students' thinking.

- What does Auggie realize about how others see him in this scene?
- How do you think he feels about that realization?
- Why does he think he's getting an award?
- What do you think Auggie might like to get an award for?
- Think of Auggie in the future (at the 6th grade awards presentation, for example). How do you think this realization might change things at those ceremonies? How do you think he might feel then? What do you think he would like to happen?

• Discuss these questions together as a group. Then push students to infer themes or lessons this scene might teach about disabilities. One way to help students with this step is to present students with several lessons this awards scene could teach readers. (See below for some examples.) Then ask: Which lessons do you want readers to learn? Which lessons strike you as a problem?

- People with disabilities live a difficult life. They deserve awards for simply living.
- No one wants to imagine being someone with a disability.
- It helps to give people with disabilities praise because it makes other people feel better about their lives.
- Getting through a year of school can be hard for many different people, some with disabilities and some without.
- People with disabilities, like all people, can do extraordinary things and have talents that are deserving of awards.

• Present writing assignment choices.

- You are an editor of *Wonder*, and you've decided this awards scene doesn't show that Auggie is a full person who could deserve awards, but not for simply getting through fifth grade with his disability; you've decided Auggie does not in fact deserve the Henry Ward Beecher medal. What kind of award could Auggie win? Think of Auggie throughout the book. What might he have done that is deserving of an award? Create an award for Auggie. How would you describe the award?
- Flash forward three years. It's the end of eighth grade. Auggie is about to go to high school. He doesn't want a repeat of the fifth-grade awards ceremony, but he does want an award. Imagine what Auggie might win an award for, how he would respond, and how others might respond. Create an award for Auggie. How would you describe the award?

Discussion Questions for Teaching Wonder

- How do Auggie's sections change and/or impact the novel? How do Auggie's sections change your perception of Auggie?
- How does Auggie grow in this novel? How does he change?
- Pick two other characters who narrate part of this novel. How do they grow and change?
- Pick two other characters who narrate part of this novel. How do they change your perception of Auggie?
- Pick two characters in this novel who struggle with kindness. Why do they seem to struggle? What is difficult for them? How do they confront these difficulties? What do they learn?
- Pick the narrator of the book you understand the best. Why do you understand this character? How do you see this character changing in this novel? Are these changes you have experienced or recognize in others?
- By the end of the book, many characters want Auggie as a friend. Why? What makes him a good friend or someone you would want to hang out with?
- What other stories would you like to see for Auggie? If you were to keep writing the book, what else would you like to see happen?
- Auggie makes fun of his face a lot in this book. Find at least two instances of Auggie putting himself down as a joke. How do others respond to these jokes? Find evidence that suggests Auggie doesn't actually think these jokes are funny. Why do you think he tells them?
- Does the book want you, the reader, to feel sorry for Auggie? Does Auggie want you to feel sorry for him? Why or why not?

Resources for Teaching *Marcelo*

Lesson Plan: What is the Real World?

Objective

Identify how the "real world" is a construction in the novel. Examine how the concept changes depending on the point of view.

CCSS Standards

Key Ideas and Details
CCSS.ELA-Literacy.RL.9–12.1

CCSS.ELA-Literacy.RL.9–12.2
CCSS.ELA-Literacy.RL.9–12.3

Rationale

Students need to recognize how the novel does not support one idea of the "real world," but rather shows that people define the "real world" differently. There is not a world that is more "real" and thus more "worthy" than others. This idea is especially important in considering the lives and worlds of people with disabilities. In order to examine the construction of the "real world" in the novel, students isolate textual evidence that helps them infer individual characters' beliefs and perspectives. Ultimately, this exercise allows students to question characters' beliefs while considering how Marcelo grows as a character. This ending point connects to our lesson on the language of growth and disability (see below).

Resources

- Books for students
- Tool for recording classroom brainstorm (doc cam, white board, chalk board, poster)

Lesson

- At a midpoint in their reading of the novel, ask students to quick-write about the "real world." Where do they hear that phrase? Who uses it? What or whom do they associate it with?
- Briefly discuss as a class. Common responses include *independence, adulthood, having a job, life after school,* and *making your own money.* We typically associate this phrase with authority figures: parents, adults, and teachers teaching young people about responsibility. You might ask students how disability relates to this phrase. Are people with disabilities typically considered to be part of the real world? Given how people with disabilities are often assumed to be unable to work or make money, students may identify how they are excluded from "real world" concerns.
- Break students into groups. Assign each group a character (thought-provoking characters for this exercise include Arturo, Jasmine, Marcelo, and Wendell).
- Post questions for each group. What are the "rules" of the real world that your character believes in and follows? What does the real world look like or mean to your character?
- As you walk around to help groups, encourage them to use the text

to locate characters' beliefs. Remind them also that their answers will not be the same. The rules Arturo follows in the real world are not the same rules that Marcelo or even Wendell choose to follow, for example. Try to encourage students to write these in "rule" form. For example, Wendell follows the rule "Act on instincts without fear of repercussions," and Arturo believes in the rule "Act as is customary" (p. 42).

- Share rules as a group and generate a list you can return to at the end of the novel.
- Discuss the list. Where are the most notable contrasts? Look at differences between Marcelo and Arturo, for example, or Jasmine and Wendell.
- Ask students if there is a list that is "more real" or "more right"? If time, let students brainstorm what their own list might look like.

At a later date:

- When you've finished the novel, pass out a copy of this list to each student.
- Divide students into groups, assign them a character, and ask them to revise their rule list to reflect their character at the end of the novel. What new rules do we become aware of, for example, by the end of the book? Or, have the rules of your character changed? Marcelo is the character's whose rules most notably change, but as we find out more about other characters, which can suggest new rules.
- As a whole class, update the list of rules. Invite students to pay special attention to Marcelo's list. Ask students to reflect in writing. How has Marcelo changed? What has he learned? How has he not changed? How is his "real world" different from Arturo's? Ultimately, did Arturo succeed in his experiment? Did he teach him rules of the "real world"? Were they the rules he intended to teach?

Discussion Questions for Teaching Marcelo

- How is Marcelo aware of others' responses to him? How does he react to these responses?
- What tools does Marcelo have to navigate social interactions? (What tools do you use in your own social interactions?)
- Marcelo often expresses pride in his differences. Why should he be proud?

- Think about some of the other principal characters in the novel. How do those characters see Marcelo? (Arturo, Aurora, Jasmine, Wendell, for example)? If you think those characters do not see Marcelo fully, what are they missing?
- Think about some of the minor characters Marcelo interacts with— Juliet, a secretary at the law firm; Robert Steely, the lawyer who is fired at the law firm; Jerry Garcia, Ixtel's lawyer; Rabbi Heschel; and Ixtel. How do these different characters talk to Marcelo? How does Marcelo respond to them? How would you characterize these characters' approaches or attitudes towards someone with a disability?
- Why does Jasmine fall for Marcelo? What does she see in him?
- Identity is complex in this book. Though Marcelo has a disability, he is not "only" a disabled person. What other features of Marcelo's life define him? Think about larger identity categories such as race and class but also those of interests and hobbies. Do the same for Jasmine. What does this book seem to suggest about identity in general?
- Why does Marcelo decide to act against his father and hand over the picture of Ixtel? How might his disability play into that decision?
- How would this book be different if someone else were telling the story, or if we didn't hear Marcelo's thoughts directly from him? What would we lose? What would we gain?
- How does Marcelo grow in this novel?
- Does he "overcome" his disability (to become cured)? If so, does that mean he never had a disability?

NOTES

1. A number of contemporary children's and young adult novels have used the freak characters; frequently taught and discussed texts include *Sweet Whispers, Brother Rush* (1983) by Virginia Hamilton, *Becoming Naomi León* (2005) by Pam Muñoz Ryan, and *Freak the Mighty* (1993) by Rodman Philbrick. A young adult novel that radically uses, challenges, and changes the trope of disabled freak characters is Ron Koertge's *Stoner & Spaz* (2002).

REFERENCES

Appleman, D. (2009). *Critical Encounters in High School English.* New York: Teachers College Press and National Council of Teachers of English.
Bartholomae, D., Petrosky, T., & Waite, S. (2014). *Ways of Reading: An Anthology for Writers.* Boston: Bedford/St. Martin's.

Carey, A.C. (2009). *On the Margins of Citizenship: Intellectual Disability and Civil Rights in Twentieth-Century America*. Philadelphia: Temple University Press.

Davis, L.J. (2006). *The End of Identity Politics and the Beginning of Dismodernism.* In L.J. Davis (ed.), *The Disability Studies Reader* (231–242). New York: Routledge.

Garland-Thomson, R. (1996). Introduction: From wonder to error—A genealogy of freak discourse in modernity. In R. Garland-Thomson (ed.), *Freakery: Cultural Spectacles of the Extraordinary Body* (1–19). New York: New York University Press.

_____. (1997). *Extraordinary Bodies: Figuring Physical Disability in American Culture and Literature*. New York: Columbia University Press.

Johnson, H.M. (2005). *Unspeakable Conversations.* In *Too Late to Die Young: Nearly True Tales from a Life* (201–228). New York: Henry Holt.

_____. (2006). *Accidents of Nature*. New York: Henry Holt.

Manning, E., & Massumi, B. (2014). *Thought in the Act: Passages in the Ecology of Experience*. Minneapolis: Minnesota University Press.

Mollow, A., & McRuer, R. (2012). Introduction. In A. Mollow & R. McRuer (eds.), *Sex and Disability* (1–34). Durham: Duke University Press.

Our All-Time Favorite Books for Young Readers. (2015, January 19). *Time.*

Palacio, R.J. (2012). *Wonder*. New York: Knopf.

Paul, L. (1998). *Reading Otherways.* Portland, ME: Calendar Islands.

Schneider Family Book Award. (2015, February 10). American Library Association (ALA). Retrieved from http://www.ala.org/awardsgrants/schneider-family-book-award.

Stork, F. (2011). *Author's Note.* In *Marcelo in the Real World* (314–315). New York: Scholastic.

_____. (2011). *Marcelo in the Real World.* New York: Scholastic.

Thein, A., Sulzer, M., & Schmidt, R. (2013). Evaluating the Democratic merit of young adult literature: Lessons from two versions of Wes Moore's memoir. *English Journal, 103(2)*, 53–59.

Wheeler, E.A. (2013). No monsters in this fairy tale: *Wonder* and the new children's literature. *Children's Literature Association Quarterly, 38(3)*, 335–350.

(Re)Defining Disability with the Schneider Family Book Award and Community Engagement

Jacob Stratman

This essay chronicles the fall 2012 semester where I asked students in a first-year seminar course titled "Disability Fiction" to define disability on the first day of the course, while I, under an anti-foundational theoretical lens, spent the rest of the semester encouraging students, through literary analysis, scholarly research, reflective journaling, and community engagement, to explore (or interrogate) their original definition and to question their initial assumptions and beliefs about disability.

Because of my background in teaching young adult literature and conducting community engagement projects, I found that the best way to help students question and interrogate their own understanding and assumptions about disability and adolescents was to read a selection of Schneider Family Book Award winners, and by requiring community engagement hours by partnering with a local non-profit that provides services for families with disabilities. The course description for this particular seminar reads as follows:

> In the world of Young Adult Literature, the Schneider Family Book Award "honors an author or illustrator for a book that embodies an artistic expression of the disability experience for child and adolescent audiences." In this class, we will read and discuss several of these novels as we begin to explore the growing world of Disability Studies; additionally, the class will be introduced to key terms and concepts in Disability Studies through a variety of academic essays. This is a perfect course for future educators, counselors, lobbyists, and church-workers, as well as avid readers. As a complement to the course, each student will be required to work with Ability Tree (a local,

non-profit that "helps grow able families and accessible organizations by providing R.E.S.T. (recreation, education, support & training)" for at least fifteen hours during the semester.

By organizing the essay chronologically, I want readers to see how students' thoughts changed throughout the semester as they read fiction and scholarly literature, as they engaged with the community, and as they reflected on these experiences. Essentially, while this essay does not provide thorough textual explication on particular novels as its focus, nor does the essay organize itself around particular theoretical concepts, the chronological organization (or course chronicle) if taken as a whole attempts to argue that the intentional combination and relationship of all of the above pedagogical tools (reading, journaling, and engaging with the community) are necessary and beneficial to effectively invite students into an empathetic relationship with people who live with disabilities— that in order to encourage students to interrogate their own assumptions about people with disabilities, then they must read, think, write, talk, listen, and act within the world of disability.

Antifoundational Theory

A note on my theoretical approach is important to understand the pedagogical trajectory of the course: what I appreciate most about a deconstructionist approach to literature is that it recognizes and insists that language is a poor way to communicate—a system fraught with complexities and contradictions. This tension has led me recently to what service-learning theorists and practitioners call an "antifoundational" approach: "there is no neutral, objective, or contentless 'foundation' by which we can ever know the 'truth' unmediated by our particular condition" (Butin, 2010, p. 12). This approach is very useful for students who believe that dictionary definitions are unbiased, inflexible lenses to view the world. According to Dan Butin (2010), "Antifoundationalism makes us aware of the always contingent character of our presumptions and truths ... it is committed to denying us the (seeming) firmness of our commonsensical assumptions" (p. 13). An antifoundational approach to literature, at some level, allows me to empower students, through literary analysis and community engagement, to recognize the flaws and complexities with the language we use concerning disability.

At the end of the semester, after spending time engaging with the community, reading scholarly works in disability studies, reading and discussing YA fiction, and then reflecting and processing on these experiences in the journals, I required students, on the final exam, to define disability; yet, I also ask them to explain how they came to their definition. Along with one of the assigned reflective journals, this exam becomes the central place for students to analyze the literature as it connects with their community engagement and thoughts on the secondary material. This type of exam, and the actual results, usually reveals the complexity of defining a word. After reading, writing, reflecting, conversing, and meeting lots of people, students struggled to rest on one definitive definition of disability that encapsulated all of their experiences. Lastly, I found that the antifoundational approach to the course encouraged students to think more critically about particular models of disability as they attempted to analyze the literature and engage with the children at Ability Tree.

Day One: The Definition

In an effort to give me and each student a starting place, on the first day of the course, I asked students to define disability and share a brief narrative of their experience(s) with disability. Below are a few excerpts from this assignment:

- "sickness, not able, doing things differently, accommodations, being different, work harder for success, strive to be accepted, expensive medical bills."
- "Any kind of impairment or handicap that keeps a person from completing a task at a normal rate, or at all."
- "unable to function under normal, everyday circumstances ... they are not able to function in the way the average person does."
- "the lack of power, either physically or mentally, to accomplish tasks."
- "prevents someone or something from participating in certain activities."
- "is being 'dis' 'able' to do something."
- "a disability is a hindrance in one's life which affects what society would call 'typical' ability, whether it be a mental or physical hindrance."

What I noticed immediately was that most students put the onus of disability on the individual with the impairment. Either implied or explicitly stated, my students defined disability as a particular problem of an individual, or they suggested that disability was the individual's responsibility to overcome. Not knowing it, these students were committed to thinking about disability as a "personal tragedy." According to Colin Barnes and Geof Mercer (2008), this approach or model regards disability "as a problem at the individual (body-mind) level; second, it is equated with individual functional limitations or other 'defects'; and third, medical knowledge and practice determines treatment options" (p. 2). Moreover, the Oxford English Dictionary supports my students' understandings of disability. Its definition reads "lack of ability; inability, incapacity, weakness." Only the last student in the excerpts above hints at the idea that society might have a role to play in defining disability for an individual, as she places the word typical in quotation marks.

After reading these definitions, my primary objective for the class became more focused. Now I planned to use the literature, reflective and analytical writing, and community engagement to disrupt these all too easily achieved definitions, while also exploring (at an introductory level) the variety of models of disability discussed in the scholarship: personal tragedy, moral, medical, and social. To many of my students, the conversation seemed closed: "You asked us to define disability. We did it on the first day. Now what are we going to do for fourteen more weeks?" To borrow more language from the antifoundationalists, I now desired the "focus to be as much on the process of undercutting dualistic ways of thinking as on the product of deliberative and sustainable transformational change" (Butin, 2010, p. 13). The pedagogical process of empowering students to question definitions became as important to me as the end goal of potential intellectual or behavioral change.

Even though, after the day one assignment, my intention through the semester was to use particular theories, novels, and experiences to disrupt assumptions and "dualistic ways of thinking," my plan was never to leave students in an utter state of confusion and questioning. My pedagogical plan was to teach students how to question and interrogate the terms we use to frame debates and label people, and also to make room for another model of thinking about disability: the social model. According to the Union of the Physically Impaired Against Segregation (UPIAS) in Britain, "In our view it is society which disables physically impaired people. Disability is something imposed on top of our impairments by the way we are unnecessarily isolated and excluded from full participation in society. Disabled people are therefore an oppressed group in society" (as cited in Barnes and Mercer, 2003, p. 11). This is where the antifoundational approach becomes important for students to critically consider how they come to think of disability in particular ways—that, in fact, all language, according to Stanley Fish, "is a function or extension of history, convention, and local practice" (as cited in Butin, 2010, pp. 12–13). Thus, we begin an arduous adventure in defining, redefining, undefining, and redefining disability, as we also begin living out these assumptions and interrogations through reading YA novels, grappling with scholarship, journaling reflectively, and engaging with the community.[1]

The Novels

In this section, I plan to discuss the themes of each novel, as well as the key disability concepts that each novel allowed the class to explore. Again, the focus on this section is to illustrate how theoretical terms associated with Disability Studies can be used to help teachers and students analyze literature from a particular lens. Honestly, any of the Schneider Family Award winners would have allowed the class to explore disability, so I invited students to choose the books we read in order to create more student-ownership in the course. During the first week of the semester, I gave students a list of the Schneider Family Book Award winners with brief plot synopses. They voted, and I chose four novels to explore over a four-week period.[2] During the first week, I introduced students to Lennard Davis' "Constructing Normalcy" and Christine Pohl's work on hospitality and the Christian tradition. The driving questions of the week (and for the rest of the semester) were "What does it mean to be normal?" and "What does it mean to be a host/guest?" Below are the novels we read, brief explorations of how these novels treat disability, and sample student responses from both the journal and the final exam. In the following section, I will return to the intersection between the novels and two particular models of disability: social and medical.

Cynthia Lord's *Rules* follows twelve-year-old Catherine and her relationship with her brother David, who has autism, and her new friend Jason, who is nonverbal and uses a wheelchair, as she attempts to define what "normal" looks like. Essentially, Catherine sees disability as a personal tragedy; therefore, she sees people (including her brother and Jason) as people that either need to be fixed or that need to find more normative ways of behaving. As soon as readers open the book, they are introduced to a list: "Chew with your mouth closed. Say 'thank you' when someone gives you a present (even if you don't like it). If someone says 'hi,' you say 'hi' back." In general, the rules that Catherine provides for her brother throughout the novel are attempts for him to assimilate into normalcy, and they are also attempt for Catherine to come to grips with her own assumptions about normalcy.

I admit that I thought *Rules* might be too *simple* of a text; however, student reflections later proved this assumption to be false. One student comes to the conclusion that Catherine's wish to fix Jason does not add to either of their abilities to flourish as humans: "For Catherine, people with disabilities, like her brother, are seen as something that needs to be fixed... . When her relationship with Jason begins to develop, she starts to accept people as they are, not how she can fix them or make them better. Hospitality is about meeting people where they are, not where you want them to be." Another student spent her reflective journal analyzing the end of the novel when Catherine writes a letter about her summer to her friend Melissa, who has spent the summer away. And, when she refers to Jason, she uses the word "boy." My student responds, "By giving Jason the classification of 'a boy,' and not any other label, Catherine has hospitably welcomed Jason in the world of normalcy, so to speak." Not only did these classroom conversations start to question the idea of normalcy, but they also introduced students to issues of identity.

Wendy Mass' *A Mango-Shaped Space* explores learning disabilities and the social stigma as it follows Mia's love-hate relationship with her synesthesia. I used this novel to disrupt the metaphor that describes people that "suffer" from a particular condition. As one student noticed,

> When you are faced with it [disability], it hinders you, prevents you from reading your full potential as an individual. In Mia's case, it did hinder her in some aspects of her life. In many ways, though, her synesthesia helped her, and it is even arguable that her life was made better through her difference. Mia does not just deal with her disability; she owns it.

With this novel, students began to come to terms with how they tend to define people with disabilities—that they expect them to act in certain ways, and they assume that the disability is the controlling force in their lives.

Secondly, I used this novel to continue our conversation revolving around identity; more specifically, I used this week to introduce students to "stigma" and Lerita M. Coleman Brown's "Stigma: An Enigma Demystified." What I desire students to recognize is how disability, in some ways and in some cases, is more about perception than reality. As Brown suggests, "Perceptually, stigma becomes the master status, the attribute that colors the perception of the entire person. All other aspects of the person are ignored except those that fit the stereotype associated with the stigma" (Davis, 2010, p. 184). As one example, at one point in the middle of the novel, after Mia's synesthesia becomes more public at school, she finds that her differences give her celebrity status. Although she is not called "freak" (opening line of the novel) anymore, stigma does not go away. Mia confesses, "I have to admit it [attention] isn't all bad. Kids who totally ignored me before are clamoring to talk to me now. It would be more rewarding if it didn't have the overtones of a circus sideshow" (Mass, 2003, p. 98). Her use of the circus metaphor is telling here, as classmates gaze upon her with wonderment and excitement. Whether freak or celebrity, Mia's synesthesia is not just one part of her; it is perceived as the sole component of her identity. To be stigmatized is to be categorized and devalued. One student observed how stigma functions in the novel: "People look at her synesthesia and see just that. She is the girl who sees colors. They cannot see any of her good qualities, because, to society, she is nothing; nothing but the girl who sees color. Her mother is adamant about trying to find a way to 'fix' Mia's problem." Reading this novel, students are invited to consider how stigmas oversimplify how they see people with disabilities.

In an effort to address societal stigmas, disability advocates address the pressures many people living with disabilities feel to compensate for differences and work toward normalcy. To explore another way that society potentially disables people, I use Simi Linton's (2010) wonderfully convicting article on language society uses to talk about disability: "Reassigning Meaning." One of the metaphors that Linton explores is "overcoming." Many of my students find Linton's argument intriguing, namely that "it is physically impossible to *overcome* a disability, [so] it seems that what is *overcome* is the social stigma of having a disability" (p. 229). Generally, YA novels that explore disability focus on a character's (in)ability to come to terms with his/her identity, and to come to terms with how others view him/her.

One novel that explores "overcoming" is **Wendelin Van Draanen's *The Running Dream.*** The novel tells the story of Jessica, a high school runner who believes that her life is over after she loses a leg in a tragic bus accident. After the incident, she begins to explore her new beginnings and the complexity of identity as an amputee. As a star track athlete, Jessica identifies herself primarily as a runner: "I am a runner. That's what I do. That's who I am" (p. 6). Notice that she also attaches her entire identity by what she can do—how she can act. With the loss of a leg, Jessica must explore the complexities and nuances of identity, and she must wrestle with the notion that one cannot actually "overcome a disability." The skewed notions of normalcy are so embedded in Jessica's psyche at the beginning of the novel that she cannot see her new self as "normal." Overcoming for Jessica is paramount, because, as students observed, overcoming disabilities bring people closer to normalcy, and it is normalcy that Jessica desperately desires. Even in the first third of the novel, Jessica begins to have a breakthrough: "Yes, I'm missing a leg, but the rest of me is ... well, it's *normal*" (p. 106). While the use of ellipses allow for hesitation or reluctance, the use of italics provides needed emphasis.

"Overcoming" became the most difficult concept in the class for much of the same reasons that Jessica struggles. Like Jessica, students generally saw normalcy as real, good and attainable. One student writes, "the power to be normal is within her [Jessica's] control. If she were to act normal and show others that she wasn't affected by all the things that in her mind make her abnormal, then maybe she wouldn't be seen as abnormal to the people around her." If only it were this easy. Some students, as this journal entry indicates, maintained a definition of disability that draws closer to the "personal tragedy" model—that disability/difference is a certainly a problem that must be fixed or at least hidden in order to be (or be perceived as) normal. Similarly, there were a few students who argued that the onus of "fitting it" or "overcoming the obstacles" still falls on the individual, instead of society. As a representative of this type of thinking, one student writes, "in order to have a disability, an individual must have an impairment and *allow* [emphasis mine] that impairment to inhibit him socially.... An impaired individual cannot hide from society but must become a part of it." To these students, the goal for Jessica (and probably for them) is to take control of one's life and become completely absorbed into community definitions of normalcy.

For these reasons, many students connected with *Running Dream*. The fact that Jessica worked very hard, along with having help from friends and family members, to overcome her impairment—not being able to run—and at the end by accomplishing her goal of running again, the novel seems to perpetuate the idea that all one with a disability has to do is work really hard in order to finish the race, win the prize, be accepted, etc. Again, the onus on acceptability is on the individual and not on society. As Simi Linton (2010) argues in "Reassigning Meaning,"

> Lest I be misunderstood, I don't see working hard, doing well, or striving for health, fitness, and well-being as contradictory to the aims of the disability rights movement.... However, we shouldn't be impelled to do these because we have a disability, to prove to some social overseer that we can perform,

but we should pursue them because they deliver their own rewards and satisfactions [p. 229].

What Van Draanen does very well with Jessica's character is that she explores how a teenager might fear social isolation, singleness, and ridicule after becoming "disabled." However, the tension of the novel and the goal of the reader are to decide whether Jessica wants the prosthesis in order to stave off social isolation and ridicule or to simply better herself through her love of running.

Reading **Jonathan Friesen's *Jerk, California*,** while also introducing students to a social understanding of disability, students witness the ugliness and desperation of Sam, a young man diagnosed with Tourette Syndrome, as he struggles with social stigma, frustration, anger, and a desire for "normalcy." One of the integral critiques of the term "disability" is its etymological make-up. As Linton suggests, "the prefix creates a barrier, cleaving in two ability and its absence, its opposite. Disability is the 'not' condition, the repudiation of ability" (p. 235). And, this approach is exactly what keeps Sam in a marginal position; people only look at what he cannot do or cannot be. However, unlike many YA novels that highlight disability, Sam's "problem" is not necessarily Tourette's. Yes, he has been diagnosed, and, yes, his classmates' and step-father's responses to the syndrome cause Sam a lot of problems and anxieties, but Sam also deals with other, maybe bigger, issues: an abusive step-father, an ineffectual mother, a complex relationship with a complex girl, and many mysteries about his biological father and his own name (he later learns that his father's given name is Jack). Sam cannot overcome Tourette's; Sam is stigmatized by his step-father and a few classmates; and Sam, due to his dysfunctional family, has no idea what normal is or what it can look like. As Sam narrates the end of the first chapter, readers get a sense of the weight he must carry: "Old Bill turned his back, Mom closed her eyes, and even at six years old I knew I was alone" (p. 3). In this line alone, students are invited to see disability as beyond a personal tragedy and begin to see how other cultural factors influence how an individual absorbs his/her difference.

After reading and discussing these novels, especially *Jerk, California*, student reflections turned to how people with disabilities identify themselves, especially when they have to fight against how others identify them. One student represents this type of thinking when she writes, "Sam understands that he does twitch, and he can't control it. However, Sam looks past that and does not let it become his whole being. Towards the end of the novel, Sam just has occasional references to his Tourette's rather than the obsession with it in the beginning. With these realizations, Jack Keegan is born again, willing to accept that an identity does not come from just one single source nor do any of the influences matter more than what the individual knows as true." Another student adds nuance to many students' depiction of "overcoming" when she writes about Sam/Jack: "Overcoming is acceptance and being comfortable in one's own skin, which Sam becomes when he states, 'my shoulder jerks, but who cares.' Sam realizes that the disease wasn't his father's fault, or anyone's fault, and it is no longer a burden that should be keeping anyone down, and through this finds his new, confident identity." What *Jerk, California* does so well is that it resists a monolithic reading about people with disabilities. Readers are not introduced to a character that "struggles" with a disability. Readers are introduced to Sam who becomes Jack.

Reading YA novels invites students into empathic relationships with fictional characters. We spent many weeks exploring significant terms associated with disability studies and hospitality: recognition, normalcy, staring, stigma, and a variety of metaphors/phrases we commonly use, like "overcoming" and "passing." These novels provided the starting point for my students to begin to rethink what it means to have a disability. Reading young adult literature became an essential way to connect the adolescent lives of the fictional characters with the real-life lives of the children they would soon meet at Ability Tree. Although I have learned over the years that reading fiction alone does not have the ability to change behavior, I have also learned that novels can be a safe place to enter foreign worlds. As Denis Donaghue (2000) writes in *The Practice of Reading*, "I believe that the purpose of reading literature is to exercise or incite one's imagination; specifically, one's ability to imagine being different" (p. 56). To incite one's imagination toward people with disabilities is to invite the reader to create mental and emotional space for the other. As the student reflections proved, this increased imagination for other ways of experiencing the world was beginning to take place. Yet, students continued to see that the responsibility of "being disabled" rested confidently on the shoulders of those with the disability. There was more work to do.

The Novels and the Models: Medical vs. Social

This section, through continued textual analysis, explores how each novel defines and depicts disability according to the medical and social models, and how students' definitions of disability on the first day of class did and did not change over the course of the semester. Partly, by introducing particular modes of thinking regarding disability, I resist the tendency to look to one place (usually a dictionary) for a definition. A term like "disability" is too complex to leave to the hands of *Merriam-Webster* alone.

In short, according to Dan Goodley (2011), the medical model "views disability as pathology (a physical, sensory or cognitive failing that tragically 'handicaps' those 'afflicted'" (p. 6). The medical model, to many theorists, is aligned with thinking of disability as personal tragedy (as I observed in students' initial writing). Goodley argues that this perspective "promote[s] an individual model of disability, reducing the problem of disability to the flawed tragedy of individual personhood treatable through the interventions of charities and healthcare professionals" (p. 6). The belief that disabilities are bad and that they need to be fixed permeates young adult literature and even the thoughts of many of my students. However, as the semester progressed, a new model became to surface through class discussions and readings: the social model. Although this is a complex model (complete with many appropriate critiques), Goodley provides a brief definition: "Disability is understood as an act of exclusion: people are *disabled* by contemporary society" (p. 8). The Disabled People's International definition of impairment and disability is helpful here: "Impairment: is the functional limitation within the individual caused by physical, mental or sensory impairment. Disability: is the los or limitation of opportunities to take part in the normal life of the community on an equal level with others due to physical and social barriers" (p. 8). In this model, the onus is on society to provide opportunities for all people to flourish. This section explores how these particular novels navigated the different models of disability, while also showcasing student responses to these novels in connection with the medical or social model. By having access to these different models of disability, not only are students asked to distance themselves from monolithic thinking about disability, but they are now given tools to analyze the novels more carefully and closely.

In support of the medical model, in three of the novels that we read, part of the plot takes place in the medical community. In Cynthia Lord's *Rules,* much of the plot occurs in the therapist's office where Catherine's brother, David, goes for occupational therapy. This is also the place where Catherine befriends Jason, a young man who uses a wheelchair and is nonverbal. Secondly, Wendy Mass's *Mango-Shaped Space* uses the medical sphere to give a name to Mia's condition, synesthesia, which she always found weird and hard to talk about with others. After Mia learns that what she has experienced all of her life has a name, she exclaims, "I stare at him for a minute trying to absorb what he just said. Somewhere in my head a chorus of voices sings hallelujah. There is a name for what I have! Not that I can pronounce it" (2003, p. 103). The tension that students discovered by exploring the medical model is that announcing a person as "disabled," on one hand allows them a language to use when discussing her impairments, while also provided much needed health services. On the other hand, disability becomes a construct, a box, a way to keep people in and out. Understanding the medical model of disability allowed me to introduce stigma where, according to Lerita M. Coleman Brown (2010), "stigma appears to be a special and insidious kid of social categorization.... People are treated categorically rather than individually, and in the process of being devalued" (p. 184). Discussing the medical model of disability alongside the novels allowed the class to explore the tensions attached to naming a condition. In a journal entry, after weeks spent at Ability Tree, one student writes, "Medical treatment has increased because of the defining of disability; more and more disabled people are being helped so they can live normal and longer lives. However, this term puts people in a category, which rarely gives them the chance to be seen as anything besides their disability."

Although the medical community plays a key role in the novel, *Mango-Shaped Space* comes closest to exploring the social model. At first, Mia keeps the fact that shapes, letters, numbers, and sounds each correspond to a particular color (synesthesia) a secret because of an earlier incident of ridicule and shame. However, through a number of interesting circumstances, Mia must address the issue with her family and a young neurologist. As I mentioned earlier, though Dr. Weiss calls the condition "harmless," he still asserts medical authority by calling it a condition and by naming it. Mia's mother, however, still holds on to the personal tragedy model as she responds to Dr. Weiss: "How can we make it go away? Mia can't very well walk around seeing colors everywhere. It's interfering with her schoolwork.... But can you help her work around it" (pp. 104, 110). Mia's mother is concerned with social perception. She fears ridicule and isolation, but above all, she desires Mia to be able to overcome the condition and become "normal." Although Dr. Weiss validates Mia by remarking, "But this is Mia's normal way of perceiving the world" (p. 110), it is up to Mia to decide how to define, describe, label, and understand her own reality.

As she internalizes these different, and sometimes opposing models, she thinks, "I do want to be able to pass my classes, and it would be nice to be like everyone else. But if I couldn't use my colors, the world would seem so bland—like vanilla ice cream without the gummy bears on top. 'I don't know,' I admit. 'I really like gummy bears.' ... I quickly correct myself. 'I mean, I can't imagine life without my colors'" (pp. 110–111). The key moment for Mia, and for my students, is that Mia has the opportunity to take control of the situation. She gets to decide how she feels about her own reality. Is synesthesia simply, and only, a medical condition? Is synesthesia a tragedy—something to work around or overcome? Or, is it simply her reality—a part of what makes her whole?

Throughout the semester, several students continued to argue that the medical field should have the authority on diagnosing and labeling people as disabled. One student writes, "Disability blurs the lines between normal and abnormal. Doctors, physicians, and medics are the ones who decide the 'normal' state of the human body, but society has taken it upon itself to label people as normal or different. In other words, society has begun to negatively stigmatize people." Another student writes, rather mechanically,

> the term disability can be defined as a human restriction that is characterized by the mental, and or physical limitations it causes. The act of being disabled is determined by medical specialists, often times due to the presence of impairments in individuals. The degree to which an individual is deemed and viewed as disabled varies according to the type of disability and its influence on the individual's day to day life.

As Barnes and Mercer (2003) point out, "twentieth-century social theory typically followed medical judgments in identifying disabled people as those individuals with physical, sensory and cognitive impairments as 'less than whole,' and then hence unable to fulfill valued social roles and obligations" (p. 2). Students that leaned on the medical definition of disability, not only come by it honestly according to Barnes and Mercer, but subsume their definition as they see the medical enterprise as the best way to help people with disabilities live "normal" lives or return to a certain level of "normality." Barnes and Mercer comment later that, "the 'well-adjusted' disabled person is someone who lives up to non-disabled peoples' expectations as brave, cheerful and grateful when being helped" (p. 7). Or, in Linton's words, "it is a demand that you be plucky and resolute, and not let the obstacles get in your way" (2010, p. 228). Yet, certain students were able to see the complexity of such a model. One student writes, "Medical treatment has increased because of the defining of disability; more and more disabled people are being helped so they can live 'normal' and longer lives. However, this term puts people in a category, which rarely gives them the chance to be seen as anything besides their disability."

At the end of the semester, many students were persuaded by some of the social-model literature, and especially by how they saw the social model played out in the literature, namely *Mango-Space Shape*; *Jerk, California*; and at Ability Tree. As one student wrote passionately,

> Disability is a term used by members of society when referring to a person that they believe has less power, strength, mental, or physical abilities than they themselves have. Disability is a fictional condition that one member of society creates for another member of society to explain difficult differences in the individuals. Members of society use the term disability as a way to be positioned above another to avoid association with an individual viewed as inferior.

Although there are problems with this definition, this student represents a turn in the way many students viewed disability. Clearly, all of us recognize that impairments are a part of life. However, it became ever present that disability had more social weight that they previously recognized or understood. One student suggests, "As a whole, society defines a disabled person by making his disability or limitation his identity. He or she is no longer a person, but instead, becomes the 'autistic kid' or the 'woman with no leg' instead of Billy or Sally." And another student agrees: "Disability is how a person is viewed, judged by what they must overcome, whether or not they could be seen as 'normal,' how they are identified, and how the world recognizes them." These comments shift disability from a personal tragedy or a condition labeled by the medical community to a civil rights issue—an identity placed upon an individual by the gaze of the community around him or her.

The social model allows students to think about language and agency. Linton (2010) also helped my students reframe the "naming" debate with these thoughts: "Although there is some agreement on terminology [of disability], there are disagreements about what it is that unites disabled people and whether disabled people should have control over the naming of their experience" (p. 224). After we discussed the moment in *Mango-Shaped Space* where Mia must come to a decision about language—the "naming" of something, I showed my class a brief clip of a press conference with Olympic sprinter, and double amputee, Oscar Pistorius. As he addresses questions about sprinting, the Olympics, and his "disability," he humorously remarks, "I grew up not really thinking that I had a disability. I grew up thinking that I had different shoes" (Pistorius, n.d.). The medical community and the law makers, and even the religious leaders in my students' lives, are not the only voices in the conversation about disability. As one of my students commented, "I am still on a journey of relating, of not buying into the world's concept of normalcy. However, my definition of disability has changed from being a measurement against a standard norm to simply being a perception held by any individual." Her definition has shifted from an assumption placed on a person to a reality perceived and named by that very person. As another student notes, "My eyes were not only opened to the fact that those with disabilities are not defined by it, but my eyes were also opened to the fact that I was a contributor in creating the problem of the disabled person. I created this by assuming that their disability was the defining factor."

It is arrogant and ignorant to believe that simply reading and discussing novels changed student behavior—that students automatically became more empathic to people with disabilities after reading a novel that portrays a character with a disability. What I desired in this class was to create an academic environment that invites empathy and a paradigm shift regarding how students think about disability. Of course, I know that reading literature can be a powerful space to explore empathy (Bracher; Stratman). This course design seeks to give students tools, and even permission, to question authority (linguistic, medical, religious, etc.) in order to come to a better understanding of truth and to create better relationships with others. Using the Schneider Family Book Award winners, through an antifoundational approach to community engagement, I worked to empower students to question, resist, and disrupt the all-too-easily constructed definitions we use to categorize and order our world. It is the community engagement aspect that is another powerful tool to invite empathy and complement the literature.

Community Engagement

In an effort to align the scholarly readings and the novels with the class discussions, each student was required to engage in one of the ministry opportunities supported by Ability Tree. Students spent fifteen hours over the semester engaging with students during after-school programs, art and creativity programs, and Friday evening "lock-ins" (to allow parents to have a date-night). Ability Tree's mission is to "envision families impacted by disability being accepted and supported in their local community; we envision individuals and families enjoying healthy relationships in their neighborhoods, schools, workplaces and churches. Our purpose is to reach out to families impacted by disability through recreation, education, support and training (R.E.S.T.); we aim to partner with individuals and organizations to raise awareness and build support networks to strengthen and grow able families." Requiring students to engage with community non-profits as a way to meet course objectives and have a better understanding of the learning that happens in the classroom comes from a belief that reading literature, while inviting students to recognize the "other," does not necessarily change behavior or create empathy.[3] As Mark Bracher (2009) reminds us, "sympathy for literary characters does not, in and of itself, benefit real people. People who feel deep sympathy for characters can be indifferent and even cruel to real people who are suffering" (p. 364).[4] Not only did working with the children at Ability Tree help connect real people to fictional narratives and scholarly theories, but it also helped students recognize that people with disabilities are not always suffering.

In their journal entries, many students remarked how spending many hours with particular children changed the way they see disability in general. One student writes, "My experience at Ability Tree created a new definition of disability for me. It showed me that these kids are not just their disability. They are their own persons, with flaws, quirks, likes and dislikes, expressions, emotions, and their own personalities." Another student comments, "At Ability Tree, I learned even more so that the kids I was working with were really just kids … Caylen is six years old, she has autism and is nonverbal, and she has some other developmental delays; but mostly, she is just Caylen. She can hum Twinkle Twinkle Little Star and blow kisses. Luke has Down Syndrome, but mostly he's just stubborn and doesn't get along with Charade, who talks to me almost entirely in quotes from the move Cars. Jonathan likes toys that spin, so we play with tops a lot.… I would be lying if I said there was nothing hard about working with them, but there are also challenges involved in working with *any* kids. And there are challenges involved in relating to *anyone.*"

What our time at Ability Tree taught me is that students need a formal, reflective vehicle to process their experiences. That simply reading and discussing literature may not allow students the type of reflective time that they need to fully process the literature and community experiences. According to Mary Stuart Hunter and Blaire L. Moody (2009) in "Civic Engagement in the First College Year," "Critical reflection should be a component of all civic engagement initiatives so that students have the benefit of awareness of the knowledge and skills they have acquired and feel empowered to use them for positive change in their communities" (pp.

82–83). Reflective journaling, then, not only provided space for students to wrestle with the semester's experiences, but they also gave me an insider's view to those processes. As you will see in the next section, I was able to track how students were thinking about the fiction, the scholarly articles, and their time spent at Ability Tree.[5] As Hunter and Moody (2009) argue, "integrative learning helps students find ways to put the pieces together and develop habits of mind that prepare them to make informed judgments in a complex fast-moving world" (p. 79). Journaling became a necessary and important aspect of the course. As I made it my job to disrupt, question, resist, and even complicate their assumptions about disability, I needed an assignment to help students mend, synthesize, restore, and even meditate.

Conclusion

Although I am a firm believer in the power of reading literature to change lives, this semester has taught me that reading cannot be an isolating experience—that, in fact, reading does not occur in a vacuum. If my students grew at all in how they treat people with disabilities, or even think about disability as a social construction, then it came as a result of a variety of influential forces: reading and talking openly in class about literary texts, namely disability fiction; playing with children and talking with parents on a weekly basis at Ability Tree; exploring scholarship introducing them to Disability Studies; and finally, having the opportunity to reflect on all of these experiences through reflective journaling. Again, teaching a group of students who did not necessarily have a "heart" for the disabled forced me to consider how much pressure I put on literature to do the heavy-lifting when it comes to increasing student empathy and concern for others. One of the anonymous reviewers of an earlier draft of this manuscript commented, "If reading by itself is not enough to prompt change, then all of us need to be engaged in service projects." Yes. This semester has taught me that our lives must be lived with others, not just with fictional characters. This might be a hard truth for all of us. Or, put better, I will end with a student response:

> Her [Mia from *Mango-Shaped Space*] synesthesia may have been a disability, but, more importantly, it was a part of her, a part of her she both hated and loved. She did not merely deal with her condition, but fully and completely owned it…. My view on disability hasn't changed so much as it has simply come to be. It's been formed through the interactions with these incredible

children and just learning how to love them. It's true that to society, these children are seen as burdens that will never contribute to the world. The way I see it is this; if they can make you smile or laugh or look at yourself or the world in a different light, then they have without a shadow of a doubt contributed something beautiful and amazing to this world.

Appendix A: Reflective Writing

In an effort to align the experiences with Ability Tree with the Schneider Family Award winners, and the discussions of hospitality, empathy, and disability in class, each student was required to keep a reflective journal. Each student wrote four journal entries over the semester. One of the major requirements for each journal was the inclusion of direct quotations from scholarly articles we explored in class. In this way, I made sure that students' reflections took key terms, concepts, and debates in mind. Below are the journal descriptions:

- **Journal #1**: How have you experienced impairment/disability in your life? Where in your life have you witnessed someone displaying hospitality (inhospitality) to those with impairments/disabilities? What was the motivation of those actions? What were the results?
- **Journal #2**: (caveat: I teach at an Interdenominational Christian Institution, and the integration of faith and learning is a key component to this introductory course). How does the Bible explore issues surrounding disability? Read the passages below. Choose several connecting pieces of Scripture to study and analyze? What truths can be gleaned from these passages? You must cite 2–3 Bible commentaries. Below is a list of possible passages.

— Leviticus 19: 14	Luke 7: 1–10	Mark 1: 40–45
— Romans 5: 1–11	Luke 8: 40–56	Mark 2: 1–12
— 2 Peter 5: 10–11	Luke 13: 10–17	Mark 7: 24–37
— 2 Corinthians 12: 7–10	Luke 14: 1–24	
— John 9	Luke 19: 2–9	

- **Journal #3**: Choose one question for reflection: How does a particular novel (that we read in class) explore issues of disability? Choose one character to analyze. How does this character define him/herself in relation to his/her impairment? Does this change? Does the novel make a political/social comment about disability? How does the novel define disability?

- **Journal #4:** Reflect on your work with Ability Tree. How has your experience helped you (re)define disability? Share stories. Be sure to engage with scholarly passages as well. How has your experience at Ability Tree helped you think about normalcy, stigma, hospitality, and other concepts that we have explored this semester?

Appendix B: Sample Student Journal Entries

As I did not want to clutter the main body of the argument with an overabundance of student responses, I have included many excerpts here from the final exam where students used the resources and experiences from the semester to (re)define disability.

- Throughout the semester, I have mainly been working with a girl named Kailyn. She is as cute as a button, she loves music, and she has an incredibly bubbly personality. She is also nonverbal. Communicating with her to begin with was a challenge. Honestly, I was a nervous wreck to begin with. However, after we both warmed up to each other, it was pretty easy to figure her out. She expresses herself through her movements and her facial expressions, and reading her this way has taught me so much more about communication. I had some previous knowledge about her love of music, so one day, she was sitting in my lap while playing with art supplies in the craft room and I began to sing "Jesus Loves Me." Halfway through the song, she turned around smiling and just stared at me. I began to sing the song again and she turned back around, started to sway back and forth and then to my amazement, she started to hum the song herself. That moment brought tears to my eyes because it was then I realized that all children are gifts from God and that we cannot let a little thing like disability get in the way of us seeing that.
- While I understand the points brought up about normalcy, hospitality, stigma, etc., I cannot really say that Ability Tree really waivered my definition of disability. I still believe that it is something that will separate people into categories, whether that is right or wrong. I believe that it is some sort of barrier and difficulty that someone has to live with going through everyday life. Whether they want to change that or not, it is still a difference. This does not make what society does right, or excuse my attitude at Ability Tree, but acting is definitely more difficult than reading and discussing.

- As I was introduced to this little boy, I will be honest in saying; I was not blinded to his disability. In fact, it was for a period of time that his disability was all I allowed myself to see. This was all I was able to see until I started observing how creative and inventive he was. Despite his outburst in temper and his occasional unwillingness to obey, he was the most creative kid I had ever spent time with. At one point he tried to create a four-way call with plastic cups and string by using what he had learned in science about plastic cups and string. Not only that, but he later constructed a haunted house with large hopscotch squares. Once I saw his *ability* to create and invent, I realized he was just like any other kid. And he saw himself as any other kid. He was not defined by this disability. I was the one who made him out to be different and assumed he was different. But he proved my assumptions to be false. He allowed me to see that there was so much to him that his disability.
- One of the little girls at Ability Tree, Sarah, is in a wheelchair, and on my first night of Recess, I thought to myself, "Poor thing! What can she do here?" I did not mean it in a mean way, but as I started to watch Sarah, and how she interacted with the other kids at Ability Tree, I saw that she was able to paint, create, play basketball, "cook" at the kitchen, and even jump on the trampoline! She, of all kids, did not meet my definition of disabled! Sarah's siblings felt completely comfortable taking her out of her wheelchair and placing her on the trampoline that I started to understand that I too did not need to be afraid of hurting her. If I let myself form a relationship with her, I could discover how gifted she is, and how she is able to do everything any "normal" child could do, just in a different way.
- Before I began taking these volunteer programs, I considered disability simply to be a physical limitation. Now that I've met and talked with these kids and personally got to know them, I know it's more complex than that. I've learned it is difficult if not impossible to give a simple, straightforward definition to disability, and that disability does not necessarily mean limitations either. These kids are just like any other children: loud, boisterous, and innocent. They enjoy running around and playing, which brings me to the topic of normal. "Normal," for these kids, is playing with everyone, or—in some cases—roughhousing with everyone. They don't see very many differences beyond girl or boy. They're all kids and they play with friends.

- It is true; Drew is clinically defined as being disabled. However, that single word does not have to consume every aspect of his life. Rather a trait that is equal among all the other. His hindrances may seem larger than ours, but we are all, in some aspect, disabled.... However, I do not feel that a disability is limited to only those who are medically diagnosed as disabled. When in a large group, I also back away and tend not to open up. I also consider this a disability. Although Drew physically looks different from the mass majority, he and I both are hindered by large groups of people. I feel like this shyness is acting as a disability in our lives.
- I think that defining disability starts within our hearts and actions, and our words will follow. There is a problem with using offensive language. The bigger problem, though, is having offensive mindsets and treating people offensively. People can have a very tactful definition full of euphemisms and controlled words, and still act wrongly toward the disabled. Defining disability within our hearts is more important than defining it on paper.
- I have also figured out that helping children with disabilities isn't charity work. At the beginning of the semester, we were asked who was the host when we worked at Ability Tree. I believe that both parties in some aspects play the host role. I see myself as a host when I help a child see what they can do. Drew could play the games that other kids were playing on the computer; he just needed some help. The children at Ability Tree also host us as they show us little bits of how they live in the world with their disability(ies). When both parties are hosts, I don't think the two groups cancel each other out. The more I went to serve at Ability Tree, the more I saw it as just going to play with kids.

NOTES

1. I will use appendixes to spell out specific assignments: Appendix A for reflective journaling and Appendix B for other student responses to the final exam (redefining disability).

2. The nature of our first-year seminar is such that professors only get six or seven weeks to explore their particular topic. And, each week is only two 50-minute periods.

3. For more on my work regarding the intersections between reading literature and empathy, I invite you to read the 2013 essay Toward a pedagogy of hospitality: Empathy, literature, and community engagement," *Journal of Christian Education and Belief, 17(1)*; the 2012 essay "Tell them im strong tell them im a man": Seeking empathy in Ernest J. Gaines' *A Lesson Before Dying, Integrite: A Journal of Faith and*

Learning, 11(2), and the Fall 2010/Winter 2011 essay Using YAL to teach sympathy and social change: War in Iraq/Afghanistan, *SIGNAL Journal 34(1)*.

4. For more general work on empathy and literature, I invite you to read Hoffman, M.L. (2000). *Empathy and Moral Development: Implications for Caring and Justice.* Cambridge: Cambridge University Press; Keen, S. (2010). *Empathy and the Novel.* New York: Oxford University Press; and Nussbaum, M.C. (1997). *Cultivating Humanity: A Classical Defense of Reform in Liberal Education.* Cambridge: Harvard University Press.

5. See Appendix D for more samples of student journals.

REFERENCES

Altieri, J. (2008). Fictional characters with dyslexia: What are we seeing in books? *Teaching Exceptional Children, 41(1)*, 48–54.

Barnes, C., & Mercer, G. (2003). *Disability.* Cambridge, UK: Polity Press.

Bracher, M. How to teach for social justice: Lessons from *Uncle Tom's Cabin* and cognitive science. *College English, 71(4)*, March 2009.

Brown, L.M.C. (2010). Stigma: An enigma demystified. In L.J. Davis (ed.), *Disability Studies: A Reader* (179–192). New York: Routledge.

Butin, D.W. (2010). *Service-Learning in Theory and Practice: The Future of Community Engagement in Higher Education.* New York: Palgrave Macmillan.

Census Bureau, United States. (2012). https://www.census.gov/newsroom/releases/archives/miscellaneous/cb12-134.html.

Davis, L.J. (2010). Constructing normalcy. In L.J. Davis (ed.), *Disability Studies: A Reader* (3–19). New York: Routledge.

Donaghue, Denis. (2000). *The Practice of Reading.* New Haven: Yale University Press.

Friesen, J. (2008). *Jerk, California.* New York: Speak.

Garland-Thomson, Rosemarie. (2010). Beholding. In L.J. Davis (ed.), *Disability Studies: A Reader* (199–208). New York: Routledge.

Gavigan, K., & Kurtts, S. (2008). Using children's and young adult literature in teaching acceptance and understanding of individual differences. *Delta Kappa Gamma Bulletin, 77(2)*, 11–16.

Hoffman, M. (2000). *Empathy and Moral Development: Implications for Caring and Justice.* Cambridge: Cambridge University Press.

Hunter, M.S., & Moody, B.L. (2009). Civic engagement in the first college year. In B. Jacoby (ed.), *Civic Engagement in Higher Education: Concepts and Practices* (74–83). San Francisco: Jossey-Bass.

Keen, S. (2010). *Empathy and the Novel.* New York: Oxford University Press.

Klipper, B. (2011). Great reads, intriguing characters: The Schneider Family Book Award winners. *Young Adult Library Services, 9(3)*, 6–7.

Kurtts, S., & Gavigan, K. (2008). Understanding (dis)abilities through children's literature. *Education Libraries, 31(1)*, 23–31.

Linton, S. (2010). Reassigning meaning. In L.J. Davis (ed.), *Disability Studies: A Reader* (223–236). New York: Routledge.

Lord, C. (2006). *Rules.* New York: Scholastic.

Mairs, N. (1996). *Waist-High in the World*. Boston: Beacon Press.

Mass, W. (2003). *A Mango-Shaped Space*. Boston: Little, Brown.

Mills, R. (2008). It's just a nuisance: Improving college student reflective journal writing. *College Student Journal, 42(2)*, 684–690.

Nussbaum, M. (1997). *Cultivating Humanity: A Classical Defense of Reform in Liberal Education*. Cambridge: Harvard University Press.

Pistorius, O. (n.d.). Interview. http://www.youtube.com/watch?v=C3yZxCMoIf.4

Prater, M. (2003). Learning disabilities in children's and adolescent literature: How are characters portrayed? *Learning Disability Quarterly, 26(1)*, 47.

Schneider Family Book Award. American Library Association. http://www.ala.org/awardsgrants/schneider-family-book-award.

Stratman, J. (2013). Toward a pedagogy of hospitality: Empathy, literature, and community engagement. *Journal of Christian Education and Belief, 17(1)*, 25–60.

_____. (2012). "Tell them im strong tell them im a man": Seeking empathy in Ernest J. Gaines' *A Lesson Before Dying*. *Integrite: A Journal of Faith and Learning, 11(2)*, 46–56.

_____. (2011). Using YAL to teach sympathy and social change: War in Iraq/Afghanistan. *SIGNAL Journal, 34(1)*, 4–9.

Van Draanen, W. (2011). *The Running Dream*. New York: Ember.

Wopperer, E. (2011). Inclusive literature in the library and the classroom: The importance of young adult and children's books that portray characters with disabilities. *Knowledge Quest, 39(3)*, 26–34.

Using YA Literature
That Portrays Disabilities
as Canonical Companions

Janine J. Darragh

This essay takes the stance that young adult (YA) novels that portray characters with disabilities should be included in the curriculum as a vehicle to represent the diverse society in which we live, not *solely* as a didactic disability awareness tool. While it is important to help students unpack the representations of disability that are presented in the novels in order to challenge thinking and combat potential misconceptions and stereotypical beliefs students may have, it is equally important, if not more so, to help students see that while disability may mean *different*, it does not mean *less*. In fact, in helping students to make text-to-self and text-to-text connections that focus on similarities rather than differences, teachers allow space for students to reject society's construct of "normal" with regards to ability. Therefore, this chapter will first address ways in which to examine the text(s) that portray a character with a disability, focusing on helping students explore what it means to be "disabled," ways in which to reconsider disability, and ideas by which to look at the term disability as a social construct. Next, strategies by which to discuss and examine the pair (YA novel and classic), focusing on similarities in characters, settings, and themes along with other literary elements will be identified, and discussion prompts and lesson plan ideas will be provided to help support teachers in exploring the potential for pairing Erskine's *mockingbird* (2010) with Lee's *To Kill a Mockingbird* (1960), Nuzum's *A Small White Scar* (2006) with Steinbeck's *Of Mice and Men* (1937), and Berry's *All the Truth That's in Me* (2013) with Hawthorne's *The Scarlet Letter* (1850). In all cases, the pairs presented have been chosen not because the character has a disability and therefore presents a didactic teaching opportunity, but because they are quality, thought-provoking pieces of literature with strong, interesting, and complex characters who happen to have a disability, and, as such, represent the diverse society in which we live.

Pairing YA Literature with the Classics

Several scholars have written extensively on the benefits of incorporating young adult (YA) literature into the English classroom in general, and on pairing YA texts with the classics in particular. Joan Kaywell, author of multiple volumes of *Adolescent Literature as a Complement to the Classics* (1995), says, "By using young adult novels in conjunction with the classics, teachers can expose students to reading that becomes relevant and meaningful. Additionally, the reading levels of most young adult books are within a range of ease that most students can master" (p. ix). Similarly, Herz and Gallo (1996) posit, "By linking YA with the classics, we can see our students become developing readers, connecting, comparing, and drawing parallels about the elements of literature they discover independently" (p. 26). Former teacher-now-librarian Pauline Schmidt (2014) concurs: "As teachers we must seek and establish opportunities to connect students to canonical texts through books that they might select to read on their own. This way, we can use contemporary YA fiction to bridge the gap between academic reading and reading for pleasure" (p. 116). Using a YA text to introduce a classical work can provide scaffolding for students, as both yield ample opportunities to practice analyzing texts in all of the ways we want students to do. Explains Gallo (2001), "Like classics, contemporary books for teenagers have plots that can be charted, settings that play significant roles, and characters whose personalities, actions, and interactions can be analyzed. There are figurative language, foreshadowing, irony, and other literary elements in the best of the newer works" (p. 36). By having students practice these skills first with a YA text, and then again with a perhaps more challenging work from the canon we can provide not only scaffolding and practice, but also a point of comparison and analysis, building upon students' schema, and yielding a rich enjoyable learning experience for all.

Whether YA literature is "bridging the gap" (Schmidt, 2014), "complementing the classics" (Kaywell, 1993, 1995, 1997), or serving as a ladder (Herz & Gallo, 1996; Lesesne, 2010) or slipstream (Schmidt, 2014), it is clear that there is great potential for using YA literature to help students connect to characters, plots, and themes that are developed in the more traditional (and often more challenging) canonical texts (Gallo, 2001; Herz & Gallo, 1996; Kittle, 2013; Schmidt, 2014). Therefore, if pairing YA literature with the classics can help students better understand, relate to, and enjoy those works, the next logical step is finding the perfect companion texts, specifically choosing book pairings that will help students explore, interrogate, and vicariously experience the lives of those who may be different from them, including people with disabilities.

Disability Studies

The Society for Disability Studies' mission "seeks to augment understanding of disability in all cultures and historical periods to promote greater awareness of the experiences of disabled people, and to advocate for social change" (Society). Similarly, Linton (1998) defines the purpose of disability studies as "not simply the variations that exist in human behavior, appearance, functioning, sensory acuity, and cognitive processing but, more crucially, the meaning we make of those variations" (p. 2). She continues in challenging the idea of what is "normal," a construct that "centers and privileges certain types of behavior, function and appearance" (p. 6). This concept of challenging that which is privileged in society today can encourage and support the development of the higher order critical thinking skills that we want our students to have, and using YA literature that portrays disabilities as an entry to the classics is one means by which to do so. In looking specifically at YA novels that portray people with disabilities, reading these texts in school may have the potential to yield dual benefits. First, students with disabilities may benefit from seeing themselves represented in the literature presented (Landrum, 1998–1999, 2001; Pirofski, 2001; Rhodes & Milby, 2007; Saad, 2004; Stelle, 1999). This may, consequently, impact their self-concept and/or emotional well-being (Cartledge, Gardner, & Ford, 2009). Secondly, students without disabilities may better understand the challenges of being different through reading books portraying characters with exceptionalities. Landrum (2001) says that reading YA literature is an "avenue by which students gain a more complex perception of themselves and others" (p. 252) and that "multiple studies have demonstrated that literature featuring characters with disabilities can spark a healthy acceptance of self and others in young readers" (p. 252). Similarly, Stelle (1999) though speaking of children's literature, not YA literature, writes that books "can be used to develop positive attitudes toward people with disabilities and to encourage positive peer relationships among children of differing abilities" (p. 123). It follows, then, that using YA novels that portray characters with disabilities as entry into the classics can provide students with scaffolding to explore that which might simultaneously challenge their critical thinking and their literacy skills.

Depending on their experiences, students will be in different places regarding both their knowledge of disability and their comfort in discussing what it means to live as a "disabled person" in society today. The English classroom can be a safe place to encourage student growth and understanding, regardless of where students may be. In an interview for *Wordgathering: A Journal of Disability Poetry*, Heather Garrison posits that there are stages of growth with regards to students' understanding about disability, "from looking at differences to looking at similarities to acceptance (simply being)." In this same conversation, Therése Halscheid explains it this way:

> In general, I think of this process in terms of a slow shifting in consciousness—one which begins with separateness, sometimes a cruel separateness (i.e., I stay away because they are so different from me) from which there is suffering from which we morph. I see an early stage of morphing as one which begins to look at others with kindness in terms of differences (whatever they may be), which then morphs into a state of not looking at differences at all but noting what is the same. I see the final stage as not looking for differences or sameness, but simply being. And I think to move from a narrow view to this highest state of consciousness takes time [Dialogue, 2009].

The English classroom in general, and discussions of literature in particular, can provide guided space for students to explore, grapple with, and question the ways in which they think about disability and difference. Regarding making connections to literature, Williams, Inkster and Blaska (2005) explain, "Reading books about characters with disabilities and chronic illnesses opens the door for children to ask questions and facilitates discussion about these types of likenesses and differences. This helps to build a foundation for acceptance of people who may look or act differently" (p. 71). This interrogation of the concept of "normalcy" and how it is played out in communities and schools provides deep critical thinking opportunities, and YA literature provides a safe vehicle by which to explore these challenging concepts. Not only may students find it easier to talk about a fictitious character rather than a "real" person, but they also most likely will not have to struggle as much with comprehending the text, so less time can be spent on elements like vocabulary and plot, giving both teachers and students the space and energy needed to really unpack what it means to be a teen with a disability in society today.

Theoretical Framework

A variety of theories that all fall under the broad heading of *sociocultural theory* will frame the novel pairings and lesson ideas presented in this chapter. At its most basic level, socio-cultural theorists believe that one's cultural and social background impact both how one will learn and how one will see and respond to others and the world (Vygotsky, 1993; Walker & Bean, 2005). This essay couples sociocultural theory with Rosenblatt's Reader Response Theory (1938, 1978), focusing on how one's background knowledge and experiences impact one's understanding of what is read and provide a foundation for making and deepening meaning. In applying that meaning to the lived experience of self and others, reading a variety of texts can aid in the process of rethinking identities, world views, beliefs and values, specifically with regards to where we position ourselves in the world with others like and unlike ourselves (Probst, 2004; Rosenblatt, 1938).

To Kill a Mockingbird and *mockingbird*

Kathryn Erskine's *mockingbird* (2010) is a beautiful, award-winning novel that can be used to introduce a study of Harper Lee's *To Kill a Mockingbird* (1960), be it as a whole class read, literature circle choice book, or a teacher read aloud. *Mockingbird* tells the story of Caitlin, a ten-year-old girl who has lost her brother due to a school shooting. In addition to navigating the world without her older brother, Caitlin, who has Asperger's Syndrome, struggles to find closure for both her father and herself.

Told from her first person perspective, the reader hears of Caitlin's challenges firsthand. "I'm not so good with people. Or emotions" (p. 138). Caitlin says. At school she relies on Mrs. Brook, her special education teacher, to help her to navigate school and social interactions. Caitlin explains, "Mrs. Brook says people have a hard time understanding me because I have Asperger's so I have to try extra hard to understand them and that means working on emotions" (p. 11). Throughout the novel, Mrs. Brook (with the assistance of the Facial Expressions Chart) helps Caitlin to understand and recognize how she is "supposed" to act and serves as not only a support to Caitlin but to Caitlin's teachers as well:

Caitlin. When a teacher says she wants you to do something that means you should do it. It's the same as saying you have to do it.

Well why didn't she say that?

It's a nice way of saying it.

No it's not. It's a confusing way of saying it. And she should say PLEASE if she's trying to be nice.

Would that have helped? If she'd said please?

Maybe. Should I share that with her?

Why don't you let me talk with her instead [p. 41].

In approaching the novel through a disability theory lens, teachers can challenge students to use passages like the one above as a vehicle to explore and question school systems in general. Is public education set up for students who have difficulties with social and emotional interactions? Should it be? What type of student does the school system privilege, and why? What might a school look like that doesn't privilege the "norm"? These are all questions that students can grapple with as they begin to analyze the novel through a disability studies lens. In doing so, they may, perhaps, see school through Caitlin's experience and challenge their previous perceptions, or at least be encouraged to think about school in a different way.

As the novel progresses, the reader struggles along with Caitlin as she tries to make sense of social interactions and behave in the ways that everyone else does—even though it does not come naturally to her.

"Emotions are evil and I hate them! Especially crying. I don't Get It.

Laughing is easier to figure out, [Mrs. Brook] says. It usually shows that you're happy.

Not always. Sometimes it shows that you're being mean [p. 42].

And later:

What we're working on Caitlin is empathy, [Mrs. Brook says].

Is that like emotion?

Sort of.

No thank you. I'm not good with emotion.

All you need to do is imagine how other people are feeling.

Why?

Then you know how to communicate with them.

What if you don't want to? Or can't.

Listen Caitlin. This is important. If they're happy you can be happy with them. If someone is very sad you should be quiet with them and maybe try to cheer them up a little bit but not start out all loud and happy because that doesn't match their emotion.

You're not matching my emotion right now.
Oh? What emotion are you feeling right now?
Kind of annoyed. And bored [p. 86].

Students may be surprised to read both of how sensing people's emotions and responding in a socially acceptable way does not come easily to all people and of how honest and blunt Caitlin is in talking to her teacher about her feelings. She isn't being rude; she is honestly answering the questions, unaware of how her frank response may not generally be deemed socially acceptable. In discussing passages like these, teachers can help students to reevaluate the social norms many of us unconsciously participate in each day and to imagine what it would be like if they did not know or understand those "rules." Students can perhaps first make connections to being in a different culture and then examine the "culture" of disability. Students might discuss questions like, Who decides what the dominant culture is and what social interactions are appropriate? With regards to Caitlin specifically, students can discuss whether there might be a way for others to work at understanding Caitlin more, to meet her in the middle, instead of her having to do all of the difficult work. They can identify the benefits of seeing the world the way Caitlin does, specifically analyzing the potential advantages as well as ramifications of rejecting social norms with regards to what is "appropriate" in order to speak the truth. In using a disability studies lens and in reading from Caitlin's first person perspective, readers can begin to empathize with the struggles of not innately understanding these "rules" and begin to question why and how these "rules" were constructed in the first place and the ways in which they are performed daily.

In the end, it is not just Caitlin's father, teachers, and classmates, but also the reader who learns a great deal about life from Caitlin. In having to struggle daily to just be accepted in the world, Caitlin is often wise beyond her years, and her simple honesty yields truth in ways that others, constrained by social norms, cannot offer. For example, in speaking with her father about Closure, she says, "You have to Work at It Dad. You have to try even if it's hard and you think you can never do it and you just want to scream and hide and shake your hands over and over and over" (p. 162), offering not just her father, but the reader some sage advice and sharing her personal coping strategies without embarrassment. Later, Caitlin offers more advice to her father, making connections between her own feelings and his, and showing the reader that despite the fact that many believe Caitlin lacks appropriate social and emotional responses to situations and others, she might just be stronger in these areas than she is given credit for. She explains to her father, "This is what happens when you have a TRM (Tantrum Rage Meltdown). You make a mess. It's okay. You just have to try harder next time" (p. 167). As readers, we learn not just some basic life lessons, but we also begin to recognize that there is so much more than what we first see in someone, physically or behaviorally. In asking and unpacking some of these questions with regards to Caitlin, a fictional character in a book, students might begin to recognize the hidden structures that are set up in society that exclude others who may perceive and interact with the world differently from the norm. In watching Caitlin struggle, face defeat, and then try again day after day to "walk in another's shoes," readers may reevaluate ways in which they could put in a little effort to see the world differently, too. And even though it might be uncomfortable, as Caitlin explains about trying to make friends, it just may be worth it in the end: "I don't think I'm going to like it at all. I think it's going to hurt. But after the hurt I think maybe something good and strong and beautiful will come out of it" (p. 171).

If students first read Erskine's *mockingbird* as a lead in to Lee's *To Kill a Mockingbird*, they will be introduced to some of the key characters and events in Lee's novel. This is done explicitly throughout *mockingbird*, as Caitlin shares the connection she, her brother, and her father have to this classic work. Students can use these bits of information to build off as they navigate the novel, and comparisons between the two books, specifically with regards to characters, literary elements, and themes can allow for higher order thinking and deeper analysis of both works. For example, Caitlin explains the similarities between herself and Scout:

> I look a little like Scout. I looked more like Scout when I was seven and Devon cut my hair like hers except Dad said not to do that ever ever again. I didn't mind the haircut. I would not like to wear a ham costume like Scout had to in the movie however but if I did I know Devon would take care of me like Jem did even if someone tried to stop him with a knife like the bad guy in the movie. I wonder if Devon was trying to help someone like me when the bad guy with the bullet stopped him [p. 79].

There are several other similarities between Caitlin of *mockingbird* and Scout from *To Kill a Mockingbird*, beyond those Caitlin herself identifies. Both girls are about the same age, with an older brother whom they admire. Both have lost their mother and are being raised by their hard-working fathers, both struggle in school and with teachers, and both are trying to make sense of the world in which they live. Students can make text-to-text connections, identifying similarities between the two characters, and speculating what their conversations might be like if Caitlin and Scout were classmates.

In addition to the female protagonists and their families and friends, in both novels the community as a whole acts as a character, with its members coming together in times of crisis and strife. For example, in *mockingbird* the community joins together at a dedication ceremony at the school to honor those who have been affected by the school shooting, and likewise, community members in *To Kill a Mockingbird* gather at the trial and in the aftermath of the trial's events to discuss it and support one another. Students may want to explore this community-as-character concept in literature and then take it one step further, discussing the types of events, historically and currently that seem to bring communities together. This may lead to an investigation of ways in which students might participate in their own local and school communities. Asking community members, school officials, or even looking at websites like the Ready Campaign (Ready) may provide some ideas for students to take the first steps in getting involved.

Finally, several themes and images are developed in both novels that students can examine. Caitlin herself explains one such theme in *mockingbird.* She says:

> The first time we watched *To Kill a Mockingbird* I waited through the whole movie for the dad to shoot a mockingbird. He'd already shot a dog. And he was a good shot. No one shot a bird for the whole entire movie. At the end I said it was the stupidest name ever for a movie. Devon said I didn't know what I was talking about. This year he read it in English and he said the title makes perfect sense and this is what it means: It's wrong to shoot someone who is innocent and was never going to hurt you in the first place. I still didn't Get It and said, "But you told me the dog was sick and he WAS going to hurt them. And Devon said, It's not about the dog! It's about people! You shouldn't hurt innocent people Scout. That's what it means" [p. 80].

In looking at this passage, students can see not only how Caitlin struggles to understand things beyond a literal level, but also how both novels demonstrate instances where the innocent are hurt, for reasons beyond their control. Teachers can help students unpack this theme of not hurting innocent people. Students can explore questions like: What are the different meanings of the word "innocent," and what does Devon mean by this? Do we protect the innocent? In what ways? Who in society is most vulnerable? Who are the "innocent" characters in both *mockingbird* and *To Kill a Mockingbird,* and in what ways are they hurt and/or protected? What is our responsibility with regards to those who are innocent, and specifically those who may navigate the world differently from us due to disability? What is the difference in speaking for and speaking up for those who are different from us? Discussing and debating questions like these can again help students deepen their understanding of the novels, while allowing space for them to evaluate the ways in which we treat others like and unlike ourselves. Furthermore, the dedication page of Erskine's *mockingbird* says, "In hopes that we may all understand each other better." Students may want to examine ways in which Lee's *To Kill a Mockingbird* relates to Erskine's dedication, brainstorming how various characters tried (or didn't try) to understand one another, and the results of doing so. Again, students can look to history and current events to see the benefits of understanding and/or the repercussions of misunderstanding people who may have different world views from the norm.

With regards to symbolism in making text-to-text comparisons, students can analyze bird imagery in general and research information about the mockingbird in particular. Tracking the bird imagery in both novels and researching the mockingbird, with attention to the ways in which this bird is incorporated into each text can lead to discussions of the role of mockingbirds in both books and speculation about why the books might be titled the way they are. Continuing with bird imagery analyses, a look at clips from the currently popular *Hunger Games* trilogy (Collins, 2008, 2009, 2010) and a reading of Pulitzer Prize winning poet Mary Oliver's (1994) poem "Mockingbirds" can also provide a format for discussion on mockingbird symbolism present in various literary works.

The pedagogical potential for pairing these two novels is great. In using *mockingbird* as an entry to both discuss some challenging questions regarding the treatment of people with disabilities and as a foundation upon which to build understanding for the novel *To Kill a Mockingbird*, student thinking and learning can be augmented. Furthermore, in focusing on ways in which the novels are similar, students can begin to consider ways in which the disability experience is just perhaps a different lived experience than their own, and to focus on looking at that which brings us together, rather than that which keeps us apart.

Of Mice and Men and *A Small White Scar*

Having similar settings, themes, and protagonists who have developmental disabilities, *Of Mice and Men* and *A Small White Scar* is another pair that complements each other well. *A Small White Scar* by K.A. Nuzum tells the story of twin brothers, Will and Denny. After their mother has died, Will is put in charge of taking care of and looking after his brother, Denny, who has Down Syndrome, while their father takes care of the ranch. In many ways a coming of age story for both characters, this novel is one of suspense, interweaving both inner and outer turmoil, as it shares Will's struggle between striking out on his own and upholding his familial responsibilities. Similarly, Steinbeck's (1937) *Of Mice and Men* tells a suspenseful story of two male traveling companions. With Lennie having a cognitive disability that makes keeping a job difficult, George finds himself, like Will from *A Small White Scar*, having to make some challenging decisions that impact both his and his travel mate's futures. Both novels take place in the West in the 1930s and 1940s when the effects of the Depression and the Dust Bowl are still being strongly felt. Lack of money is a constant worry for characters in both novels, and the male protagonists in each earn their keep by working on a farm.

A Small White Scar examines the practice of institutionalization for people with disabilities. This, unfortunately, is part of our history that is not commonly taught in schools. With the majority of students with disabilities currently being either fully included or partially included in the traditional classroom throughout the day (Gargiulo, 2009), it is possible that students will not know that learning alongside classmates with disabilities was not a common practice in public schools just forty years ago. A scene where Doc Sidders and Will are talking about Will's brother, Denny, introduces the topic to readers. The doctor explains to Will:

> "He [Will and Denny's father] asked me what I thought he should do about Dennis. I told him, I thought your brother should be institutionalized, put away." *Institutionalized?* I felt surprise sweep down my back and through my legs. I had heard of places where they kept the feebleminded, but I had never thought of babies being put there. Never thought of people quitting their own children. I had never thought of Momma and my father weighing a decision like that.... I had never thought of Denny locked away from his home, from his family [p. 119].

This conversation between Doc Sidders and Will can set the scene for students to investigate the practice of institutionalization. Excerpts from Kim E. Nielsen's *A Disability History of the United States* (2012) can be read to provide students with background information and descriptions of insane asylums and state hospitals of the past, so they have a better context for understanding why Will is surprised to hear that institutionalization was a consideration for his brother. As this pair of novels each portrays characters with cognitive disabilities, it is an especially appropriate time for teachers to help students explore the history of the treatment of people with disabilities. In researching the past practice of institutionalization and the laws that changed the way we support people with disabilities in society in general, and in public schools in particular, students can begin to discover aspects of discrimination they most likely have not learned about previously. *A Small White Scar*'s Denny provides an example readers can relate to as they think about Institutions; students can analyze all that Denny can do, identifying the ways in which he contributes to both the family and to the farm.

Likewise, Ben Mikaelsen's (1998) children's book *Petey* can provide readers with background information about the practices of Institutionalization—what daily life was like for the patients as well as the impacts on mind, body, and soul. Beginning in the year 1922 when two-year-old Petey's parents commit him to the state's insane asylum, this book tells Petey's life story. While unable to communicate verbally due to his cerebral palsy, Petey is very intelligent and aware of his surroundings. Readers live vicariously through Petey as he grows up in horrific conditions, and they rejoice with him when the state hospital is finally closed and Petey is moved to a nursing home. In first reading the fictional *Petey* and/or excerpts from Nielsen's *A Disability History of the United States* (2012), students may better understand why Institutions were not recognized as an acceptable option for neither Denny nor Lennie in *A Small White Scar* and *Of Mice and Men*, respectively.

Of Mice and Men offers some unique challenges for teachers, as students read about Lennie and the unfortunate events that lead to his death. Anecdotal evidence suggests that this novel actually can promote fear in students regarding people with disabilities. Some young readers find Lennie and his lack of understanding regarding how strong he is and the appropriate ways to touch animals and humans (so as not to harm them) scary. Knowing this potential response to the book and anticipating and addressing it and other representations of disability in literature is necessary. If not examined with the help of teachers, texts may unintentionally oversimplify, promote stereotypes, or even promulgate fear in students who do not have experiences with people with disabilities, about those who are different from them.

Pairing *A Small White Scar* with *Of Mice and Men* provides a platform for such discussions. Having first researched the historical and legislative background regarding Institutionalization and unpacking heavy issues of the often horrifying and certainly unfair treatment of people with disabilities through the lens of Will and Denny from *A Small White Scar*, students will have some schema on which to connect to the characters and events portrayed in *Of Mice and Men*. Specifically, students will first examine disability through Denny who exhibits no "scary" behavior, before they move on to the difficult events of the classic work. With regards to *Of Mice and Men* in particular, students will better understand why so many characters are surprised that Lennie and George are traveling partners, as throughout the novel the boss and other workers at the ranch comment on the unlikely traveling companions. For example, on the day of their arrival, Slim, the jerkline skinner, comments, "It jus' seems kinda funny a cuckoo like him and a smart little guy like you travelin' together" (p. 43), and on various occasions George finds himself explaining not just how and why Lennie and he are traveling together, but how Lennie is capable of working at all. Furthermore, an understanding of the treatment of people with disabilities at the time (like the forced-sterilization and restrictive immigration laws [Nielsen, 2012]) can provide readers with insight regarding why George "hadda" take Lennie's life at the end of the novel, opening up critical discussions on quality of life and euthanasia practices of both the past and today.

With regards to literary techniques, animal imagery is used extensively and symbolically in both *A Small White Scar* and *Of Mice and Men*. Students can chart these images and analyze how issues of power are connected to the animal scenes for each text, as well as how those might contribute to symbolism and theme development. For example, in *A Small White Scar*, Will kills the rattlesnake that is poised to bite Denny, and while he knows it was the right thing to do, Denny is upset:

"Thank you, brother Will. You had to shoot him."
Denny's eyes were filled with tears.
I nodded.
"You had to shoot him.... Sorry, snake," he said.
He looked up at me.
"I feel sad to see his belly up, brother Will. That is not comfortable for snakes" [p. 48].

Students can investigate the ways in which society has, historically, treated people who are different, and compare those examples to the ways in which animals are often perceived and (mis)treated in not only these two works, but in other works of literature as well. To add a third piece of literature for comparison, students might also read and use historical, literary, and disability studies lenses to analyze Robert Burns's poem "To a Mouse," the titular reference for Steinbeck's novel, drawing connections between it and both *Of Mice and Men* and *A Small White Scar*. Both novels clearly relate to the poem:

> The best laid schemes o' Mice an' Men,
> Gang aft agley,
> An' lea'e us nought but grief an' pain,
> For promis'd joy!

Adding this third piece of literature can help students to connect not just recurring images and messages in various genres of literature, but also examples from history and the world today.

While *A Small White Scar* and *Of Mice and Men* can easily be compared with regards to setting, characters, and imagery, it is equally important to guide students in making character-to-self connections to the books. Theme development is one way in which to do so. Both novels lend themselves to an exploration of the pursuit of the American Dream. Students can look at barriers to the American Dream as they play out with individual characters in each book, specifically for characters who are marginalized due to ability, socioeconomic status, and race. They can debate whether or not the American Dream even exists—and if so, for whom? To extend the theme, students can examine how the quest for the American Dream impacts the characters in these novels, characters in other works of literature, people in history, and people today. They can even consider their personal dreams, tracking the steps they will need to take to reach those goals and the potential barriers they may need to overcome. In making broad connections like these, students can practice identifying the universal feelings and experiences humans have.

Relationships are another theme that can be explored extensively through both novels. In both cases, the relationship between male protagonists is complicated. The reality is that having a family member or a friend with a disability can sometimes be challenging. However, any relationship provides challenges, and it is in recognizing the enrichment that a relationship can bring that yields satisfaction for all involved. Students might discuss questions like: What does Will gain from his relationship with his brother? What does Denny gain from his relationship with Will? The same questions can be asked regarding travel mates George and Lennie, and answers can be compared. Students might also want to debate for which individual character(s) is the relationship more complicated and why, with a follow up activity of exploring other complicated relationships in literature, history, and in their own lives. Issues of guilt, anger and fear are also evident in each novel, as is the struggle between doing what one wants to do and putting others before oneself. Grappling with questions like these can provide a stepping stone for making text-to-text and text-to-self connections.

Finally, students may want to discuss dreams and the power that having a dream or goal can have on individuals, for good and for bad. In both novels, it is the need for and pursuit of a dream that instigates all action. For example, when Will tells Denny of his plans to leave the ranch and join the rodeo circuit, his brother is devastated—and not just because his brother is leaving, but because his brother has a plan for the future: "'But, brother Will'—Denny's voice quavered, his cheeks bunched up—'I don't have a plan. Nobody said I would need a plan.' Fat tears spilled out of his eyes" (p. 69). Later in the novel Denny is offered a plan and the option of accepting or rejecting it. In being given choice, voice, and a purposeful plan, Denny finds joy. He shares with his brother:

> Will! I have a surprise to tell. I have got a plan. I am a grown-up now too. Because of my own plan. I am going to stay here. At the Doc Sidder's. For a while. Our dad and the Doc Sidder have talked it over. Then they asked me. I had to say "okay." No one else could say it. So I said it. Now I am going to do the things like at home. Chores. Like at home when I reach under the chickens for their eggs. When I put them in the blue basket. And I am going to sweep the broom for the Doc Sidder. I am going to wash the dishes. And some forks and knifes. And something new. I am going to fold the Doc Sidder's towels. For his sick people. He says he can teach me that. He says I can learn it. So, I am a grown up. Like you, Will [p. 162].

Readers can see that Denny has longed to contribute and have a purpose in life. While he may have more limitations than his brother Will with regards to the ways in which he can contribute, he is willing and able to help and is overjoyed to be given both the choice and opportunity to do so.

While less autonomous, Lennie also finds great joy in reviewing his and George's plan for the future, and the conversation about how they will have their own land and how George will tend to the rabbits is repeated throughout the novel. "'Come on, George. Tell me. Please, George. Like you done before.' 'Guys like us, that work on ranches, are the loneliest guys in the world.... They ain't got nothing to look ahead to.... With us it ain't like that. We got a future'" (p. 15). This need for a plan or dream is picked up by other characters as well. For example, upon hearing of George and Lennie's plan, Candy, another marginalized character in the novel due to his physical disability, adopts George and Lennie's dream:

"I ain't much good with on'y one hand. I lost my hand right here on this ranch.... S'pose I went in with you guys"... They fell into a silence. They looked at one another, amazed. This thing they had never really believed in was coming true. George said reverently, "Jesus Christ! I bet we could swing her." His eyes were full of wonder. "I bet we could swing her, he repeated softly" [pp. 65–66].

It is clear that the characters have not considered that positive options might be available to them, and the realization that there is potential for a different and happy life is powerful. Having a plan, hopes, dreams, and goals are universal yearnings, regardless of ability. In making text-to-self connections to this theme, students can find common ground with the various characters in the novels, regardless of historical setting and/or characters' abilities.

If including a film study is desirable, Peter Hedge's *What's Eating Gilbert Grape* (1993) can provide another comparison for students to examine. Like both Will from *A Small White Scar* and George from *Of Mice and Men*, Gilbert has to take care of and support his brother Arnie who has cognitive disabilities. The visual experience of the film allows the reader to literally see both the love and often frustration Gilbert has toward not only his brother but also his whole family and the situation into which he has been thrust due to his father's death and his mother's physical and psychological challenges. In the end, like Will, Gilbert has a choice in how and where to spend his life, and even if he chooses to stay in small town Endora with his brother, it is simply having that choice that sets him free. In fact, the power of choice is a recurring theme throughout all of the works mentioned (*A Small White Scar, Of Mice and Men, Petey, A Disability History of the United States*) and one to which all can relate.

Though the setting, characters, and many symbols and themes align and tie these two novels together, the tones of each book, specifically the ending of each novel, are in stark contrast to one another. Students may want to discuss the culminating events of each book, specifically with regards to the characters with disabilities, analyzing what exactly led to such different conclusions, and speculating how both choices and uncontrollable events along the way may have altered the endings to be more similar to each other. Furthermore, an analysis of how an author's worldview can impact his/her work would be appropriate. Students can compare the time period in which the books were written, the chosen style, and the target audience of each text in order to analyze how those factors may have influenced the writing. Using YA literature as an entry to both Steinbeck's classic novel and as an exploration of disability history can provide the schema students need to more fully engage with these difficult and important topics they need to know.

The Scarlet Letter and
All the Truth That's in Me

Unlike the other novel pairs presented in this chapter, *All the Truth That's in Me* and *The Scarlet Letter* are unique in that they provide an opportunity for readers to conduct a historical analysis of belief systems of the Colonial time, specifically the intersection of religion, disability, and physical and/or "moral" illness. *All the Truth That's in Me* shares the story of Judith, a young woman who goes missing from her Puritan community and returns two years later ... with her tongue cut out. As the novel progresses, the reader journeys with Judith as she tries to make sense of what has happened to her and to literally and figuratively find her voice, independence, and love. In addition to Judith's physical disability and challenges with her speech, her brother, Darrel, requires amputation at the knee after an accident in an unnamed battle. These representations allow for readers to look historically at the treatment of people with disabilities based on both gender and physical disability presented.

For example, the people in the town, and even Judith's own mother, treat her poorly upon her return to the village. Told from Judith's first person perspective, we see how hurtful this is:

> "[I'm] Sorry I'm like this now. *Ar-ee, sssshhar-ee.* My gruesome sounds made Mother wince.
> "Be still!" she'd say. "You sound idiotic."
> She told no one of my return for days.... When at last the secret could no more be hidden, she led me to the shed and said, "You've come back maimed. I leave it to God to judge what brought this upon you. But the village will fear you. They'll call you cursed. Some men may try to take advantage of you. I know my duty to my own flesh and blood, and I will protect you. But you'll mind me and behave as a maiden should. Utter one sound to our shame, and you'll sleep here among the rakes and shovels" [p. 48].

With no separation of Church and State, and with religion playing such a large role in all aspects of Puritan life, the community, even Judith's own mother, feels that what has happened to her is somehow justified and connected to the will of God, or, like Puritans of the time, that disability was a sign of "divine displeasure" (Nielsen, 2012, p. 27). With this in mind, the following questions can first be examined through the YA novel and then built upon when later reading *The Scarlet Letter*: What was the role of religion in the New World? What were the beliefs and laws regarding disability? What were the differences in treatment of those with disabilities depending on whether or not they could contribute economically to the New World? How, unlike the United States of today that separates Church and State, did crime and punishment intertwine with issues of religion?

While the focus of *The Scarlet Letter* is not on disability, it is clearly integrated throughout the novel. For example, when protagonist Hester is standing on the scaffold serving her punishment for her crime of committing adultery, she recognizes Chillingworth (her husband whom she has not seen for quite some time) because "one of this man's shoulders rose higher than the other ... [a] slight deformity of the figure" (p. 47) In the very next chapter, Chillingworth explains that due to his physical disability he is not worthy of love and affection, acknowledging specifically that appearance is more important than intellect. He tells Hester that because of his physical appearance, he cannot blame her for not being faithful to him: "Misshapen from my birth hour, how could I delude myself with the idea that intellectual gifts might veil physical deformity in a young girl's fantasy?" (p. 56). Moreover, as the novel progresses and the reader follows Chillingworth's obsessive quest for revenge on Dimmesdale, Hester's lover, Chillingworth's physical appearance changes, his moral sin showing itself outwardly: "Ever and anon, too, there came a glare of red light out of his eyes, as if the old man's soul were on fire ... in a word, old Roger Chillingworth was a striking evidence of man's faculty of transforming himself into a devil" (p. 123). These scenes set the stage for not only an analysis of the literary technique so popular in the 1800s, of including elements of the supernatural into writing, but also perceptions that outward appearance reflects one's heart and soul, and the pattern of using appearance to signify one's personal nature. At the end of the novel, Chillingworth is "a deformed old figure with a face that haunted men's memories longer than they liked," and he "positively withered up, shriveled away and almost vanished from mortal sight, like an uprooted weed that lies wilting in the sun" (126). Students can investigate how physical disability has historically been used to visually represent evil or wrongdoing in both literature and film. Critically viewing clips of films and books like *Rain Man, Million Dollar Baby*, and *A Christmas Carol* can help students to identify stereotypes (e.g., all people on the autism spectrum are savants, a life with a disability is not worth living, those with disabilities should be pitied) presented in media and analyze why these representations may have taken place as well as what messages are, either intentionally or unintentionally, being sent to readers and viewers. Likewise, clips from more current television shows like *Game of Thrones, Breaking Bad,* and *Push Girls* can be reviewed to illuminate ways in which characters with disabilities can and are being represented in ways that defy traditional stereotypes surrounding disability and respectfully show the lived experiences of those who are disabled.

In looking at theme, both *All the Truth That's in Me* and *The Scarlet Letter* offer messages regarding the power of friendship. In *All the Truth That's in Me* Judith feels isolated upon returning to her community, until former classmate Maria reaches out to her. Having broken her marriage betrothal to marry the man she really loves, Maria finds kinship in the also ostracized Judith and invites her to her home. In Maria's interactions with Judith, we see ways in which she respectfully accommodates for Judith's speech challenges. Judith explains:

> She has a pretty way of asking questions that don't expose my lack of speech, and it occurs to me, as she fetches the preserves from her cupboard, that she rehearsed this in her mind before I came. She wanted to spare me awkwardness. Mother and I can communicate, but not in a way that doesn't humiliate me [p. 123].

Judith yearns for friendship and social interaction, yet she is worried and embarrassed about her ability to communicate. Maria is aware of Judith's challenges and finds ways to converse with her that put her at ease, yet allow for her to be part of the conversation. This is a skill that does not come naturally for all people. Studies and anecdotal evidence show us that often students without disabilities are uncertain about or even afraid of those who are disabled, having biases against and negative attitudes about people with disabilities, not readily accepting their peers with disabilities, and preferring to spend both in and out of class time with their classmates who are not disabled (Bender, 2008; Campbell, Ferguson, Herzinger, Jackson, & Marino, 2004; Dore, Dion, Agner & Brunet, 2002; Fisher, 1999; McDougall, DeWit, King, Miller & Killip, 2004; Morton & Campbell, 2008; Nowicki & Sandieson, 2002; Swaim & Morgan, 2001). Moreover, often, in attempts to be polite, students will just ignore the disability altogether, not realizing that in doing so they are dismissing the person as well. Students need to learn that it is natural and even appropriate to "see" a difference. It is appropriate to ask a question and to include others. No one likes to feel invisible. Often those who may look a little different just need someone else to take that first step. This is clearly evident in *All the*

Truth That's in Me when looking at the friendship between Judith and Maria, not just in her initial ways of speaking to Judith as seen in the scene above, but also later as their friendship develops, and Maria addresses Judith's speech challenges directly:

> "Why don't you speak, Judith?... You can, can't you? Somewhat?... I've been thinking about it a great deal. We need to find a way for you to talk."
> "...Why?"
> "...Because I want to know you," she says. And others will want to as well."
> "*They... sshay...*" I must think hard about each sound, how each muscle of my face and throat might now combine to form it.... "*...I'hm... curshedth*."
> "...I know some say you're cursed," she says quietly. "Tell them otherwise.... Don't laugh—I've been experimenting to see what sounds can be made without ... a tongue. There's—as I said, there's no reason to dillydally about the truth, is there? Without a tongue. DO you lack all of your tongue, or only some?" [pp. 130–132].

Literature provides a safe vehicle for readers to explore the uncomfortable topic of why people often ignore or are afraid of those who are different, whether it is wearing a scarlet letter or lacking one's voice. Students can see through Judith and Maria's friendship that it is ok to acknowledge disability. They can wrestle with the idea that in ignoring one's disability, they are rejecting a part of the person—just a part of the person, not all that the person is. Judith is so much more than her physical disability; as the book progresses, she does not let it define her, and people should not define her by it either.

After completing both novels, there are numerous opportunities for students to connect the two texts to each other and to their own lives. For example, students might contemplate why the endings of the novels are so different, specifically the lives and prospects of the female protagonists, Judith and Hester. They might want to discuss the power of friendship, and, conversely, the power of loneliness. Consider the following questions: How do you reject what others think of you and be true to and believe in yourself? What happens if you do not? In what ways can guilt, shame and secrets be powerful? When should someone keep a secret? When should someone tell a secret? What happens when secrets are told? Why do some people feel like they should hide their disabilities? Is there ever a time when it is appropriate to hide one's challenges and/or strengths? These topics that can be discussed verbally, debated, or answered in writing, with students using examples from the novels, history, other literature, and/or modern day to support their claims.

Likewise, creative writing opportunities that demonstrate understanding of both novels are plentiful. For example, there is a climactic public event at the end of each novel where truths are revealed. Students can review both of those scenes then rewrite the Election Day scene in *The Scarlet Letter*, speculating what Hester would have said, if, like Judith, she had the opportunity and courage to "tell the whole story"—to find her voice and speak the truth. Students might also consider writing a dialogue between Hester and Judith, envisioning what they might say to one another if they had the chance to meet. Students could rewrite or add a scene to either novel, after dropping characters from one novel into scenes from the other. What, for example, would happen if Dimmesdale was the minister instead of the Reverend Frye in *All the Truth that's in Me*? What would happen if Judith was called on to babysit Pearl? How would Hester's life be different if, like Judith, she did not have the ability to speak? The opportunities to make text to text connections in unique ways that help students flex their creative and critical thinking muscles are endless.

Finally, at a very basic skill level, *All the Truth That's in Me* is the perfect introduction to *The Scarlet Letter* because it sets the stage for Hawthorne's challenging work. Setting, historical time period, vocabulary, symbolism, and themes are all similar. Both are suspenseful stories of love, vengeance, secrets, guilt, bullying, fear and oppression, and as such comparisons are easily made. There are potentially unfamiliar vocabulary terms specific to the historical settings that are present in both works, and reviewing the meanings of words like *Papist, Goody, pillory,* and *scaffold* when students read *All the Truth That's in Me* may lift some of the burden of the lofty language readers will encounter in *The Scarlet Letter.* Similarly, much of the background knowledge students will need to know about the time period in general and the Puritans in particular can be front loaded with Berry's novel, scaffolding the knowledge for students, building those bridges and providing those slipstreams for readers in order to ease the challenge of Hawthorne's text. In providing that support, students can more deeply engage with Hawthorne's text, going beyond plot comprehension and toward more complex analysis. Therefore, in having students read Berry's *All the Truth That's in Me* in conjunction with *The Scarlet Letter,* teachers support students in their understanding of not only this challenging literary classic, but also of the time period in which the novels were set and the views regarding disability and difference in the Colonial times and beyond.

Conclusion

These are just three examples of potential pairings of canonical literature with YA novels that portray characters with disabilities (see the Appendix for more pairing suggestions). Unlike many novels of the past (Davis, 1997), the three YA novels presented here, *mockingbird, A Small White Scar,* and *All the Truth That's in Me do* have a main character with a disability, and the depictions of those characters do not fall into any of the stereotypes often associated with representations of disability (e.g., pitiable, laughable, "super crip," sad, nonsexual) (Anti-Defamation League, 2005; Blaska, 2004; Landrum, 2001). Moreover, the characters in these novels are well-rounded, well-developed, successful, and interesting-traits that scholars say one should look for in choosing books of the disability genre (Anti-Defamation League, 2005; Blaska, 2004; Landrum, 2001).

As English teachers, we have the weighty task of helping students to build both their literary and their critical thinking skills. In pairing YA novels with canonical pieces of literature, we can intentionally address and help develop both of these. Furthermore, including YA novels that portray characters with disabilities as both the centerpieces of instructional units and the introduction to works from the canon may provide our students with the foundation to unpack the underlying issues of difference and the ways in which we treat others who are not like us. In making text-to-self connections to the protagonists with disabilities presented in these works, we can help our adolescent readers to *reject* the concept of the character with disability being an outsider, or "other," and to question what society deems as "normal." Comparing works of literature and focusing on similarities and life lessons learned is a skill that, hopefully, can transcend the classroom, as young adults begin to see that the human experience is universal, regardless of ability, and that strong, rich connections can easily be made when we set aside differences and focus on commonalities instead. Whether we call it a ladder, bridge, slipstream, or something else, YA literature that portrays characters with disabilities may be just the tool we need to connect our students to not only the classics, but also to one another, and to the world.

Appendix:
Other Possible Canonical Companions

Choldenko, G. (2004). *Al Capone Does My Shirts*
Dowd, S. (2007). *The London Eye Mystery*

Doyle, A.C. (1892). *The Adventures of Sherlock Holmes*
Draper, S. (2010). *Out of My Mind*
Fitzgerald, F.S. (1925). *The Great Gatsby*
Frank, A. (1967). *Anne Frank: The diary of a young girl*
Friesen, J. (2008). *Jerk, California*
Gibson, W. (1956). *The Miracle Worker*
Giles, G. (2014). *Girls Like Us*
Green, J. (2012). *The Fault in Our Stars*
Hesse, H. (1951). *Siddhartha*
Mazer, H. (2012). *Somebody, Please Tell Me Who I Am*
Mikaelsen, B. (1998). *Petey*
O'Brien, T. (1990). *The Things They Carried*
Salinger, J.D. (1951). *The Catcher in the Rye*
Shakespeare, W. (1892, 1993). *Romeo and Juliet*
Steinbeck, J. (1937). *Of Mice and Men*
Stork, F.X. (2009). *Marcelo in the Real World*
Walker, A. (1982). *The Color Purple*
Wein, E. (2013). *Rose Under Fire*
Wiesel, E. (1982). *Night*

References

Anti-Defamation League. (2005). Evaluating children's books that address disability. Retrieved from http://archive.adl.org/education/curriculum_connections/fall_2005/fall_2005_sb_disability.html.

Bender, W.N. (2008). *Learning Disabilities: Characteristics, Identification, and Teaching Strategies* (6th ed.). Boston: Pearson.

Berry, J. (2013). *All the Truth That's in Me.* New York: Viking.

Blaska, J.K. (2004). Children's literature that includes characters with disabilities or illnesses. *Disability Studies Quarterly, 24(1).* Retrieved from http://dsq-sds.org/article/view/854/1029.

Burns, R. (1785). To a mouse. Retrieved from http://www.robertburns.org.uk/Assets/Poems_Songs/toamouse.htm.

Campbell, J., Ferguson, J., Herzinger, C., Jackson, J., & Marino, C. (2004). Combined descriptive and explanatory information improves peers' perceptions of autism. *Research in Developmental Disabilities, 25*(4), 321–339.

Cartledge, G., Gardner, R., & Ford, D.Y. (2009). *Diverse Learners with Exceptionalities: Culturally Responsive Teaching in the Inclusive Classroom.* Upper Saddle River, NJ: Pearson.

Choldenko, G. (2004). *Al Capone Does My Shirts.* New York: Penguin.

Collins, S. (2008). *The Hunger Games.* NY: Scholastic.

_____. (2009). *Catching Fire.* New York: Scholastic.

_____. (2010). *Mockingjay.* New York: Scholastic.

Davis, L. (1997). Constructing normalcy: The bell curve, the novel, and the invention of the disabled body in the nineteenth century. In L. Davis (ed.), *The Disability Studies Reader* (9–28). New York: Routledge.

Dialogue on Teaching Disability Literature. (2009). *Wordgathering: A Journal of Disability Poetry, 3(1)*. Retrieved from http://www.wordgathering.com/past_issues/issue9/interview/dialogue.html.

Dore, R., Dion, E., Wagner, S., & Brunet, J. (2002). High school inclusion of adolescents with mental retardation: A multiple case study. *Education and Training in Mental Retardation and Developmental Disabilities, 37(3)*, 253–261.

Dowd, S. (2007). *The London Eye Mystery*. New York: Yearling.

Doyle, A.C. (1892). *The Adventures of Sherlock Holmes*. New York: Harper.

Draper, S. (2010). *Out of My Mind*. New York: Atheneum.

Erskine, K. (2010). *mockingbird*. New York: Puffin.

Fisher, D. (1999). According to their peers: Inclusion as high school students see it. *Mental Retardation, 37(6)*, 458–467.

Fitzgerald, F.S. (1925). *The Great Gatsby*. New York: Scribner.

Frank, A. (1967). *Anne Frank: The Diary of a Young Girl*. New York: Doubleday.

Friesen, J. (2008). *Jerk, California*. New York: Penguin.

Gallo, D. (2001). How classics create an alliterate society. *English Journal, 90(3)*, 33–39.

Gargiulo, R.M. (2009). *Special Education in Contemporary Society: An Introduction to Exceptionality*, 3d ed. Los Angeles: Sage.

Gibson, W. (1956). *The Miracle Worker*. New York: Simon & Schuster.

Giles, G. (2014). *Girls Like Us*. Sommerville, MA: Candlewick.

Green, J. (2012). *The Fault in Our Stars*. New York: Penguin.

Hallstrom, L. (dir). (1993). *What's Eating Gilbert Grape* [Video]. Paramount.

Hawthorne, N. (1850, 1994). *The Scarlet Letter*. New York: Dover.

Herz, S.K., & Gallo, D. (1996). *From Hinton to Hamlet: Building Bridges Between Young Adult Literature and the Classics*. Westport, CT: Greenwood Press.

Hesse, H. (1951). *Siddhartha*. New York: New Directions.

Kaywell, J. (ed.). (1993). *Adolescent Literature as a Complement to the Classics*. Norwood, MA: Christopher-Gordon.

_____ (ed.). (1995). *Adolescent Literature as a Complement to the Classics*, 2d ed. Norwood, MA: Christopher-Gordon.

_____ (ed.). (1997). *Adolescent Literature as a Complement to the Classics*, 3d ed. Norwood, MA: Christopher-Gordon.

Kittle, P. (2013). *Book Love: Developing Depth, Stamina, and Passion in Adolescent Readers*. Portsmouth, NH: Heinemann.

Landrum, J. (1998–1999). Adolescent novels that feature characters with disabilities: An annotated bibliography. *Journal of Adolescent & Adult Literacy, 42(4)*, 284–290.

_____. (2001). Selecting intermediate novels that feature characters with disabilities. *The Reading Teacher, 55(3)*, 252–258.

Lee, H. (1960, 1988). *To Kill a Mockingbird*. New York: Grand Central.

Lesesne, T. (2010). *Reading Ladders: Leading Students from Where They Are to Where We'd Like Them to Be*. Portsmouth, NH: Heinemann.

Linton, S. (1998). *Claiming Disability Knowledge and Identity.* New York: New York University Press.

Mazer, H. (2012). *Somebody, Please Tell Me Who I Am.* New York: Simon & Schuster.

McDougall, J., DeWit, D.J., King, G., Miller, L.T., & Killip, S. (2004). High school-aged youths' attitudes toward their peers with disabilities: The role of school and student interpersonal factors. *International Journal of Disability, Development and Education, 51(3)*, 287–313.

Mikaelsen, B. (1998). *Petey.* New York: Disney Hyperion.

Morton, J.F., & Campbell, J. (2008). Information source affects peers' initial attitudes toward autism. *Research in Developmental Disabilities, 29*, 189–201.

Nielse, K.E. (2012). *A Disability History of the United States.* Boston: Beacon Press.

Nowicki, E.A., & Sandieson, R. (2002). A meta-analysis of school-age children's attitudes towards persons with physical or intellectual disabilities. *International Journal of Disability, Development and Education, 49(3)*, 244–265.

Nuzum, K.A. (2006). *A Small White Scar.* New York: HarperCollins.

O'Brien, T. (1990). *The Things They Carried.* New York: Houghton Mifflin.

Oliver, M. (1994). Mockingbirds. *Atlantic Monthly, 273(2)*, 80.

Pirofski, K.I. (2001) Race, gender, and disability in today's children's literature. Retrieved from http://www.edchange.org/multicultural/papers/literature2.html.

Probst, R. (2004). *Response and Analysis: Teaching Literature in Secondary School*, 2d ed. Portsmouth, NH: Heinemann.

Ready Campaign. (2013). Retrieved from http://www.ready.gov/get-involved.

Rhodes, J., & Milby, T. (2007). Teacher-created electronic books: Integrating technology to support readers with disabilities. *Reading Teacher, 61(3)*, 255–259.

Rosenblatt, L.M. (1938). *Literature as Exploration.* New York: D. Appleton-Century.

_____. (1978). *The Reader, the Text, the Poem: The Transactional Theory of the Literary Work.* Carbondale: Southern Illinois University Press.

Saad, C. (2004). The portrayal of male and female characters with chronic illnesses in children's realistic fiction, 1970–1994. *Disability Studies Quarterly, 24(1)*.

Salinger, J.D. (1951). *The Catcher in the Rye.* Boston: Little, Brown.

Schmidt, P.S. (2014). Carpe librum: Seize the (YA) book: Literary slipstream: Using YA fiction to connect students with the canon. *English Journal, 103(3)*, 115–116.

Shakespeare, W. (1892, 1993). *Romeo and Juliet.* New York: Dover.

Society for Disability Studies. Mission and history. Retrieved from http://disstudies.org/about/mission-and-history.

Steinbeck, J. (1937). *Of Mice and Men.* New York: Bantam.

Stelle, L. (1999). Review of children's literature: Children with disabilities as main characters. *Intervention in School & Clinic, 35(2)*, 123–128.

Stork, F.X. (2009). *Marcello in the Real World.* New York: Scholastic.

Swaim, K.F., & Morgan, S.B. (2001). Children's attitudes and behavioral intentions toward a peer with Autistic behaviors: Does a brief educational intervention have an effect? *Journal of Autism and Developmental Disorders 31(2)*, 195–205.

Vygotsky, L. (1993). *The Collected Works of L.S. Vygotsky: The Fundamentals of Defectology (Abnormal Psychology and Learning Disabilities)*(Vol. 2). New York: Plenum Press.

Walker, A. (1982). *The Color Purple.* New York: Harcourt.

Walker, N., & Bean, T. (2005). Sociocultural influences in content area teachers' selection and use of multiple texts. *Reading Research and Instruction, 44(4),* 61–77.

Wein, E. (2013). *Rose Under Fire.* New York: Hyperion.

Wiesel, E. (1982). *Night.* New York: Bantam.

Williams, S.Q., Inkster, C.D., & Blaska, J.K. (2005). The Joan K. Blaska collective of children's literature featuring characters with disabilities or chronic illnesses. *Journal of Children's Literature, 31(1),* 71–78.

Part 2: Disability, Young Adult Literature and Literary Theory

Beowulf *and Aesthetic Nervousness:* *A Multidimensional Pedagogy*

Darcy Mullen

"You know where you stand with monsters, don't you?" ["The Monarch of the Glen," 2006].

This essay emerges from a self-designed/self-taught course at the University at Albany in spring 2010, intended as an introduction to Disability Studies through a survey of canonical literature.[1] I proposed the course at the request of a student who, with great frustration, asked how come college is all about *diversity* but there are not any courses that focus on literature and Disability Studies.[2] With a background in Utopian Studies, Post-Colonial Theory, and Rhetoric, I admittedly had little or relatively no prior knowledge about the field of disability studies. I was surprised at how little information there was on paradigms for the pedagogy of disability studies (as opposed to the body of literature of inclusive pedagogy, or pedagogy for students with disabilities). According to Anthony Nocella II's "Emergence of Disability Pedagogy" (2008), perhaps one of the reasons for holes in Disability Pedagogy is that the field's "brief history" is the cause of "it presently lack[ing] a clearly articulated definition of its aims, assumptions and methods" (p. 81). Nocella's assessment is spot on. The strongest resource I was able to find was *The Disability Studies Reader*, edited by Lennard J. Davis (2010). It offers an organizational principle for structuring the course, and it helped me begin to answer some of my own questions on the nature of pedagogy and Disability Studies.[3]

Each primary text we read has a central place within the foundation of literary studies, particularly the "'typical introduction'" to literary studies.[4] We began at the beginning, with *Beowulf*. Through intensive reading of these canonical texts, with an eye to representations of disability, we constructed a canon that differed from other Literature survey classes. By the time we got to *Rain Man* in week seven, we realized something bizarre was happening in terms of the form and stylistic choices in many of the texts. Ato Quayson's essay "Aesthetic Nervousness" (2007) gave us vocabulary for that strangeness. Quayson develops the concept of "aesthetic nervousness" as a reading framework in that text.[5] In *Aesthetic Nervousness*, Quayson's project is "to show that the literary domain invokes" some "attitudes" towards disability, "but dissolves them into the tapestry of representation" (20). Quayson suggests that conventions of literary aesthetics rely on representations of disability on a fundamental level. In other words, ideas (including stereotypes, fears, and misconceptions) are often subsumed, or even normalized, as a part of the literary landscape.

Readers, and pedagogy for disability studies, have a history that focuses on the "ethical dimensions" of the aesthetics of representations of disability (Quayson, p. 33–34). Quayson suggests a reading practice that reads "disability not as a discrete entity within the literary aesthetic domain, but as part of the totality of textual representation" (p. 215). Such a perspective would require that we invigorate readings of aesthetics within the canon with methods that account for representations of disability as a formative component of literature. Isolating particular texts as "the literature of disability" would, hopefully be a partially self-effacing process (in the way literature by or about women was first marginalized as "women's literature," with the qualifier of "women's" being significant but secondary to the larger domain of "literature").

For the purposes of this essay, I suggest a simplified working definition of aesthetic nervousness as when representations of disability determine structural, stylistic, thematic or formal elements of a text in such a way that activates cultural perceptions of disability. While cultural perceptions of disability need not be negative, the texts in this essay seem to activate largely negative stereotypes (which may have something to do with the fact that the villain(s) in the *Beowulf* genealogy is where disability figures most prominently). In Quayson's terms, aesthetic nervousness is often found in moments when the text has "a short circuit triggered by the representation of disability" (p. 254). As is explored in the following pages, there are many effects of these conditions—for the texts themselves, as well as for both reading and teaching practices. For student-readers and learners, there is the potential for a problematic conditioned expectation for aesthetic nervousness within reading practices, as well as reinforcing stereotypical trends within aesthetic nervousness. For example, we do not want to teach students that a character with a disability is a sign for them to anticipate conflict between characters, or within the narrative fiber of a text. As for our role as teachers, our pedagogical decisions are informed by a multitude of factors. I suggest here that our decisions might be in the best interest for both students and the field at large if we provide students with the tools for a reading practice that includes the concept of aesthetic nervousness.

This paper proposes suggestions for a pedagogy that embraces reading practices with attention to aesthetic nervousness so that we can improve our teaching of both canonical and non-canonical texts. I address this through examples of close reading; suffice it to say for now that we can paraphrase his concept as how texts break down when confronted with disability.[6] In this essay, I propose pedagogical tactics specific to Quayson's idea of aesthetic nervousness through the example of *Beowulf*-texts.[7] This essay offers close readings in the genre of *Beowulf* texts (or *Beowulfiana*), including Seamus Heaney's translation of *Beowulf* (1999), Neil Gaiman's "The Monarch of the Glen" (2006), John Gardner's *Grendel* (1971), and cinematic adaptations of *Beowulf*. The genre of *Beowulf*-texts are often taught in tandem to young adult (YA) readers, and for that reason, I suggest that we consider these texts together in order to see the layers of representation that these texts share.

The additional pedagogical move that this essay ultimately argues for is adding concepts from aesthetic nervousness to the toolkit for basic locating elements of plot (like exposition, climax, resolution, and so forth), style, and literary form. For example, if we can teach reading practices that look for literary foils, we can teach that the primary dimensions of aesthetic nervousness can also be responsible for the construction of foils. For many adaptations, Beowulf and a monster (Grendel, his mother, or the dragon, respectively), are doubles of themselves, not only in how they are described but also in representational modes and codes.

The method of this essay (close readings that highlight dimensions of aesthetic nervousness and its operation in the genealogy of this genre) is intended as an example for reading practices to show the necessity of extending these lenses throughout other canonical texts and their affiliate progenies. While it is difficult to find a single figure of how many students read *Beowulf* in advanced middle school classes, high school, and/or college, the text is generally considered to be the first and most important text in the canon of English Literature, as evidenced by its continued adoption by Norton anthologies.

Monstrosity

As interlocutors ourselves (i.e., teachers, instructors, professors, teaching assistants, and adjuncts alike) making *Beowulf* accessible or identifiable in a general survey or introduction to literature often means incorporating contemporary texts into the conversation—such as *Beowulf* and John Gardner's *Grendel*, or the 2007 film *Beowulf*. If aesthetic nervousness shows us moments of short-circuiting in the canon, then how does that shape our responsibility in introducing YA readers to the canon and popular texts that are retellings of it? The many representations of the monstrous figures of Grendel and Grendel's Mother, I argue, share codes of representation with characters that have disabilities. For YA readers in particular, this is an important factor to consider in these texts. *Beowulf* is often the model for practical application of the tools of textual analysis, and for how to operate in the rhetorical situation of the world of serious literary study. We are therefore implicated in the ethics of what YA readers learn about disability in the canon *because of* this particular textual entryway, as well as other gateway texts. Furthermore, we have a responsibility to recognize that our means of introduction to the canon may continue to activate aesthetic nervousness.

To paint with sweepingly broad strokes, *Beowulf* is considered by most to be the oldest surviving poem in English (thus securing its hold as an important piece of English literature that recalls myth, legend and history).[8] While original sources and dates of authorship are unclear, the general consensus is that the poem comes from sometime between 600 and 900 AD. Beowulf, the man, is an outsider (a Geat and a warrior) come to save the Danes (and their mead hall) against an initially-unnamed monster. The monster terrorizes the Danes at night in their mead hall.

Contemporary readings of the poem have encouraged a focus on the aesthetics of the poem (even if the poem is largely read in translation). The combination of recent readings that interrogate both aesthetics and monstrosity give occasion to ask how monsters in the poem shape its aesthetics, and how do the poem's aesthetics create the monsters. Nickolas Haydock, in his 2014 article "Meat Puzzles: *Beowulf* and Horror Film" explains the trend "in recent *Beowulf* scholarship" of "an increasing willingness to put monsters at the center of our reactions to the poem" (p. 145). He describes how "in some ways parallel is the rash of recent *Beowulf*-inspired films that have adapted the poem according to stereotypes, commonplaces, and plotting devices of the horror film" (p. 145). He notes that the genre of horror film strongly and directly influenced these films, in addition to "works such as John Gardener's *Grendel* and Michael Crichton's *Eaters of the Dead* as well as the saturation of popular and academic cultures" (pp. 145–146). The desire to "put monsters at the center of our reactions to the poem" speaks to our own expectations for how plots, archetypes and aesthetics function.

Aesthetic Nervousness

To focus on the monstrous in *Beowulf* retellings shows the trend to place the primary dimension of aesthetic nervousness at the center of narrative practices. My focus here is primarily on the role of Grendel as a figuration of disability within the *Beowulf* stories. In Quayson's method for reading practices that locate aesthetic nervousness, he adopts the phrase "constitutive points" as opposed to starting points "to signal the fact that the social deformation does not always show itself at the beginning of the plot" (p. 35). In other words, that aesthetic issues connected to disability do not necessarily avail themselves in the beginning of a text. The "constitutive point" for many of the *Beowulf*-texts center around Grendel rather than an opening move of the plot. While Quayson's method is to read and identify forms of aesthetic nervousness in texts, those reading practices and taxonomies are easily extended to reading film and other cultural objects that can be analyzed.

In addition to noting where aesthetic nervousness occurs, Quayson explains the different dimensions it can take: primary (between characters), structural (within the text), and final (between the reader and the text). Additionally, these three dimensions of aesthetic nervousness often overlap or have interconnection within a text. Quayson furthermore explains that it is more likely for a text to have multiple dimensions of aesthetic nervousness when a character with a disability is vital, or dominant in the text (p. 49). *Beowulf*-texts are a great sample set to read in terms of aesthetic nervousness due to Grendel's vital role as (generally speaking) antagonist or plot-catalyst.

We find the primary dimension "in the interaction between a disabled and nondisabled character, where a variety of tensions may be identified" (p. 30). This dimension of aesthetic nervousness manifests as tension between characters within the text resulting from representations of disability. This primary level is important to note as a pedagogical issue, as many YA readers are taught to identify with and empathize with characters as their first way into a text. If the interactions between characters have, for example, aesthetic nervousness at their core, then readers-as-identifiers are pushed into a certain paradigm. Readers then learn to identify or dis-identify with a certain "side" of experiencing that tension. Reinforcing a binary like this is problematic at best, if not outright antithetical to critical thinking and reading skills.

As a constitutive point, Grendel thus registers in the primary (and structural dimension, which I will return to in a moment) of aesthetic nervousness. Heaney writes in his introduction to his translation of the poem that Grendel and his mother serve two specific needs: one for the poet and one for the poem. He writes, "the poet may need them as figures who do the devil's work, but the poem needs them more as figures who call up and show off Beowulf's physical might and his superb gifts as a warrior" (p. xviii). This encapsulates the elements of aesthetic nervousness that need to be flagged in *Beowulf.* Both the poem and poet here need a monstrous figure. They need a character that does "the devil's work" and allows Beowulf to show his full strength turns us to the primary dimension of aesthetic nervousness. We need the monster as a site of conflict between characters. The conflict that results is the catalyst for the epic tale, and the monstrous figure gives a foundation to the plot.

The next dimension of aesthetic nervousness, according to Quayson, is when the aesthetic structure of a text contains tension as a result of representations of disability. While Quayson does not give a concrete term for this form of aesthetic nervousness, for my purposes, I apply the phrase "structural dimension." Like the primary level of aesthetic nervousness, there are pedagogical issues to take note of in the structural level as well. YA readers are taught to identify, define, and explain a variety of literary devices, including those mentioned by Quayson: "symbols and motifs," "narrative or dramatic perspective," and "plot structure" (p. 30). If it becomes commonplace for YA readers to expect or predict literary devices in relation to aesthetic nervousness, then critical reading skills may begin to normalize literary devices that refract tensions with the representations of disability. There is the further possibility that aesthetic nervousness could be learned as an expected convention within literature.

The "final dimension" of aesthetic nervousness refers to the tension created between readers and the text because of representations of disability. The primary level and structural levels can contribute to this final dimension, but that is not necessarily the case (p. 254). As with the primary and structural dimensions, pedagogies heavily reliant on reader-response to a text must take note of aesthetic nervousness as a tension existent between the reader and course mater. This "final dimension," when tension emerges between reader and text, is often the one focused on in cultivating empathy in readers. The reading model here presumes that readers are, on the whole, readers without disabilities. The concerns of aesthetic nervousness extend to all categories of readers, however, because this reading model illustrates dominant cultural codes and modes of representation.[9]

Beowulf

In the original *Beowulf*, the first major description of Grendel is where we learn the motivation for his violence and see the constitutive point for aesthetic nervousness. The following passage also sets the standard for the three dimensions of aesthetic nervousness in the poem. The passage reads:

> Then a powerful demon, a prowler through the dark,
> nursed a hard grievance. It harrowed him to hear the din of the loud banquet
> every day in the hall, the harp being struck and the clear song of a skilled poet
> telling with mastery of man's beginnings, how the Almighty had made the earth [2001, lines 86–92, page 9].

The "grievance" comes from the cacophony that accompanies the telling of the creation story and the history of "man's beginnings." His particular circumstance (of monster, peripheral, and damned creature) is an extricable narrative element of the poet's song. This first description of him focuses on his internal world and the tension resulting from his unholy lineage. We learn that he is "a powerful demon," that "prowls." Thus, the first description connects his body—and both the actions and manner in which he can act—as the result of his lineage. This form of aesthetic nervousness is structural—the catalyst for the plot is the attacks. Without that conflict, the poem would offer an aesthetic presentation of genealogy and history, but the action would be limited to a dialogue-driven description of past battles, rather than a plot-driven narrative about story-telling.

The poem continues, and quite clearly describes the Monster as punished by God, and that accounts for his monstrosity. In terms of the cultural context of the poem, early attitudes towards disability were "closely aligned to disease and disease was often interpreted as a form of plague and punishment for past sins, along with the encouragement to charity there also persisted an idea of disability as a sign of divine disfavor"

(Quayson, p. 22). In the Middle Ages, representations of disability, monstrosity, and criminality, historically, have conferred meaning upon and between each other (Quayson, p. 20).[10] I argue that we must read Grendel as a composite of monstrosity and disability.[11] Grendel, as a product of "divine disfavor" is a clear archetype of a character facing continued punishment as a result of his disability.

It is still a common motif to see both monsters and characters with disability alike having back-stories that result from forbidden unions, and those monsters still share narrative conventions of representations with characterizations of disability. As Haydock writes in "Meat Puzzles: *Beowulf* and Horror Film" (2014), the slippage between these categories of representation are not confined to characters with disabilities in Medieval texts. Furthermore, forbidden unions, allegedly, produced "monstrous forms that embody forbidden desires and hybrid offspring," including "the Sphinx, the Medusa, the Minotaur, [and] Lilith" (p. 133). In the case of *Beowulf*, Grendel's mother appears as one of these archetypical sites of "forbidden desire and hybrid offspring."[12] These unions as penultimate narrative sites of the primary dimension of aesthetic nervousness carry through *Beowulf* and the canon, alike.

Moreover, writers in the Middle Ages, such as Isidore of Seville (560–636), had categories that correlate disability and monstrosity. Quayson paraphrases Isidore of Seville to outline the "taxonom(ies) of monstrosity in which the disabled take their place beside monsters" (p. 21).[13] There are striking similarities to contemporary "taxonomies" of representation of characters with disabilities.[14] As foundational archetypes of figures with disability, the original poem illustrates them as (in Isidore's words) hypertrophic and atrophic, excrescent, superfluous and deprived of bodily parts, with a mixture of animal and human parts. These are the markings of the "embodied impairment-as-monstrosity" as a result of the moral trap that Grendel and his mother are victims of in the poem.

Haydock further explains that focusing on the function of horror in the poem is a reading practice that remains at the periphery of discourse on the poem. This is, according to Haydock, "despite the warnings of Tolkien and his successors, namely, that the monsters—not genealogy, archeology, history, or religion—are the center of the poem (p. 125). Haydock's call to bring the monsters from the periphery to the center of *Beowulf* scholarship echoes other now well-known calls to bring marginalized discourses and the questions inherent in the representations of peripheral subjectivities. In retellings of *Beowulf*, we are reminded "to refocus our attention back unto the garish, nightmarish qualities of the poem" (p. 125). If the films keep turning back to the "nightmarish" elements of the poem, then those elements and their consequences deserve further consideration.

Grendel, the Catalyst

For "nightmarish" elements to depend on representations of disfiguration, then the particular forms of aesthetic nervousness present in a given *Beowulf*-text reinforce disability as the catalyst for dimensions of aesthetic nervousness. Haydock's article offers a comprehensive scope of how genre conventions in horror film have influenced representations and tropes in *Beowulf*-stories. Culturally, we come to the *Beowulf* story with an affective disposition shaped by ideas of monstrosity that are the legacy of horror films, beginning in the 1970s.[15] Placing Grendel and his mother at the center of the poem is a reading practice that we have normalized by historical equivocation with monstrosity and disability (p. 125). Haydock gives the example of "phantom-of-the-opera-type disfigurement" lurking behind a mask as a prime example of disability as a form of monstrosity that causes aesthetic nervousness almost to the level of cliché (p. 124). The "nightmarish" disfigurement is precisely the type of narrative tensions that result in the primary and final dimensions of aesthetic nervousness.

Following the first description of the monster, we learn that "times were pleasant for the people there/ until finally one, a fiend out of hell/ began to work his evil in the world" (line 99–101, p. 9). Following this, the "evil," "fiend out of hell" is finally named; "Grendel was the name of this grim demon" (line 102, p. 9). The affective concern at this point in the poem is with Grendel's evil as the result of "divine disfavor." As stated above, Grendel is the result of a forbidden union, and this plot point is a narrative site of the primary dimension of aesthetic nervousness. Grendel "had dwelt for a time / in misery among the banished monsters, / Cain's clan, whom the Creator had outlawed / and condemned as outcasts.... (lines 104–107, p. 9) As descendants of Cain, Grendel and his kin are monsters that are human-not-human.[16] The passage continues:

> For the killing of Abel
> the Eternal Lord had exacted a price:
> Cain got no good from committing that murder
> Because the Almighty made him anathema
> and out of the curse of his exile there sprang

ogres and elves and evil phantoms
and the giants too who strove with God
time and again until He gave them their reward [lines 107–114, p. 9].

We know that Grendel lives "in misery among the banished monsters": ogres, elves, evil phantoms and giants, but we still do not know much about his physical form—only that he is evil. Grendel's "banishment," "monstrosity," and "hard grievance" are his punishment, and God's will. Grendel's physical form here is a secondary concern to the structure set up by the poem. For example, the passage where we get a description of the mother-son pair repeats as a story-telling practice, even though they no longer pose a threat (through, as the gloss reads, "the country people's tales about the monsters" [p. 95]). Grendel and his mother "prowl the moors":

> One of these things,
> as far as anyone ever can discern,
> looks like a woman; the other, warped
> in the shape of a man, moves beyond the pale
> bigger than any man, an unnatural birth
> called Grendel by country people
> in former days [lines 1345–1361, p. 95].

First, the retelling by the country-people emphasizes that Grendel and his mother appear both human in some ways. She appears to be "a woman," and he is "in the shape of a man." While his mother "looks like a woman," rather than *is a woman*, Grendel's monstrosity definitively qualifies him and the rest of their story telling. His monstrous qualities are the entire focus of the story's retelling. As we examine the rest of the passage, this pattern continues:

> They are fatherless creatures,
> and their whole ancestry is hidden in a past
> of demons and ghosts. They dwell apart
> among wolves on the hills, on windswept crags
> and treacherous keshes, where cold streams
> pour down the mountain and disappear
> under mist and moorland [lines 1345–1361, p. 95].

The theme of flawed genealogy (as the result of divine disfavor) results in their isolation amongst animals in harsh climate and terrain. This reiteration of their biography long after they are no longer a threat in the text further shows the function of Grendel and his mother as figures that both serve to move the story along, and literally provide narrative material. As shown in the next discussions of *Beowulf*-texts, the category of representation—disability as monstrosity—seems to be the one relied upon most strongly and the one continues to be responsible for dimensions of aesthetic nervousness.

John Gardner's *Grendel* (1971)

John Gardner's *Grendel* (1971) retells *Beowulf* to give Grendel a voice, and, in doing so, shows Grendel's break-down due to his relationship with aesthetics. I would suggest the acknowledgement and revising of aesthetic nervousness in the original poem is part of *Grendel's* endurance and popularity.[17] *Grendel* makes aesthetic choices that can be read as repairing, or reworking, the primary dimension of aesthetic nervousness that *Beowulf* has imparted to the canon by reworking aesthetic nervousness as an aesthetic tool. Specifically, the primary dimension of aesthetic nervousness emerges in passages where we see Grendel's isolation. Moreover, we can see how the structural dimension of aesthetic nervousness emerges in passages where Grendel recognizes that the Shaper treats him as a literary device. Lastly, the reader bears witness to Grendel's escalating violence and self-destruction, which results in the final dimension of aesthetic nervousness. Unlike the original poem, Grendel tells his own story of his demise, even though he is forced to sing his own death as it happens. He becomes what he has always wanted to be, the storyteller of his own story. Unfortunately, when he takes on that role, he breaks the rules of the archetype (so to speak) of Grendel, the disabled monster. The narrative cannot contain his existence outside of that form, and his death is the resulting and final instance of the structural dimension of aesthetic nervousness.

Through the first-person point of view, we get Grendel's history and a window into his curious and thoughtful internal landscape. Grendel's childhood is comparable to Frankenstein's monster; he learns language, its powers and problems, and we watch him marvel at a painful and unjust world. The first time he hears the harpist/poet that sings the history that will be remembered, and therefore shapes reality (this character being named "the Shaper"), he has a visceral and pained reaction. The description of his gut reaction to hearing the Shaper shows the violent effects of the Shaper's aesthetics on Grendel:

> I too crept away, my mind aswim in ringing phrases, magnificent, golden, and all of them, incredibly, lies…. Thus I fled, ridiculous hair creature torn

apart by poetry—crawling, whimpering, streaming tears, across the world like a two-headed beast, like mixed-up lamb and kid at the tail of a baffled, indifferent ewe—and I gnashed my teeth and clutched the sides of my head as if to heal the split but I couldn't [pp. 43–44].

Grendel takes on characteristics of Isidore's taxonomy, including excrescence and superfluity of bodily parts, as well as deprivation of bodily parts, to a mixture of animal and human. Upon hearing the Shaper's song, Grendel experiences something akin to the overwhelming power of Stendhal Syndrome—where one is emotionally overwhelmed and faces a breakdown of sorts when confronted with powerful art (or aesthetics).

Grendel embodies the structural dimension of aesthetic nervousness. He begins to unravel at seeing his own aesthetic form in the Shaper's text, and likewise, standard narrative conventions begin to loosen as well. In an attempt at solace, Grendel talks to the forest, trying to work through how and what the Shaper does. He thinks to himself, "If the ideas of art were beautiful, that was art's fault, not the Shaper's" (p. 49). Grendel understands that aesthetic power lies within the codes of art, not a magical power unique to the Shaper. Rather, the Shaper is "a blind selector, almost mindless: a bird" (p. 49). Aesthetics and their power are compared to nature—something that birds just do "mindlessly." This evokes a slippery slope about the logic of aesthetics, and something we try to make our students aware of; if aesthetics, and thereby aesthetic nervousness are part of a natural process, then tension in a text, or between characters, due to disability becomes *naturalized*.

Grendel seems to think through the problem of aesthetics being naturalized. Following his above quoted thoughts, he continues thinking,

Yet I wasn't satisfied. [The Shaper's] fingers picked infallibly, as if moved by something beyond his power, and the words stitched together out of ancient songs, the scenes interwoven out of dreary tales, made a vision without seams, an image of himself yet not-himself, beyond the need of any shaggy old gold-friends pay: the projected possible [p. 49].

The primary dimension of aesthetic nervousness emerges in Grendel's discursive isolation. The feelings brought on by the Shaper are, for Grendel, fueled by the aesthetic codes and modes that the Shaper works and reworks. These aesthetic codes and modes are the result of cultural formations and history, not a natural part of life. Thus, in creating "the projected possible," Grendel experiences cognitive dissonance and conflict over how to deal with representations of himself and the history of representation that he belongs to in the Shaper's culture.

Grendel, however, is betrayed by both the Shaper and aesthetics. The dragon explains to him that the Shaper prevents men from having an existential crisis and that that Grendel's very existence is essentially a literary device (p. 65). The passage reads:

> "Ah, Grendel!" he said. He seemed that instant almost to rise to pity. "You improve them, my boy! Can't you see that yourself? You stimulate them! You make them think and scheme. You drive them to poetry, science, religion, all that makes them what they are for as long as they last. You are, so to speak, the brute existent by which they learn to define themselves. The exile, captivity, death they shrink from—the blunt facts of their mortality, their abandonment—that's what you make them recognize, embrace!" [p. 73].

Here disability functions as an ethical reminder, a memento mori, an Other with which to define ones' self against, and an exercise in philosophy. This critique of Grendel's purpose, to "drive them to poetry," flags Grendel's role as the first dimension of aesthetic nervousness that allows the structural dimension to emerge. Grendel is a literary device with particular aesthetic dimensions, as both a muse and plot catalyst—as in the original poem. This is painful for Grendel, and something he neither reconciles nor accepts because he sees himself as both an artist and appreciator of art, not a prisoner of it. Disability in the structural dimension removes Grendel's agency while allowing the narrative to continue with a purpose.

Grendel's own existential crisis begins when he realizes that he is frozen in a particular aesthetic role, and this is exacerbated with feelings of anger and betrayal when he learns that the Shaper misrepresents him (p. 54). Furthermore, the Shaper's art can only prevent an existential crisis for the Geats and the Danes, not for descendants of Cain. The moment in the text when Grendel fully accepts both that his enemies define themselves against him, and he is a toy in their aesthetic world, is the information that the novel opens with (in a nonlinear move), and ultimately moves towards. At this constitutive point in the text, there is an aesthetic shift. Grendel becomes a poet, speaking and thinking in verse. For example, he thinks,

> *Pity poor Hrothgar*
> *Grendel's foe!*
> *Pity poor Grendel,*
> *O, O, O!*
> Winter soon.
> (whispering, whispering. Grendel, has it occurred to you my dear that you are crazy?)

(He clasps hands delicately over his head, points the toes of one foot—
aaie! horrible nails!!—takes a step, does a turn:
Grendel is crazy,
O, O, O! [p. 92].

Grendel asks of his own shift in aesthetics if he himself has not gone
"crazy" (p. 92). When Grendel steps out of the aesthetic role he is meant
to inhabit his relations with other characters begin to break-down—to the
point of violence.

For example, Grendel reacts to Weathlow's beauty the way he once
reacted to the Shaper's poetry. He sees her beauty as the only kind of real
beauty uncorrupted by cultural codes. The Anglo-ideal that she represents
has long defined an ideal archetype; however, this is problematic in that
we know that there is no universal standard for beauty. Grendel does not
see her beauty as a culturally constructed ideal. Instead, he sees her beauty
as the only truth that remains. Before attacking her, Grendel decides to

> count my numberless blessings one by one.
> I. My teeth are sound.
> I. The roof of my cave is sound.
> I. I have not committed the ultimate act of nihilism: I have not killed the
> queen.
> I. Yet [p. 93].

To kill Weathlow would, for Grendel, be "the ultimate act of nihilism"; it
would show his ultimate break with the world. Eventually, Grendel does
assault Weathlow (p. 100–102). Grendel's attack on Weathlow is the manifestation of the primary dimension of aesthetic nervousness. This near-
rape further extends the dimension of aesthetic nervousness between the
characters in the text and between the readers and the text itself.

The turn to violence and rape that the text takes at this point is likely
to trigger discomfort for readers (both for being forced to bear witness to
the assault, and dis-identification with Grendel, who had been an identifiable, if not lovable, hamlet-type character), thus resulting in the final
dimension of aesthetic nervousness. At this point, the narrative structure
breaks down and is full of tension between characters (the primary dimension), within the prose, verse and dramatic script (the structural dimension), and for readers watching Grendel's escalating violence and self-
destruction (the final dimension). Grendel's demise and a conclusion that
falls apart and away from aesthetic conventions illustrates the problems
inherent in assigning aesthetic conventions—and aesthetic nervousness—
natural roles.

Neil Gaiman's
"The Monarch of the Glen" (2006)

Neil Gaiman's "The Monarch of the Glen" (2006) is a novella included in his collection of stories *Fragile Things*: *Short Fictions and Wonders*. In "The Monarch of the Glen," the protagonist from his epic novel *American Gods* (2001), Shadow, is somewhat stranded in a small, Northern Scottish town. There, Shadow makes a series of strange acquaintances. The first is a little man named Doctor Gaskell who offers Shadow a job as a bouncer of sorts at a posh party for "the locals." He meets a bar-keep, Jennie, who becomes his quasi-love interest, and who also turns out to be a Norwegian mountain creature (a *hulder*) (p. 313). At dinner in the hotel restaurant, Shadow encounters a mother-son duo that we expect to be the "fractal" iterations of Grendel and his mother (given that the introduction of *Fragile Things* flags this novella to be a retelling of *Beowulf*) (p. 303, 316).

First, the primary dimension emerges when Shadow encounters a mother-son team, which we expect to be Grendel and his mother. Second, the novella uses the final dimension of aesthetic nervousness as a device to critique "the oldest fight ever" (p. 347). Finally, the conclusion of the novella releases tension back into the text, at the primary level, like the gods now freed from the ship made from the fingernails of dead men. Like in *Grendel*, this use of aesthetic nervousness aims to be generative. For example, the novella ends with the archetypes of Beowulf (aka Shadow) and Grendel refusing to fight each other, and thus changing the balance of good and evil energy in the world. Nevertheless, the monsters and representations of disability still carry ethical burdens that reinforce moral modes of disability and the secondary dimension of aesthetic nervousness.

We see the primary dimension of aesthetic nervousness when Shadow comes upon mother-son pair having dinner. Given that we know this is a retelling of *Beowulf*, we expect the pair of characters to develop into Grendel and his mother. The description is as follows:

> Two people were sitting at a table in the corner, two people who seemed different in every way that people could be different: a small woman who looked to be in her late fifties, hunched and birdlike at the table, and a young man, big and awkward and perfectly bald. Shadow decided that they were mother and son [p. 316].

Here the descriptions of mother and son rely on indicating what is different, as in the example of the woman being "hunched and birdlike." Here the woman is described as atrophic and in animal-like terms. The two begin eating their soup, and Shadow continues watching them—to the point of noting that the mother hit her son on his hand with her spoon for blowing on the soup before eating it. The son and Shadow exchange a look (p. 317). Later in conversation, Doctor Gaskell says,

> "Anyway. He's a monster," he said gesturing across the room with a mostly chewed lamb chop. The bald man was eating some kind of white pudding with a spoon. So's his mother."
>
> "They don't look like monsters to me," said Shadow.
>
> "I'm teasing you, I'm afraid. Local sense of humor" [pp. 318–319].

Doctor Gaskell conflates human and monster. Although Shadow disagrees, his own observations eventually evoke representations of disability that rely on aesthetic codes that refer to monstrosity. For example, while having after-dinner coffee in the bar, the young man comes in and Shadow further observes him. The passage reads,

> The bald young man came in. He nodded a nervous greeting to Shadow. Shadow nodded back. The man had no hair that Shadow could see: no eyebrows, no eyelashes. It made him look babyish, and unformed. Shadow wondered if it was a disease, or if it was perhaps a side effect of chemotherapy. He smelled of damp [p. 319].

The primary dimension emerges in the emphasis on excrescence (i.e., "pudding" and "damp"), and deprivation (i.e., "no hair"). Shadow perceives the young man as disabled (the "medical" category). The young man enters nervously ("He nodded a nervous greeting") and here we see the primary dimension of aesthetic nervousness. While Shadow presents not a specific outward reaction to the young man, his thoughts focus on what makes the young man different and what disease could account for that difference. The interaction between the young man and Shadow is held in tension from the first look they exchange and transforms from tension-as-suspension to tension-as-nervousness in the example of the young man with his "nervous greeting," and Shadow's preoccupation with excrescence and deprivation. This passage is foregrounded with a general dark and stormy setting in an old, dank establishment. These aesthetic choices converge to create a heightened feeling of suspense before Shadow's trip to the party (where he will eventually be asked to fight the archetypical Beowulf-Grendel fight).

The introduction of this young man and his mother has no other role in the text other than as a constitutive point of tension for Shadow and Gaskell. This scene and the interaction with the mother and son function to create tension for the upcoming fight. It is important to note that the category of medical disability of the son, or the atrophic, admixture of animal and human parts for the mother, are aesthetic components that further the idea that disability (and its conflation with monstrosity) is a normalized, narrative process meant to create tension between the characters.

As the plot continues, Shadow is led to the party under false pretenses—his purpose there is to fight a Grendel-figure. Shadow does not want to fight; he knows "he had been set up," and does not want to participate, stating, "I'm not your hero," and "I don't want to fight you" (pp. 333, 344–346). Described as "the oldest fight ever," aesthetic nervousness is used as a structural form to show the futility of this never-ending fight between good and evil, or man and other. We are privy to Shadow's thoughts, and he specifically describes the fight as man vs. monster:

> This fight was old, Shadow thought.... It was the fight of man against monster, and it was old as time: it was Theseus battling the Minotaur, it was Beowulf and Grendel, it was the fight of every hero who had ever stood between the firelight and the darkness and wiped the blood of something inhuman from his sword [p. 347].

Grendel, and other famous monsters (or monstrous archetypes), are ultimately "something inhuman" to slay. When the creature falls, the locals attack it with their clubs, and are set on killing the monster then Shadow (p. 348). Shadow calls Jennie, and she saves him and the monster from the locals. Then the monster's mother comes from the water, and Shadow hands her son to her, remarking that it is a "nice change" that the monster is not dead, but only hurt (p. 349).

The fact that the monster is still alive is a "nice change" in the paradigm, and it reworks the structural dimension of aesthetic nervousness in the *Beowulf*-story. Smith, the man that brings Shadow to the party, says, "'Shadow,' he said, shaking his head. 'Shadow, Shadow, Shadow, Shadow, Shadow. This was not how things were meant to turn out'" (p. 350). Shadow has broken the fractal cycle of the oldest fight and disrupted the order of things. In this sense, "The Monarch of the Glen" reworks aesthetic nervousness on the structural level of the plot. However, as we see in the descriptions of the young man and his mother, the primary dimension of aesthetic nervousness is a tool the text uses in order to get us to the paradigm-shift.

In this novella, the three noted instances of aesthetic nervousness are in the primary dimension (in the encounter with the mother-son duo, and the fight still being between man and monster-as-disabled figure), and the structural dimension (in rewriting the "the oldest fight ever"). Like in *Grendel*, this use of aesthetic nervousness aims to be generative, while the monsters and representations of disability still carry ethical burdens.[18] Still, like the original poem, disability is used as a narrative site for meditations on storytelling. The ambiguous physical otherness of the mother and son work as recognized tropes or clichés (akin to "dark and stormy nights") that contribute to the tension that leads up to the rewriting of the *Beowulf*-story.

This essay could easily devote itself to Neil Gaiman's Beowulfiana alone. In *Smoke and Mirrors: Short Fictions and Illusions* (1998), Gaiman notes that while he was working on that adaptation and explaining the project to others, he often had to repeat himself because people often mistakenly heard him say he was adapting *Bay Watch* (p. 25). The prose short story, "Bay Wolf," in *Smoke and Mirrors*, is a satiric homage to the process of making *Beowulf* accessible to Hollywood, in addition to Hollywood's influence on the ideas in *Beowulf*. In "Bay Wolf," the monster, Grand Al, is a "movie monster," rising from the surf (pp. 193–194). This is another instance that shows even when we take the monster out of the movie, we cannot take the movie out of the monster. The representational modes persist.

Robert Zemeckis's *Beowulf* (2011)

One benefit to including filmic adaptations in a discussion on the aesthetic use of disability in retellings of *Beowulf* is that representations of disability are perhaps more accessible (or blatant) for YA readers that are still developing critical reading and thinking skills. In this discussion, I focus on Robert Zemeckis's *Beowulf* (2011) as a visual text that employs the primary and structural dimensions of aesthetic nervousness. In doing so, it lends itself to teaching tool that very clearly poses questions, themes, and representational patterns that we might hope our students could learn from and transfer onto other instances of reading when encountering disability in texts.

According to Kelly Ann Fitzpatrick's article, "Ond Hyre Seax Geteah Brad ond Brunecg": Failing Swords and Angelina's Heels in Robert Zemeckis's *Beowulf*" (2011), Neil Gaiman and Roger Avery's cinemagraphic adaptation of *Beowulf* sticks fairly closely to ideas and impulses of the original poem. I quote Fitzpatrick's plot summary at length here (as it is a strong summation of the first battle within the film):

Up until the episode with Grendel's mother, the film follows the main action of the poem fairly accurately. In both poem and film, Beowulf, himself a Geat, arrives in Denmark to aid Hrothgar in eradicating the monster, Grendel, who has plagued Hrothgar's grand mead hall, Heorot, and claimed the lives of many of his people. After a proper reception by Hrothgar, Beowulf counters the boasts of Hrothgar's retainer, Unferth, by relating a story of his own experience slaying a number of sea monsters, thus establishing the earliest tokens of Beowulf's abilities as monster-slayer and hero. That night, Hrothgar and his retainers withdraw from the hall, leaving Beowulf and his men to await Grendel's attack. When he arrives, Beowulf faces him unarmed. Although Grendel escapes, Beowulf deals him a mortal wound when he tears Grendel's arm from his body [p. 213].

The film, according to Fitzpatrick, updates the motifs (i.e., the warrior motif, and dangerous female sexuality) to a contemporarily, culturally relevant representation. I suggest we can extend this to include the motif as Grendel as a constitutive point where aesthetic nervousness emerges.

In the opening scene, Grendel's exposed eardrum resembles a chartreuse and crimson, rippling eye sans lid. He claws into himself as the pain from the noise increases. This opening scene gives us our very first instance of aesthetic nervousness. Tension between the Geats and Grendel are the primary instance of aesthetic nervousness, and the tension is the result of Grendel's atrophic and excrescent ear. Grendel's malformed ear is the explanation for his ensuing violence.

During Beowulf's battle with Grendel, we have the next major occurrence of aesthetic nervousness, and this time in the structural dimension. The text begins a pattern of representation that disrupts the narrative, quite literally, with a strobe effect. First, Grendel hits the side of the hall, pieces of it splinter, and his breath (presumably) blows out all the fires. He enters the dark hall and screams in response to a woman screaming at his appearance. Grendel's representation recalls Isidore's fifth category (deprivation of bodily parts). We see his figure in full, and the woman's screams make his exposed left eardrum throb. Grendel screams in response to the pain her screams cause him, and a single fire (where a pig had been roasting) reignites, showing a flickering blue flame that casts a strobe-effect throughout the hall. This mystical, blue fire swirls and grows, and it provides the strobe-effect for the duration of Grendel's attack. The simultaneous change in fire, and Grendel's disposition, creates a new visual pattern that shows the structural dimension of aesthetic nervousness.

Strobes, as a visual rhetorical tool, are literally disruptive. The function is to simultaneously illuminate and obfuscate. The introduction of a
disruptive visual queue concurrent with Grendel's entrance is where the
structural dimension emerges. Grendel does not strike or kill prior to
the fire turning blue, and the lighting of the hall transition into the
strobe. The blue fire propels him back out through the ceiling of the hall
when he leaves (after refusing to fight his father, Hrothgar), and then the
fire goes out. The next scene begins with someone lighting a torch with
a standard yellow, not-blue, fire. When Grendel returns to his home with
his mother, the color of the water glows a blue that is the same color as
the strobe-fire. The strobe-fire and Grendel's underworld/otherworldly
home are the only places where this color occurs. This blue-fire likely
recalls the original poem's description of Grendel's home: "At night there,
something uncanny happens: / the water burns" (2001, lines 1366–1367,
p. 95). The pairing of these two scenes is significant because they are
indicative of the visual language the film uses both to indicate Grendel
(and Grendel's mother), and the disruption that their presences cause the
Geats.

Both Grendel's super-human strength (as a categorical representation
of Isidore) and the visual disruption are concurrent with the duration of
the strobe-fire. The strobe effect does not appear at any other moment in
the film, and it is the constitutive point in this text.[19] When Grendel enters
the hall the second time (where a naked Beowulf and his men are waiting),
the same thing happens—the regular fire goes out and reignites with the
magical blue strobe fire. Beowulf kicks the mead tub over the blue fire; it
turns back to yellow fire, the strobe effect stops, and the first sword strikes
Grendel. The fight ensues, and Beowulf realizes Grendel's ear is his weak
spot. He maneuvers his way onto Grendel's back, punches him repeatedly
in his bad ear, until it ruptures and sprays yellow bile. That is when Beowulf
takes Grendel's arm. The important things to note here are that Grendel's
presence and his screaming result in the strobe effect from the fire that
creates the structural dimension of aesthetic nervousness. As a tool of
visual rhetoric, a strobe illuminates and obfuscates, thus causing narrative
disruption. Once the strobe stops, that is when Beowulf is able to defeat
him. Thus, we see support for the notion that the strobe is a narrative tool
that signifies Grendel, and disruption in general. When order is restored
(by eliminating Grendel), the strobe is eliminated as well.

An additional instance of aesthetic nervousness is in the reenactment
of Beowulf's fight with Grendel in the years following the battle. In the
dramatization and retelling of the fight, a little person (or a person that

appears to have some form of dwarfism) plays the part of Beowulf (1:15). The choice to use a little person is an aesthetic one that emphasizes the size difference between Beowulf and Grendel. This reenactment causes Beowulf great guilt and shame, because in actuality he is not the virtuous defeater that his people imagine him to be. Specifically, he feels shame about his liaison with Grendel's mother in exchange for the power she bestows upon him. The primary dimension of aesthetic nervousness—where a representation of disability embodies and acts of the site of tension in the text—is found, in double, here. First, a character with a disability stands in for the anxious Beowulf (the shamed character), and secondly, the cause of Beowulf's tension comes from his relationship with Grendel's mother who (like the mother in *Monarch of the Glen*) is an admixture of animal and human parts, as well as copious excrescence and hytrophy. Without these aesthetic choices, the film—like the texts discussed throughout this essay—would have to find another way to move the plot structure forward.

Conclusion

If aesthetic nervousness makes us construct a certain kind of knowledge—and therefore a certain kind of way of approaching/teaching that knowledge in the classroom, then we need a pedagogy that confronts the knowledge constructed through social and linguistic codes that carries that knowledge. The introduction of reading skills informed by a lens of aesthetic nervousness at the introductory and formative level of *Beowulf* allows students to navigate the canon with more tools for engaging the standards and practices they encounter. These critical thinking skills have direct application for operating in life. In Quayson's conclusion, he returns us to the importance of what these reading practices do for us, as social beings, with this reminder:

> Language and cultural stereotypes are the most deadly instruments for denying the humanity of people. To provide the tools for unmasking the essentially violent dimensions of such stereotypes from a close reading of literary texts is to go some way toward at least rectifying the attitudes behind such stereotyping practices. More important, it helps to show that our ultimate obligation as literary critics must be addressing the particularities of injustice of the world in which we live [p. 218].

In addition to the obviously major task of addressing the injustices in the world, as teachers we have a responsibility to equip our students to read into the deep histories of our injustices, and the aesthetics that have developed in response. Moreover, we must impart our students with the critical thinking and reading tools to engage with emergent aesthetic and social forms, and the deep diachronic histories of those forms.

For the pedagogy of disability studies (particular to literary, film or cultural studies), there seems to be a caesura in pedagogical methods to address the difficulties with very prominent occurrences of aesthetic nervousness. I originally approached teaching these texts with a Constructivist perspective. Deborah J. Gallagher identifies the methodology for the Constructivist perspective in her article "The Importance of Constructivism and Constructivist Pedagogy for Disability Studies in Education" (2004). Gallagher explains a constructivist perspective as the following: "Start with a Problem, Teach Skills in a Conceptual Context, Treat Errors as Useful Information, Let Them Seek Solutions, Know Your Students' Interests." A limit with this approach presumes that "solutions" to "problems" exist. What do we do when "treating errors as useful information" allows readers to circumvent, or normalize, the final dimension of aesthetic nervousness? How do we read when "problems" are a function of a structural dimension of aesthetic nervousness; or if "errors" result from the primary or final dimensions of aesthetic nervousness? So, what is there to do when texts or constructivist mistakes cannot be made "useable" to a productive end? I suggest that pedagogies that account for aesthetic nervousness can add to Constructivist pedagogical approach.

The utility of "errors as useful information" is challenged when students, or readers, are constructing information that perpetuates attitudes towards disability and normativity that create the dimensions of aesthetic nervousness. Gallagher addresses the potential difficulty of teaching texts that short circuit as the result of aesthetic nervousness as sites for utility in the classroom. The problem remains, however, of how to deal with the construction of text as a culturally conditioned process. Gallagher explains that many approaches within disability studies "approach disability as a culturally constructed experience, owing its existence to the beliefs and practices built around how any given society responds to human difference" (2004). This paradigm relies on the maxim that "knowledge is socially constructed" (2004). Additionally, "constructivism affirms that because knowledge is constructed (made) rather than discovered (found), therefore all knowledge is inseparable from the individual learner's language, cultural values, experiences, and interests" (2004).

Language and Our Practices with It Construct Aesthetic Nervousness

Pedagogical approaches that rely on the creation of identification for readers are often ill equipped to respond to how disability is represented for two reasons. First, an approach that relies on identification can obscure the focus of discussion from textual operations and, counterproductively, put students on the spot as either textual authorities or outsiders based on their subject positions. We all read from where and whom we are, and that is a valuable part of imparting self-efficacy to students. As teachers of literature, we have the responsibility to foster reading practices that allow students to build upon, and extend beyond identification as a reading practice, into participation within the discourse of literature.

Secondly, and perhaps more significantly, aesthetic nervousness can result in the inability to identify with a text when a text has moments that do not seem to "work" (such as the introduction of the mother and son in "The Monarch of the Glen"). In those cases, "devices of aesthetic collapse that occur within the literary frameworks themselves" (p. 40). For that reason, it behooves us to teach reading practices that further address the reliance of literary frameworks on aesthetic nervousness.

Quayson further explains that aesthetic nervousness occurs simultaneously "with the nervousness regarding the disabled in the real world" (p. 34). Specifically, "the embarrassment, fear, and confusion that attend the disabled in their everyday reality is translated in literature and the aesthetic field into a series of structural devices that betray themselves when the disability representation is seen predominantly from the perspective of the disabled rather than from the normative position of the nondisabled" (p. 34). He later clarifies that "the aesthetic nervousness of the literary-aesthetic domain cannot by any means be said to be equivalent to the responses to disabled persons in reality" (p. 44). Or, put another way, aesthetic correlation does not equal social causation. His practice is for close reading with the desire that we "lift our eyes from the reading of literature to attend more closely to the implications of the social universe around us" (p. 45). No matter where we stand on the fraught history of "the humanities" and moral education, there is no responsible way to advocate for pedagogy that abdicates a link between what we read and the world around and before us.

Moreover, if we can teach students to read for motifs, for example, then we can teach them to read for moments when motifs overlap with other literary devices. Moreover, teaching the concept of "constitutive points," alongside, provides a more textured understanding of not only how, but also *why* a narrative follows a particular arc. Reading exercises that focus on personal identification or responses to texts can be framed as interrogations of the final dimension of aesthetic nervousness. Additionally, teaching to read for dimensions of aesthetic nervousness contributes to fuller understandings of foundations in reading practices (for example, basics of narratology, representation and cultural contextualization, and so on) to more complex synthesis of critical thinking.

NOTES

1. From that course followed a subsequent conference presentation at NEMLA 2012 (Rochester, New York).

2. I owe vast and warm thanks to the student that asked this important question, and my students in ENG 226 at SUNY Albany. Additionally, KellyAnn Fitzpatrick, Eric Madsen and Dr. Sami Schalk were invaluable in helping me navigate the historical, structural and conceptual challenges in this project.

3. Spring 2015, *Disability Studies Quarterly*, special issue: Interventions in Disability Studies Pedagogy (jointly co-edited by the Disability Studies Program at University of Toledo: Liat Ben-Moshe, Kim Nielsen, Jim Ferris and Ally Day).

4. The course plan included many canonical texts that are popular in both high school and college curricula, including; *Beowulf* (trans. Heaney), *The Cure at Troy; A Version of Sophocles' Philoctets* (Heaney), *Richard III* (Shakespeare), *Frankenstein* (Shelly), and *Of Mice and Men* (Steinbeck). We concluded with J. M Coetzee's *Waiting For the Barbarians*, and Katherine Dunn's *Geek Love*. In addition to literature, the course also included influential and popular films: *Freaks, 300, Rain Main, Forrest Gump, Daredevil, Quid Pro Quo,* and *Stuck on You.* In addition to these primary texts, the course was supplemented by Lennard Davis' *The Disability Studies Reader,* Rene Descartes's *Discourse on Method* (1637/1998, trans. Cress), selections from *Disability and the Media* (Riley, 2005), *Exploring Disability: A Sociological Introduction* (1999), *Why I Burned My Book and Other Essays on Disability* (Longmore, 2003), and *Disability* (2003).

5. Quayson's *Aesthetic Nervousness* (2007) is the text I reference throughout this essay.

6. Quayson builds his "notion of aesthetic nervousness" in response to two main sources: Rosemarie Garland-Thomson's "highly suggestive concept of the normate," and Lennard Davis' and Mitchell and Snyders' "reformulations of literary history from a disability studies perspective" (Quayson 30). Quayson states, "Thomson proposes the notion of the "normate" to explicate the cluster of attitudes that govern the nondisabled's perception of themselves and their relations to the various "others" of corporeal normativity," and that "Thomson's notion of the relations between the normate and the disabled derives ultimately from a symbolic interactionism model" (31–33). Mitchell and Snyder's *Narrative Prosthesis* (2003) "follow David Wills (1995) in trying to define literary discourse as essentially performing certain prosthetic

functions" (Quayson 38). Thus Mitchell and Snyder's idea of the shutting down or stumbling of the literary operation is extrinsic to the literary field itself and is to be determined by setting the literary representations of disability against sociocultural understandings (Quayson 39). Quayson's approach differs from Mitchel and Snyder's in that he instead turns his "attention on the devices of aesthetic collapse that occur within the literary frameworks themselves. Also, I would like to disagree with them on their view of the programmatic identity assigned to the disable, because, as I will try to show by reading the disabled character within the wider discursive structure of relations among different levels of the text, we find that even if programmatic roles were originally assigned, these roles can shift quite suddenly, thus leading to the stumbling they speak of" (Quayson 40).

7. The same project certainly could model reading and teaching practices that follows Thompson's *normate,* or Mitchell and Snyder's *prosthesis.*

8. This essay uses Seamus Heaney's 1999 translation, widely adopted by instructors in many levels of instruction.

9. Literary aesthetics matter to all readers, as Quayson states, because our aesthetic models reflect "the construction of a universe of apparent corporeal normativity both within the literary text and outside it" (Quayson, 2007, p. 30).

10. Although the term Middle Ages (or Medieval) is fraught with debate as to when exactly that period starts and stops, I take it here as a relevant temporal marker from understanding representations of disability in the poem.

11. For further reading on this I suggest Stiker, H-J. (1999). *A History of Disability,* Metzler, I. (2013). *A Social History of Disability in the Middle Ages: Cultural Considerations of Physical Impairment;* Eyler, J.R. (ed). (2010). *Disability in the Middle Ages: Reconsiderations and Reverberations;* and Garland-Thompson, R. (ed.). (1996). *Freakery: Cultural Spectacles of the Extraordinary Body.*

12. Grendel's mother, / monstrous hell-bride, brooded on her wrongs. / She had been forced down into fearful waters, / the cold depths, after Cain had killed / his father's son, felled his own / brother with a sword. Branded an outlaw, / marked by having murdered, he moved into the wilds, / shunned company and joy. And from Cain there sprang / misbegotten spirits, among them Grendel, / the banished and accursed, due to come to grips / with that watcher in Heorot waiting to do battle [lines 1255–1268; 89].

13. According to Quayson, "His twelve-part taxonomic grid starts off as follows: (1) hypertrophy of the body, (2) atrophy of the body, (3) excrescence of bodily parts, (4) superfluity of bodily parts, (5) deprivation of bodily parts, and then through various gradations on to the mixture of animal and human parts and to monsters proper..... the degrees of embodied impairment-as-monstrosity are inherently part of a moral map of the corporeal body itself and the ways in which society might relate to it. Though his taxonomy seems extreme to modern eyes, the assumed ethical implications of impairment are also discernable in literary texts of different periods and cultures" (p. 21).

14. In *Exploring Disability: A Sociological Introduction* (1999), the work of Clogson (1990) and Haller (1995) is combined to provide a reference of categories of representation of both characters, and media representations of people with dis-

abilities. The list is as follows: "1. medical: disability as illness or malfunction; 2. social pathology: disabled people as disadvantaged, needing support; 3. 'supercrip': disabled people as deviants, achieving super human feats in spite of impairment; 4. civil rights: disabled people having legitimate grievances, as members of a minority group; 5. cultural pluralism: disabled people as multi-faceted, impairments not the only issue....; 6. business: disabled people as costly to society, particularly to commerce; 7. legal: disable people possessing legal rights; 8. consumer: disabled people as an untapped market" (p. 195).

The fourth, fifth, seventh and eight categories are suggested as "positive representations" (p. 195). To this, we can add a ninth model, from Quayson "disability as signifier of ritual insight" (Quayson 61). Disability as a signifier of ritual insight is a mode of representation common in texts that straddle post-colonial politics or metatemporal texts.

15. The scope and focus of Haydock's research in this article is so strong that I would highly recommend his article for any instructor teaching either any retelling of *Beowulf*, or any retelling of medieval texts through a contemporary lens.

16. Furthermore, many misguided historical justifications for racism (and specifically American slavery) extend from the curse placed upon Cain's descendants.

17. John Gardner's *Grendel* is certainly worth comparing with Matt Wegner's Grendel graphic novels. For the sake of space, I table that discussion for now.

18. There are certainly other sites in *Monarch of the Glen* where we could examine how aesthetic nervousness constructs the narrative (in the character of the "Hulder," or Smith's dialect). Ultimately, this form of aesthetic nervousness aims to be generative, while the monsters and representations of disability still carry ethical burdens.

19. In addition to the discussion of this film, it is worth a brief mention of the 1999 futuristic, quasi-steam-punk adaptation of Beowulf, and the 2005 adaptation of Beowulf and Grendel. While the 1999 and 2005 adaptations also have unique presentations of aesthetic nervousness, I will not discuss that here due to the unlikelihood that they would be taught in the YA classroom. First, these adaptations are both rated R, while the 2006 adaptation is rated PG-13. Secondly, there are significant departures from the original *Beowulf* text that would likely be both distracting and challenging to overcome in order for them to be productive teaching tools. Suffice it to mention now, the 1999 adaptation struggles with representations of prosthesis and disability in its aesthetic fiber. The narrative in the 2006 adaptation, on the other hand, makes aesthetic choices to incorporate deafness, and muteness as the result of an atavistic and feral childhood, as well as a composite-figure of autism that sacrifices himself in service of the group. These choices result in aesthetic nervousness between a variety of social groups in the film, and place very great moral imperatives on the characters with disabilities.

References

Baker, G. (1999). *Beowulf.* Dimension Films, Miramax Films.

Beowulf: A New Verse Translation (Bilingual Edition). (2001). S. Heaney (trans.) New York: Norton.

Bowman, M.R. (2014). "Words, swords, and truth: Competing visions of heroism in Beowulf on screen." In K. Fugelso (ed.), *Studies in medievalism XXIII: Ethics and medievalism* (147–166). Cambridge, UK: D.S. Brewer.

Butler, G., Skarsgård, S., Polley, S., Ingvar, S., Endgame Entertainment (Firm), Film Works, & Warner Home Video (Firm). (2006). *Beowulf & Grendel*. Equinoxe Films.

Carroll, N. (1990). *The Philosophy of Horror: Or, Paradoxes of the Heart*. New York: Routledge.

Davis, L.J. (2010). *The Disability Studies Reader*, 3d ed. London: Taylor and Francis.

Descartes, R. (1637, 1998). *Discourse on Method*. Indianapolis: Hackett.

Disability. (2003). Cambridge, UK: Barners and Mercer Polity Press.

Disability Studies Quarterly. (Spring 2015). Special Issue: Interventions in Disability Studies Pedagogy. Jointly co-edited by the Disability Studies Program at University of Toledo, Liat Ben-Moshe, Kim Nielsen, Jim Ferris and Ally Day.

Exploring Disability: A Sociological Introduction. (1999). Malden, MA: Polity Press.

Eyler, J.R. (2010). *Disability in the Middle Ages: Reconsiderations and Reverberations*. Farnham, Surrey: Ashgate.

Fitzpatrick, K. (2011). "Ond Hyre Seax Geteah Brad ond Brunecg": Failing swords and Angelina's heels in Robert Zemeckis's Beowulf. In K. McDonald (ed.), *Americanization of history of time and culture in film and television* (212–230). Cambridge: Cambridge Scholars.

Gaiman, N. (1998). *Smoke and Mirrors: Short Fictions and Illusions*. New York: HarperCollins.

_____. (2001). *American Gods*. London: Headline.

_____. (2006). *Fragile Things: Short Fictions and Wonders*. New York: HarperCollins.

Gallagher, D.J. (2004). "The importance of constructivism and constructivist pedagogy for disability studies in education." *Disability Studies Quarterly, 24(2)*, Spring 2004.

Gardner, J. (1989). *Grendel*. New York: Vintage.

Haydock, N. (2014). "Meat puzzles: *Beowulf* and horror film." In K. Fugelso (ed.), *Studies in Medievalism XXIII: Ethics and Medievalism* (123–146). Cambridge, UK: D.S. Brewer.

Heaney, S. (1991). *The Cure at Troy: A Version of Sophocles' Philoctets*. New York: Farrar, Straus and Giroux.

Longmore, P.K. (2003). *Why I Burned My Book and Other Essays on Disability*. Philadelphia: Temple University Press.

Metzler, I. (2013). *A Social History of Disability in the Middle Ages: Cultural Considerations of Physical Impairment*. New York: Routledge.

Mullen, D. (2010). Self-designed course. University at Albany.

_____. (2012). Conference presentation at NEMLA 2012, Rochester, NY, "Grendel eats Freire! Proposing a pedagogy of Aesthetic Nervousness." Panel: "Re-presenting (dis)Ability."

Nocella, A., II. (2008). "Emergence of disability pedagogy." *Journal for Critical Education Policy Studies, 6(2)*, 77–94.

Quayson, A. (2007). *Aesthetic Nervousness: Disability and the Crisis of Representation.* New York: Columbia University Press.

Riley, C.A., II (eds.). (2005). *Disability and the Media.* Hanover, NH: University Press of New England.

Stiker, H.J. (1999). *A History of Disability.* Ann Arbor: University of Michigan Press.

Thompson, R.G. (1996). *Freakery: Cultural Spectacles of the Extraordinary Body.* New York: New York University Press.

Zemeckis, R., Bing, S., Rapke, J. Starkley, S. & Zemeckis, R., Gaiman, N., Avary, R. (2007). *Beowulf.* Paramount Pictures and Warner Bros. Pictures.

"So tough, so brave, the consummate survivor": War, Trauma and Disability in the Harry Potter Series

MARC NAPOLITANO

In a subtle yet important scene in J.K. Rowling's (2003) *Harry Potter and the Order of the Phoenix*, Alastor "Mad-Eye" Moody shows the title hero a photograph of the original members of the Order of the Phoenix, a secret society of highly-trained wizards and witches dedicated to thwarting the machinations of the dark wizard Lord Voldemort. Mad-Eye grimly recounts how many of these individuals ultimately died at the hands of Voldemort and his henchmen (pp. 173–174). The photograph unnerves Harry, who is left wondering why Mad-Eye chose to share this artifact, though at the end of the book, following the death of Harry's beloved godfather, Sirius Black (one of the few surviving members of the original Order), the photograph's significance becomes clear. It will become even clearer in the final two books, as many more heroic characters, including Albus Dumbledore, Severus Snape, Remus Lupin, Nymphadora Tonks, Fred Weasley, Colin Creevey, Dobby the house-elf, and Mad-Eye Moody himself, die in the war against Voldemort. The photograph is a poignant reminder that every war has casualties, and Mad-Eye's interactions with Harry in the abovementioned scene are roughly analogous to those of a weary veteran conversing with a naive recruit, warning him of what is to come.

The *Harry Potter* series is typically classified as "children's literature," "young adult literature," or "fantasy literature," yet it is interesting to consider just how heavily the series revolves around war. In fact, war forms the backbone of the entire narrative: the first book, *Harry Potter and the Philosopher's Stone* (1997), opens with the conclusion of a brutal war and a chronological jump of ten years, while the last book, *Harry Potter and the Deathly Hallows* (2007), closes with the conclusion of a brutal war and a chronological jump of nineteen years. It is likewise important to consider that the 9/11 terrorist attacks marked a defining moment for the "*Harry Potter* generation,"[1] and that the latter half of the series, which deals explicitly with the topic of war, overlapped with two major international wars in Afghanistan and Iraq as well as the larger Global War on Terror. Harry's distress and suffering in *Order of the Phoenix* (the first *Harry Potter* book published after September 11, 2001) stem from the realization that the world he knew has completely changed following Voldemort's return. The overlap between this character's trauma and the trauma that affected his countless fans in the wake of 9/11 may very well have cemented his status as the chief literary representative of the millennial generation ... even as his adventures provided millennials with an escape from the reality of living in a post–9/11 world.[2]

In *Re-Reading Harry Potter*, Suman Gupta (2003) asserts "that the Magic world that these books focus on is deliberately and self-consciously used to play with, allude to, comment on, interrogate and take positions with regard to social and political issues that are relevant to our world" (p. 91), and certainly, literary and cultural critics have debated how Rowling's universe deals with issues of race, class, gender, and various other real-world topics. Surprisingly, there has been little analysis of the portrayal of war in the *Harry Potter* series.[3] I am particularly interested in Rowling's commentary on the physical and mental costs of war as epitomized by her portrayal of characters who have been left disabled as a result of combat experiences. In fact, some of the most prominent characters with disabilities in the series are combat veterans, the primary example being Mad-Eye Moody.[4]

Given that the topic of injuries sustained in war complicates the already multifaceted issue of disability, Rowling's characters offer opportunities for teachers and their students to analyze "the meaning of disability in the context of injury and illness sustained in behalf of state and nation" (Gerber, 2012, "Preface," ix). In this essay, I will examine the depiction of disability in the *Harry Potter* books in relation to the series' emphasis on war. As the most prominent disabled veteran in the series, Mad-Eye Moody will serve as the primary subject of my inquiry. Mad-Eye's most enduring trait throughout the series is his otherness, as shaped by his disabilities and the way in which characters respond to them. Notably, his primary disability is so pronounced that it has usurped the place of his first name as his central designation. In spite of Rowling's tendency to celebrate otherness, to promote tolerance, and to question normativity throughout the *Harry Potter* series,[5] her portrayal of Mad-Eye is steeped in many of the stereotypical traits associated with the depiction of disabled veterans, including the sense of fear and pity that typically surrounds them (Gerber, 2012, "Introduction," p. 6).[6] However, Rowling likewise implies that Mad-Eye's marginalization and failure to reintegrate following his service are defined partly by his conflict with the Ministry of Magic, an institution whose authority and integrity are eventually questioned by virtually all of the heroic characters in the *Harry Potter* series, including the title hero. In this sense, Mad-Eye's otherness might be indicative of his connection to the group of marginalized characters who provide the most tenable support to Harry (including the Muggle-born Hermione, the impoverished Ron, the sickly and downtrodden Remus, and "racial" others such as Dobby and Hagrid). Still, Mad-Eye is ultimately incapable of reaching the levels of transcendent heroism reserved exclusively for Harry and his closest allies, not because of his physical and mental disabilities, but because of what these disabilities signify. Mad-Eye's physical scars, prostheses, and hypervigilance are presented as indicators of his status as a disabled soldier, and though the series builds toward an epic war between good and evil, that war cannot be won "on the ground" through the physical and emotional sacrifices of soldiers. Rather, it can only be won through the unearthly, spiritual journey of the series' title character, a journey that fundamentally separates him from the soldiers on the battlefield and from the struggles of disabled veterans.

Mad-Eye or Alastor?
Disability as Defining Characteristic

In defining Mad-Eye's otherness, it is first useful to consider Rose-marie Garland Thomson's (1997) writings on the depiction of disability in literature; Thomson observes that "literary representation sets up static encounters between disabled figures and normate readers" (p. 11). These "static encounters" oftentimes prove useful to writers who wish to restrict their disabled characters to specific roles and thematic functions within the text: "The plot or the work's rhetorical potential usually benefits from the disabled figure remaining other to the reader—identifiably human but resolutely different.... Thus the rhetorical function of the highly charged trait fixes relations between disabled figures and their readers" (Thomson, 1997, pp. 11–12). Typically, this situation facilitates the melding of a disability with some other defining and static trait; for example, David Mitchell and Susan Snyder (2000) analyze the connection between Ahab's status as an amputee and his "monomania" in Melville's *Moby-Dick* (pp. 119–121). Snyder and Mitchell (2000) devote an entire chapter of their book to analyzing how this "straightforward" explanation of the root of Ahab's madness runs counter to *Moby-Dick*'s emphasis on indeterminacy (pp. 120–121), noting that the text unquestioningly accepts the "yok[ing] [of] disability to insanity, obsessive revenge, and the alterity of bodily variation" (p. 121). Mad-Eye shares several traits with Ahab (including a prosthetic leg), and, like Ahab, he remains a static character whose physical disabilities are ultimately connected with his most dominant personality trait: his hypervigilance.

Still, the conflating of the physical disability with the deviant characteristic is complicated somewhat in Mad-Eye's case by the fact that both of these traits trace back to his career as a soldier: Mad-Eye's physical disabilities are the result of his battlefield wounds, and his hypervigilance is a common symptom of Post-Traumatic Stress Disorder (PTSD). Indeed, Nathan Ainspan and Walter Penk's (2008) description of hypervigilance, as stemming from PTSD, is immediately applicable to Mad-Eye: "Feeling on duty all the time is exhausting. Veterans may find themselves jumpy, irritable, or awaking frequently during the night and being reactive to loud noises" (p. 34).[7] Notably, the very first mention of Mad-Eye in the *Harry Potter* series involves this exact scenario: two characters recount how Mad-Eye created a major disturbance upon waking to the noise of a possible intruder (Rowling, 2000, pp. 159–160). While Thomson stresses the tendency to characterize a disabled literary figure entirely by his or her disability through the conflation of that disability with the defining, rigid (and frequently aberrant) character trait—thus freezing the character in the role of "other"—Mad-Eye presents a variation on this conflation in that he is defined entirely by his status as a disabled *veteran*. However, the same sort of "static" encounter described by Thomson applies in the case of Moody, as the complex issue of disability in relation to military service is simplified by the consolidating of the visible physical injuries and the emotional instability; these two components ultimately reinforce one another in the construction of Mad-Eye's otherness. Furthermore, the physical and mental conditions supplement one another in the fear that they inspire in other characters.

The sheer conspicuousness of Mad-Eye's horrific physical wounds is central to this same fear, though it is yet another indication that his disabled veteran status is his defining characteristic; David A. Gerber (2012) writes that certain noticeable disfigurements or physical disabilities can serve as "markers" that define "an individual's or group's social identity and self-understanding. Especially traumatic, visible injuries have tended to become the primary way in which the general population of disabled veterans often seems to have been conceived in the minds of experts, artists, and the general citizenry" ("Introduction," p. 2). The prominence of visual wounds in the representation of the disabled veteran takes on further importance in the context of Thomson's (2002) analysis of the politics of staring at the disabled: "Starers gawk with abandon at the prosthetic hook, the empty sleeve, the scarred flesh, the unfocused eye, the twitching limb, but seldom does looking broaden to envelop the whole body of the person with a disability" (p. 57). In keeping with Gerber's assertion, Thomson's allusions to the "prosthetic hook, the empty sleeve, [and] the scarred flesh" immediately evoke images of disabled veterans, despite the fact that these wounds are not exclusive to soldiers nor do they account for the multitude of non-visible injuries—including PTSD—that affect wounded warriors.

Nevertheless, Thomson's assertion regarding the tendency of the starer to fixate on deviations from what is considered normative and to so define the disabled person is certainly applicable in the case of Mad-Eye's introduction to the students and faculty at Hogwarts: "Everyone else seemed too transfixed by Moody's bizarre appearance to do more than stare at him" (Rowling, 2000, p. 185). Intriguingly, the reader is encouraged to participate in this act of staring based on the comprehensive description of Mad-Eye's physical wounds and prostheses:

> [Mad-Eye's face] was a face unlike any Harry had ever seen. It looked as though it had been carved out of weathered wood by someone who had only the vaguest idea of what human faces are supposed to look like, and was none too skilled with a chisel. Every inch of skin seemed to be scarred. The mouth looked like a diagonal gash, and a large chunk of the nose was missing. But it was the man's eyes that made him frightening.
>
> One of them was small, dark, and beady. The other was large, round as a coin, and a vivid, electric blue. The blue eye was moving ceaselessly, without blinking, and was rolling up, down, and from side to side, quite independently of the normal eye [Rowling, 2000, pp. 184–185].

Here, Mad-Eye is presented, quite literally, as the "battle-scarred" veteran, though it is his ocular prosthesis, which can spin 360° and see through solid objects including the back of his own skull that dominates the perception of him by other people. It is, by far, the more notable of his two prostheses, the other being his artificial leg, though even here, there is an emphasis on otherness: "Harry saw, below the table, several inches of carved wooden leg, ending in a clawed foot" (Rowling, 2000, p. 186). The two prostheses deliberately call attention to their non-normativity, for they are crafted in such a way as to accentuate their dissimilarity to their intact twins: Mad-Eye's electric blue eye stands in utter contrast to his uninjured brown eye, and his clawed foot is meant to draw attention to this prosthetic limb as opposed to its simply serving as a nondescript and utilitarian replacement to the missing appendage. As in the case of his scars, Mad-Eye's nontraditional prostheses contribute to the overall sense of discomfort that his appearance provokes.

In keeping with his observation regarding the emphasis on physical injury in the popular impression of disabled veterans, Gerber notes the amputee's unique status as the most "prominent" example of the disabled serviceman (Gerber, 2012, "Introduction," p. 2), and it is not surprising that Rowling heavily emphasizes her disabled veteran character's prostheses. The aforementioned merger of the physical disability and the deviant personality trait is notably manifested through the always dominant ocular prosthesis; as stated, this object grants Mad-Eye the power of complete visual perception of his surroundings, which is in keeping with Mad-Eye's desire to be aware of what is happening around him at all times. However, there is another conflation here, as the visible combat injury merges with the traditionally invisible PTSD: the ocular prosthesis is the result of the physical maiming that took place in combat, but its incessant swiveling about within Mad-Eye's skull is a physical manifestation of the hypervigilance (the eye essentially allows him to be "on duty" at all times by giving him complete spatial and environmental awareness).[8] Fundamentally, Mad-Eye's magical eye allows him to fully live by his own guiding principle (and personal catchphrase) of "constant vigilance" (Rowling, 2000, p. 213) as repeated throughout the novel.

However, Mad-Eye's actions frequently go beyond vigilance and into the intrusive realm of surveillance, as the students and professors at Hogwarts gradually come to fear that Mad-Eye is spying on them. Harry repeatedly falls under Mad-Eye's gaze, even at the celebratory Yule Ball, and his date, Parvati Patil, is left shaken upon learning of Mad-Eye's spying: "'He is so *creepy!*' Parvati whispered as Moody clunked away. 'I don't think that eye should be *allowed*'" (Rowling, 2001, p. 420, Rowling's italics). Parvati's comments could easily be read as a minor example of the negative response to Mad-Eye's unusual appearance: it is not Mad-Eye's "eye" that is "creepy," but Mad-Eye himself. However, Parvati's assertion should also be scrutinized as a concrete representation of the merging of the physical disability and the aberrant personality trait in the construction of the disabled veteran's otherness: the eye facilitates the trait that makes him "creepy," his surveillance of people. Parvati claims that the eye should be prohibited, not because it is unpleasant to behold, but because it allows Mad-Eye to spy on her and the other students. Ironically, this results in the students becoming more and more edgy over the course of the novel. In a humorous moment, Ron reflects on Mad-Eye: "'Talk about paranoid...' Ron glanced nervously over his shoulder to check that Moody was definitely out of earshot and went on" (Rowling, 2000, pp. 232–233). While Mad-Eye repeatedly instructs the students to be vigilant, he is in fact the source of much of the paranoia that consumes the student body, a fact which ultimately accentuates his estrangement and otherness.

The link between Mad-Eye's ocular prosthesis and his hypervigilance forges a strong connection between the character traits that delineate his otherness and the resulting fear that stems from that otherness. The ways in which these two traits work together reinforce the notion that Mad-Eye's disabilities define him, though it is again important to consider that both the prostheses and the PTSD are the result of his prior combat experiences. Mad-Eye was severely injured while fighting on behalf of his society, and his scars and prostheses could theoretically be scrutinized as testaments to his courage, or as proof of his selfless service.[9] However, Gerber (2012) observes that injuries sustained in war, which initially serve as "the 'red badge of courage' of a warrior engaged in a cause worthy of his sacrifice" may lose this heroic significance over time: "When war ends, however, and memories of it begin to fade in the general desire to return to a normal peacetime existence, the warrior hero gradually loses his luster and is reduced in stature to a beleaguered disabled man" ("Introduction," pp. 5–6).[10] Moreover, the fact that Mad-Eye provokes fear in other characters, despite his heroic sacrifice, is not without historical precedent; Gerber (2012) maintains that fear has consistently been one of the customary responses to the disabled veteran in Western culture ("Introduction," p. 6), even in the case of "popular" wars such as World War II ("Heroes," p. 71). Specifically, Gerber (2012) cites the writings of Willard Waller, a professor at Columbia University who feared that wounded veterans returning home from fighting in Europe might adopt a fascistic, violent, Nazi-like mentality due to their bitterness: "They had given up so much that they had nothing to lose in following a violent, antisocial path as civilians" ("Heroes," p. 72). Even in less extreme examples, the anxiety over the reintegration of the wounded soldier following his return to civilian life is part of the overall sense of fear that customarily frames the disabled veteran. In Mad-Eye's case, reintegration is unfeasible given the static nature of his character and the overarching emphasis on his otherness; as a result, the disabled veteran—like the traditional disabled literary figure as described by Thomson—remains a marginalized and aberrant other.

From Fear to Pity:
Mad-Eye as Plot Device

Though the issue of reintegration warrants closer scrutiny, it is first helpful to address the second major emotion that Gerber associates with the disabled veteran narrative: pity. In the case of Mad-Eye, this sense of pity has less to do with how various characters view or treat him and more to do with his loss of agency as a result of *Goblet of Fire*'s sudden and unexpected plot twists. The centrality of the disabled character in the execution of the key plot twist (and in the general destabilization of the narrative) is worth scrutinizing in detail, particularly in the context of Mitchell and Snyder's (2000) theories in their groundbreaking *Narrative Prosthesis*.[11] While the merging of the physical disability with the deviant personality trait renders Mad-Eye a static character, he is actually the source of several dynamic narrative transitions.[12] However, given the circumstances of this development, he is ultimately robbed of much of his power and thus rendered pitiable.

By this point, fans of the *Harry Potter* series will likely have noted a major oversight in my prior analysis of *Goblet of Fire*, namely, the revelation that Mad-Eye Moody is not who he seems to be. Following the climactic rebirth of Lord Voldemort in chapter 32, Harry and Professor Dumbledore eventually discover that the villainous Bartemius Crouch, Jr., abducted the real Mad-Eye shortly before the start of term and assumed his identity through the use of a shape-shifting potion. The disguised Crouch mentors Harry throughout the school year; however, he does so as part of a complicated conspiracy to hand Harry over to Voldemort following the conclusion of the Tri-Wizard Tournament. This unexpected and convoluted plot twist fundamentally changes the overall narrative of *Goblet of Fire*; indeed, one could argue that it changes the overall narrative of the entire *Harry Potter* series in as much as the fourth book marks a turning point in the overarching storyline.[13] It is intriguing that a disabled character serves as the crutch upon which the shift ultimately rests. In *Aesthetic Nervousness*, Ato Quayson (2007) proposes a typology of nine different representations of disability; his third representation is arguably the most complex and the most intriguing, as he analyzes how disability can be "used as a means of establishing multiple and often contradictory values. There is often a disjuncture between the content and the narrative structure, and the level at which this disjuncture manifests itself is around the disabled character" (p. 41). This presentation of *"disability as articulation of disjuncture between thematic and narrative vectors"* (p. 41, Quayson's italics) seems strikingly relevant to any discussion of Mad-Eye's character in *Goblet of Fire*, given the contradictions between his ostensible role as Harry's mentor in the Tri-Wizard Tournament and his actual role as the site of narrative destabilization.

In spite of the overarching centrality of Albus Dumbledore as Harry's moral and spiritual guide throughout the series, *Goblet of Fire* presents Mad-Eye as Harry's most involved and diligent teacher. The mentor-protégé bond that forms between Mad-Eye and Harry in *Goblet of Fire* heavily contributes to Harry's success while competing in the Tri-Wizard Tournament. Fundamentally, Harry is presented as the quintessential underdog, while Mad-Eye steps in as the grizzled, surly, dedicated coach who might recapture his own former greatness through his mentorship of said underdog. Picking up where Remus Lupin left off in *Harry Potter and the Prisoner of Azkaban*, Mad-Eye helps Harry to become a more powerful and competent wizard; Mad-Eye is likewise the first character to suggest that Harry consider becoming an Auror, the very vocation that Harry pursues in the later books. The revelation that this Mad-Eye is in fact Bartemius Crouch, Jr., and the equally shocking revelation that by training Harry for success in the Tri-Wizard Tournament, Crouch has in fact been leading him like a lamb to slaughter, completely contradicts the thematic and narrative vectors that have defined Mad-Eye's role.

It is ironic, however, that while Mad-Eye is at the center of this narrative instability, his role in this plot twist proves debilitating. By the end of *Goblet of* Fire, the actual character of Mad-Eye Moody has been robbed of virtually any potential dignity and power, and the discovery of the real Mad-Eye in chapter 35 is noteworthy for its emphasis on the character's profound impotence: "His wooden leg was gone, the socket that should have held the magical eye looked empty beneath its lid, and chunks of his grizzled hair were missing" (Rowling, 2000, p. 681). For the majority of the novel, Mad-Eye's ocular prosthetic and the dull, clunking sound of his wooden leg elicit feelings of fear and paranoia, but in this climactic scene, it is the *absence* of the prostheses and the corresponding sense of help-lessness that provoke discomfort.

In her assessment of Melville's Ahab, Thomson (1997) reflects on the notion that disabled literary figures ostensibly threaten Western ideals such as autonomy and self-determination:

> According to such logic, physical alterations caused by time or the environ-ment—the changes we call disability—are hostile incursions from the outside, the effects of cruel contingencies that an individual does not adequately resist. Seen as a victim of alien forces, the disabled figure appears not as transformed, supple, or unique but as violated.... [T]he disabled figure rep-resents the incomplete, unbounded, compromised, and subjected body sus-ceptible to external forces: property badly managed, a fortress inadequately defended, a self helplessly violated [p. 45].

The disabled veteran problematizes this depiction (not to mention Thom-son's metaphors regarding "hostile incursions from the outside" and "inad-equately defended" strongholds), for, traditionally, the body of the disabled soldier is not a reminder of the universal vulnerability of the human form, but rather, a reminder of the ravages of war. Still, the sense of helplessness and violation in the above-quoted scene is palpable, and the notion of "badly managed" property takes on an ironic dimension when one con-siders that Mad-Eye's property—his prostheses—were stolen by the sin-ister Crouch.

Even after the restoration of his magical eye and prosthetic leg, how-ever, Mad-Eye seems far more damaged than his fake predecessor: "He was extremely twitchy, jumping every time someone spoke to him. Harry couldn't blame him; Moody's fear of attack was bound to have been increased by his ten-month imprisonment in his own trunk" (Rowling, 2000, p. 720). The notion of the bold and heroic warrior having been held prisoner in his own trunk for ten months seems a sad and unfitting con-clusion to his story. When we finally meet the real Mad-Eye Moody, he has been reduced to an object of Harry's pity.

Tellingly, the real Mad-Eye is not given a single line of spoken dialogue in the text, perhaps the ultimate indication of his helplessness and mar-ginalization, though he returns in the subsequent books and is finally granted an opportunity to move beyond the stereotypical realms of fear and pity. Notably, Moody finally speaks his first line in *Order of the Phoenix*, a text that places him among a group of characters far less inclined to react to him with fear, namely his fellow soldiers in the Order of the Phoenix who turn to him for guidance and leadership. Still, Mad-

Eye is a static character throughout, and the emphasis on the supplemental relationship between the physical disabilities and the hypervigilance in the construction of the disabled veteran remains; even his protégés, such as Nymphadora Tonks, express frustration with his obsessive vigilance at various moments in the text (Rowling, 2003, pp. 55–57). Furthermore, the question of the disabled veteran's reintegration is completely dismissed, for the Order of the Phoenix is reactivated only after Voldemort returns. In other words, the Order of the Phoenix cannot help Mad-Eye readjust to civilian life because the Order of the Phoenix only exists in a time of war.

Resisting Reintegration:
Mad-Eye, the State and Prostheses

This issue of reintegration can serve as a useful transition point regarding Mad-Eye's inability to adapt to civilian life following his combat experiences. In spite of his marginalization, it is important to note that the Ministry of Magic remains aware of the debt that it owes to Mad-Eye and wrestles with the central tension that Gerber (2012) outlines regarding the societal view of the returning veteran: "On the one hand, the veteran's heroism and sacrifices are celebrated and memorialized, and debts of gratitude, both symbolic and material, are paid to him. On the other hand, the veteran also inspires anxiety and fear and is seen as a threat to social order and political stability" ("Heroes," p. 71). Prior to his first appearance before the students at Hogwarts in *Goblet of Fire*, Mad-Eye is mentioned in a conversation between government employees Amos Diggory and Arthur Weasley, both of whom fear that he will be prosecuted for misuse of magic following a violent outburst in his home; the two men, though frustrated by his actions (which are the latest in a string of incidents dating back several years), make plans "to get him off on a minor charge" (Rowling, 2000, p. 160). Clearly, both wizards respect Mad-Eye's service and wish to accommodate him, though they simultaneously fear that his tendency toward hypervigilance and violence will create severe problems within the Wizarding world.

The emphasis on Mad-Eye's tumultuous relationship with the government that he fought for is significant, as Gerber (2012) analyzes the disabled veteran as a fundamentally public figure with a "singular and broadly ramifying relationship to the state" ("Introduction," p. 25) that runs contrary to the more private and less direct relationship between the state and the disabled civilian. Notably, this contrast can sometimes promote hierarchical tensions between the two groups, as the state's accommodation of the disabled veteran frequently takes the form of material benefits that are not available to disabled civilians; Gerber (2012) quotes an American soldier who, while awaiting an expensive and advanced prosthetic leg, boasted, "Civilians get crappy legs but ours is going to be top of the line" ("Preface," p. xiii). Though Gerber frames the somewhat tactless statement in the context of the civilian/military divide over disability, it is likewise possible to scrutinize this assertion in relation to technology and the state's desire to provide veterans with the most technically sophisticated prostheses available so as to facilitate their readjustment to civilian life.[14]

While Mad-Eye's wooden leg is decidedly old-fashioned, his magical eye can be compared to the modern prosthesis, which ostensibly blurs the line between sci-fi/fantasy and reality and which can serve as a potent example of state power; David Serlin (2006) writes that "the association between amputees and state-of-the-art prosthetics research may have been an intentional strategy to link disabled veterans with the cutting edge of new scientific discoveries" (p. 55). Granted, the origin of Mad-Eye's magical eye is never explicitly stated, and it should not be assumed that the device was provided to him by the Ministry of Magic. Still, its purpose is roughly analogous to that of the technologically advanced prostheses that the modern state has sought to provide amputees since World War I. Specifically, the modern prosthesis restores a sense of normality to the veteran's life due to its functionality, which in turn promotes reintegration through a return to the workforce and to the general community (Gerber, 2012, "Introduction," p. 8). Though the visually disturbing characteristics of Mad-Eye's prostheses seemingly contradict the notion of normativity, it is important to note that serviceability frequently eclipses aestheticism in the discourse on the prostheses that are provided to disabled veterans by state governments; Gerber (2012) cites the proliferation of pictures and films on the use of metal hooks as replacements for hands in the years following World War I and World War II, noting that these prostheses were far more functional than traditionally "cosmetic" prosthetic limbs and oftentimes allowed disabled veterans to regain a great deal of their manual dexterity ("Introduction," pp. 8–9). Mad-Eye's ocular prosthesis not only allows him to continue his work as an Auror (and later, as a member of the Order of the Phoenix) but simultaneously enhances his success in these endeavors given the powers granted to him by this device.

Still, the attempt at reintegration is, in the end, unsuccessful given

Mad-Eye's aforementioned tendencies toward disruptive behavior follow-ing his combat experiences. Perhaps this is not surprising in as much as the eye, which should theoretically promote reintegration by restoring functionality, ultimately fuels Mad-Eye's hypervigilance and simultane-ously promotes the aforementioned conflation of the mental and physical disabilities that signify his otherness. Mad-Eye's eventual break with the Ministry is arguably his most pronounced rejection of reintegration given the state's desire for him to quietly acclimate to civilian life. Still, although this rejection of the state and its efforts toward readjustment reinforces Mad-Eye's marginalization, it is important to recall that the Ministry of Magic is never portrayed in a particularly favorable light in the *Harry Pot-ter* series.

At its best, the Ministry is well-meaning but ineffective, and at its worst, it is prejudiced and oppressive. Notably, Harry forms antagonistic relationships with the two major governments depicted in the series; in *Order of the Phoenix*, Harry criticizes the Fudge government, which would rather ignore direct threats to its existence than face the reality of an inevitable war, while in *Half-Blood Prince*, he criticizes the Scrimgeour government for its overzealous (yet inefficient) mobilization against Volde-mort and for treading upon people's civil rights for the sake of preserving safety. Mad-Eye has already broken with the government upon his intro-duction in *Goblet of Fire*, and his primary role in the later books is as a member of the Order of the Phoenix as opposed to an official Auror.

This depiction is not surprising given that the Ministry ultimately falls under Voldemort's control in the final book, though even before this "coup," Rowling has subtly been linking the two.[15] Sarah Fiona Winters (2010) offers one of the best commentaries on this issue by documenting how the Nazi-like qualities of Voldemort's followers find their parallel in the "banal evil" (p. 64) of the officials in the Ministry of Magic (p. 64–67).[16] Conversely, Mad-Eye is praised for avoiding the temptation to adopt the brutal practices of Voldemort and his followers, even when the gov-ernment licenses him to do so: "[Mad-Eye] never killed if he could help it. Always brought people in alive where possible. He was tough, but he never descended to the level of the Death Eaters" (Rowling, 2000, p. 532). In the context of the Ministry's incompetence and corruption, Mad-Eye's inability to reintegrate becomes a potentially celebratory characteristic and serves as something of a rebuttal to Waller's argument; throughout the series, it is the government itself, as opposed to the disabled veteran, that poses a threat to society.

Mad-Eye's prostheses add yet another dimension to this issue, however. Recalling Serlin's assertion, in spite of the ostensibly noble efforts on the part of real-life governments to promote rehabilitation and reintegration through the use of state-of-the-art prostheses, there is something disconcerting and perhaps even sinister about a nation's desire to showcase its technological prowess via the body of the wounded soldier.[17] Given the state's power in defining the social identity of the disabled veteran, it is disturbing to consider how easily the government-issued prosthesis can turn the private body of the soldier into a public representation (or, in the case of Mad-Eye, tool) of state power. Granted, the notion of the magical eye as a representation of the power of the Ministry of Magic diminishes significantly upon Mad-Eye's forsaking Ministry policy. This break with the government simultaneously reinforces Mad-Eye's ownership of the object that has become his namesake, though the overbearing and authoritarian Ministry of Magic—which becomes infinitely more overbearing and authoritarian upon Voldemort's rise to power—repossesses it in *Deathly Hallows* following Mad-Eye's death.

In chapter 13, Harry discovers that the loathsome Ministry bureaucrat Dolores Umbridge has attached Mad-Eye's eye to her office door as a means of spying on other people (Rowling, 2007, p. 249). The revelation that Umbridge is exploiting Mad-Eye's prosthesis is a rather surprising plot twist, though her doing so hints toward the troubling view of the prosthesis as a piece of state property that is temporarily attached to the body of the wounded soldier for the purpose of reintegrating that soldier into the social order and restoring his functionality within that society. Mad-Eye's resistance toward that order (and toward reintegration) prefigures the government's repossession of the prosthesis following his death; while Mad-Eye had ceased to be "functional" for the state, the prosthesis—which retains its functionality—is put to use. Ironically, this is a less extreme example of the fate that befalls another prominent amputee, the villainous Peter "Wormtail" Pettigrew. Wormtail willingly sacrifices his hand while facilitating Lord Voldemort's second rise to power, and he is later granted a magical prosthetic as a reward for his service (Rowling, 2000, p. 649). In the final book, however, Wormtail is brutally strangled by his own artificial hand when he acts against Voldemort's wishes; apparently, the hand is magically "programmed" to destroy him the moment he defies his master (Rowling, 2007, p. 470). This connection between Wormtail and Mad-Eye is another significant example of the numerous parallels between Voldemort's forces and the Ministry of Magic; in both cases, the prosthesis serves as a symbol of power that simultaneously facilitates the disabled veteran's regaining functionality so as to facilitate his continued work/service. However, the conscription of the prosthetic body part for sinister purposes by those who issued it following the veteran's "rebellion" underscores the disquieting notion that the private body of the disabled veteran, upon being equipped with a prosthesis, becomes a sort of public property that is expected to perform specific tasks.[18]

Hero or Survivor? Mad-Eye vs. Harry

The exploitation of Mad-Eye's prosthesis by the Voldemort-controlled Ministry greatly disturbs Harry, who steals back the eye and buries it in the hope of giving the deceased warrior a proper internment (Rowling, 2007, p. 284). This scene reinforces the bond between Harry and Mad-Eye,[19] and it is important to note that both of these characters reject the Ministry's authority in favor of the anti-authoritarian leadership of Albus Dumbledore; just as Mad-Eye takes on a primary leadership role in Dumbledore's Order of the Phoenix, Harry forms his own secret society, "Dumbledore's Army." However, Harry's role in the coming war (and the war storyline) diminishes in the final two books, which introduce the otherworldly objects that eventually dominate his story arc: Voldemort's horcruxes and the Deathly Hallows. Harry's divine destiny thus diverts him away from the battlefield, and it is left up to Mad-Eye and the other soldiers to fight the ground war against Voldemort while Harry walks the unearthly path blazed for him by Dumbledore. Though Harry and Mad-Eye are both "battle-scarred," their scars denote their widely divergent roles in the series: Harry's single (and singular) lightning-bolt scar marks him as the "chosen one"—the hero destined to vanquish the infamous Lord Voldemort. Conversely, Mad-Eye's countless scars denote his innumerable battles against dark wizards and witches. These contrasts carry even larger implications regarding their contradictory roles; while reeling from Mad-Eye's death in *Deathly Hallows*, Harry reflects on the deceased wizard as "the consummate survivor" (Rowling, 2007, p. 78). It is intriguing to note, however, that this designation is actually more applicable to Harry himself, whose role as "survivor" is established in the opening chapter of the first book, a chapter entitled "The Boy Who Lived": against all logic, Harry survived Voldemort's attempt to kill him. Though Mad-Eye has survived a brutal war (despite suffering horrific injuries), his actions go beyond "survival." Rather, Mad-Eye has achieved many heroic results in the battles against Voldemort's forces—Charlie Weasley reflects that "Half the cells in Azkaban are full because of him" (Rowling, 2000, pp. 161–162). Unlike the infant Harry, Mad-Eye is not merely a survivor but a heroic, victorious wounded warrior.

In a controversial article published in the early stages of Operation Iraqi Freedom, Jonathan Eig (2003) addressed the contrast between "heroism" and "survival" in the context of the Iraq war, assessing the contemporary tendency to "venerate survivors more than aggressors, the injured more than those who inflict injuries" (p. A1). Here, Eig quotes John A. Lynn of the University of Illinois at Urbana-Champaign, who affirms "a funny shift.... We want to fight wars but we don't want any of our people to die and we don't really want to hurt anybody else. So Pvt. [Jessica] Lynch, who suffers, is a hero even if she doesn't do much. She suffered for us" (qtd. in Eig, p. A1). Granted, my comparison does not take into consideration Harry's transition from passive survival and suffering toward a more active role in combat as the novels progress (nor does it consider Mad-Eye's fame as an Auror, which stands in contrast to the obscurity that Eig ascribes to the "actively heroic" soldiers in the Iraq War). Still, even up through the final moments in the series, Harry takes a passive approach to combat. Notably, his signature spell is the nonviolent "Expelliarmus," a disarming charm used to knock an opponent's wand from his or her hand. In his two major duels with Voldemort (in *Goblet of Fire* and *Deathly Hallows*), Harry instinctively invokes this spell in spite of Voldemort's use of the deadly "Avada Kedavra" killing curse. In both instances, Harry miraculously *survives* the battles, much as he survived Voldemort's attempt to kill him as an infant. Mad-Eye's battles not only lack the prophetic, miraculous contexts that ensure Harry's survival (as evidenced by his own death) but simultaneously present a much more violent and brutal vision of active combat; in *Order of the Phoenix*, Mad-Eye suffers a bloody head wound and briefly loses his prosthetic eye while bravely dueling one of Voldemort's most dangerous henchmen, Antonin Dolohov (p. 802). Still, Harry's passive and "divinely sanctioned" battles are idealized in as much as they are connected to the overarching theme of his spiritual journey/maturation; Mad-Eye's gritty duels, and indeed, the two "Wizarding Wars," in general, provide the backdrop against which Harry's spiritual maturation unfolds.

This fact relegates Mad-Eye, the wounded warrior, to the background as well, which is a common occurrence in real life; Gerber (2012) claims that "disabled veterans are neglected figures in the histories of war and peace" ("Introduction," p. 1). Though Dumbledore, the spiritual mentor, is given an extensive back-story in the final book (despite his having died in the penultimate novel), Mad-Eye, the soldierly mentor, remains an obscure and static character who never comes close to achieving the same level of character depth, the same bond with Harry, or the same heights of heroism in the war against Voldemort. Intriguingly, Harry connects his two mentors in death, as both men fall from horrific heights after being struck by curses. Harry finds himself morbidly reflecting on Mad-Eye's missing corpse: "For the first time, Harry imagined Mad-Eye's body, broken as Dumbledore's had been, yet with that one eye still whizzing in its socket. He felt a stab of revulsion mixed with a bizarre desire to laugh" (Rowling, 2007, p. 94). The title hero's admittedly "bizarre" reaction to this grotesque image is in keeping with the both the overarching fascination with Mad-Eye's wounded and disfigured body throughout the series and with the emphasis on Mad-Eye's otherness, as established from the moment he is introduced in *Goblet of Fire*. Conversely, Dumbledore transcends the physical realities of war, not only through his spiritual mentorship of Harry, but also through his spiritual reunion with his former pupil in one of the most important and memorable chapters in *Deathly Hallows*, "King's Cross." Mad-Eye, so defined by his physicality throughout the entire series, lacks this transcendence, though this is partially due to the fact that that same physicality invariably defines him by his combat experiences; as noted, the pronounced emphasis on Mad-Eye's visible, physical wounds is in keeping with the tendency to define veterans by such disabilities. The physical war is ultimately of secondary importance to Harry's story, and the physically disabled warrior is thus marginalized.

In the end, this relegation of Mad-Eye to the background has more to do with the general trajectory of the series' narrative and Harry's personal development than with any limitations inherent in the disabled veteran character, and despite Rowling's emphasis on her title character's mystical journey, she nevertheless values the bravery of characters like Mad-Eye who participate in the more physical and harsh realities of war (Rowling, 2007, p. 79).[20] Still, the fact that Mad-Eye and the war storyline are on the periphery of the central narrative precludes the character's being given sufficient development to fully transcend the typical (and stereotypical) depiction of disabled veterans, or to achieve a sense of appreciation. This lack of understanding is all too common in the real world, even with soldiers who are not suffering from PTSD; Anne Demers (2011) recounts the struggle of soldiers to reintegrate into civilian life and the fact that many veterans feel as though "*No one understands us*" (p. 170, Demers's italics). She insists that there must be "support groups for veterans, in which they would have the opportunity to share their stories"

(p. 175), and perhaps the most unfortunate element of Mad-Eye's characterization is that he is never given the chance to do so.[21]

Conclusion

The scene with which I began this chapter—Mad-Eye's showing Harry a picture of the original Order of the Phoenix—ends abruptly as Harry, too disturbed by the photograph, looks for an excuse to leave the room. Though Harry's sadness and discomfort are understandable, he notably ignores the fact that Mad-Eye knew and fought with these deceased individuals, whom Harry knows only by name and reputation (his parents excepted). Mad-Eye likely feels their loss far more significantly than Harry, however much his surface-level gruffness might obscure the fact, and Harry's abandonment of Mad-Eye at this critical moment is a sign of the younger wizard's irresponsibility in this early stage of the fifth novel. While some readers might view the scene as an indication that Harry needs to "toughen up," it is actually a reminder that Harry should think about the feelings of soldiers who have suffered losses and who may wish to speak about their experiences. It is an especially important lesson for him to learn given his own struggle to try and articulate his feelings of depression and anxiety in *Order of the Phoenix*. However, the movement away from the war storyline in the final two novels, and the reframing of Harry's journey around the spiritual quest that awaits him, allows the protagonist to move forward without ever having to listen to Mad-Eye's war stories. As was the case in *Goblet of Fire*, the disabled veteran remains silent.

NOTES

1. I have been unable to trace the precise origins of this phrase. Furthermore, the term may be a bit misleading in as much as the readership of the novels was never confined to a single age group. In 2013, a blogger on the prominent fan website *Mugglenet* analyzed the term's significance to the millennial generation based on the fact that many millennials "[grew] up alongside Harry" (Jenette, 2013) in the sense that they were about the same age as the protagonist when the first book came out. An article on the website *Millennial Manifesto* likewise notes that "if there is one piece of pop culture that united the Millennial generation, it was 'Harry Potter'" (Panek, 2014).

2. In a *New York Times* article, David Browne (2009) hypothesized that the millennial generation embraced a fervent nostalgia for the late 90s and early 2000s as a way of coping with the trauma of the September 11 attacks, and that the pervasive and enduring millennial passion for *Harry Potter* was just one manifestation of this wistfulness.

3. The few critics and scholars who have addressed this topic have focused mainly on the merging of the war story arc with the more mythic "good vs. evil" story arc, assessing it in the context of cultural discussions of World War II and the post-9/11 wars. Several critics and scholars have observed that Rowling metaphorically links the "pureblood supremacist" wizards such as Voldemort, Grindelwald, and their followers to Nazis. Rowling has discussed the connection in various interviews and commentaries (see J.K. Rowling's 2007 Carnegie Hall interview and her 2000 BBC Newsround interview). The metaphor is somewhat loose, and Nancy R. Reagin (2011) eloquently notes that "the Nazis are a sort of historical shorthand that all readers would understand; [Rowling] thus invoked a fictional scenario with particular ideas about power and social hierarchies, good and evil, and political movements" (p. 129). The basic result is that Harry's "war" against Voldemort is presented as a war against an evil that *must* be fought, but the fact that the *Harry Potter* novels overlapped with widely controversial wars such as Operation Enduring Freedom and Operation Iraqi Freedom problematizes this depiction for some scholars. Marc Bousquet (2009) has analyzed the series "in the context of the Reagan-Bush-Thacher-Blair 'war against evil' and an intensifying reliance on melodrama in political culture" (p. 177); he is critical of the application of "melodramatic ethics" (p. 177) (as presented in the *Harry Potter* novels) to contemporary wars. It is worth noting, however, that Rowling does not present as unambiguous a binary as some critics have implied; in her 2007 Carnegie Hall interview, she notes that the issues of social hierarchy and prejudice presented in the series are not attributed solely to Voldemort and his followers, but are part of the Wizarding world even before Voldemort's second rise to power ("J.K. Rowling at Carnegie Hall").

4. In defining Mad-Eye as a soldier, I should acknowledge that Mad-Eye's formal vocation is an "Auror," or "Dark wizard catcher" (Rowling, 2000, p. 161). Aurors are typically presented as law-enforcement officials as opposed to military personnel, but they are also on the frontlines of the two Wizarding Wars. Thus, I do not think it inappropriate to characterize Mad-Eye as a soldier/veteran.

5. Returning to Gupta's (2003) emphasis on the metaphorical function of Rowling's universe, he notes that the books "appear to be fairly unambiguously against intolerant and extremist ideologies" (p. 104). Rowling (2007) has likewise stated that her overarching "thesis" throughout the series is a message of universal tolerance ("J.K. Rowling at Carnegie Hall").

6. Gerber (2012) asserts that "pity and fear are responses to disability and to the disabled veteran that are continuous over many centuries" ("Introduction," p. 6), and he traces the evolution of these feelings toward disabled veterans throughout the introduction to *Disabled Veterans in History*, and in his essay on *The Best Years of Our Lives*.

7. Hypervigilance is just one of the numerous symptoms of Post Traumatic Stress Disorder (PTSD) that Mad-Eye exhibits throughout the series; he is frequently characterized as possessing many of the personality traits that define this condition, most notably furtiveness, dominating behavior, a desire to be armed, aggressiveness, anxiety, jumpiness and watchfulness, petulance, insomnia, and morbid thoughts (Ainspan and Penk, 2008, pp. 33–42).

8. This conflation presents a problematic oversimplification in that the physical/visible disability is always given priority, and even when the psychological disability is acknowledged, the acknowledgment unfolds through a merger with the physical; conversely, in real life "many veterans develop PTSD whether or not they have been physical injured" (Geiling, Rosen, and Edwards, 2012, p. 1239). In the United States, the Intrepid Fallen Heroes Fund recently began airing commercials in which several veterans who lost limbs in Operation Iraqi Freedom are juxtaposed against a soldier who suffered no visible injuries in the war but who is dealing with PTSD. The commercial implies that amputees, by virtue of their highly visible wounds, receive more attention and support from the public, and it concludes by promoting the aptly named website, *makeitvisible.org*. Nevertheless, the oversimplification of Mad-Eye's status as a disabled veteran through the combining of the physical and mental wounds is in keeping with Thomson's observations about the traditional portrayal of disability in literature; in the case of Mad-Eye, the merger allows for a straightforward depiction of his defining character traits (which remain unchanging throughout the *Harry Potter* series.)

9. Fleur Delacour adopts this perspective in *Harry Potter and the Half-Blood Prince* (2005) when her fiancée, Bill Weasley, is left permanently disfigured due to combat injuries: "What do I care how he looks? I am good-looking enough for both of us, I theenk! All these scars show is zat my husband is brave!" (Rowling, 2005, p. 623).

10. Most of the discussions of Mad-Eye frame him as fundamentally "beleaguered," as characters focus on his tendency toward paranoia. George Weasley tactlessly observes that Mad-Eye is regarded as a "nutter" (Rowling, 2000, p. 161), while his brother Charlie takes a more understanding view, noting that Mad-Eye's anxieties are likely the result of his having made so many enemies during his years of service. Still, Charlie admits "I heard he's been getting really paranoid in his old age" (Rowling, 2000, p. 162). This transition from emphasizing Mad-Eye's service to viewing his paranoia as a sign of "old age" is telling, as the wounded warrior's heroism is obscured when set against his "beleaguered" status as an unreasonable, harassed old man.

11. Mitchell and Snyder's (2000) concept of "narrative prosthesis" addresses the idea that literary narratives depend upon some sort of deviance to initiate their existence, and that "disability has functioned throughout history as one of the most marked and remarked upon differences that originates the act of storytelling" (p. 54). They use Hans Christian Andersen's faerie tale, "The Steadfast Tin Soldier," as their example, noting that the revelation of the tin soldier's missing leg basically creates the narrative: "Narrative interest solidifies only in the identification and pursuit of an anomaly that inaugurates the exceptional tale or the tale of exception.... [T]he outward flaw 'attracts' the storytellers'—and by extension the reader's—interest" (p. 54). Mad-Eye's role in *Goblet of Fire* diverges from this example in that he is not introduced until the twelfth chapter (nearly two hundred pages into the text), though it is worthwhile to note that he is introduced in the same chapter that presents the central plot point of the novel: the Triwizard Tournament. Still, the revelation of the fake Mad-Eye at the end of the novel is the true moment of deviance,

as the entire story suddenly changes, and the narrative never truly resolves this deviance.

12. Granted, there are instabilities in the *Harry Potter* narrative well before Mad-Eye's introduction. Throughout the early books, the various "Voldemort climaxes" that oftentimes shape the denouements are not always even. In his assessment of the first four books in the series, Colin Manlove (2003) sees this element as the major weakness in Rowling's plotting of her novels: "Without adequate preparation, the two levels of narrative, of school life and Voldemort, can produce too violent a jerk when brought together, as in *The Goblet* when, in the moment of his winning the Tri-Wizard Tournament, the victory goblet transports Harry to the lair of Voldemort, and suddenly we are in another plot" (190). In his critique of Rowling's plot twists, Manlove (2003) makes a rather glaring mistake when he notes that, in *Prisoner of Azkaban*, our suspicions alternate between Sirius Black and Remus Lupin before Mad-Eye is ultimately revealed as the true villain (p. 190). Mad-Eye is not even introduced until *Goblet of Fire*, though Manlove's error reinforces his confusion in tracing the various plot twists that define the early books.

13. The sudden shift from Harry's participation in a school competition to Harry's fighting for his very survival against the ultimate evil anticipates the larger shift in the series from Books 1–3 (which focus on Harry's moral and intellectual growth at Hogwarts) to Books 5–7 (which focus on the war against Voldemort and Harry's mythical quest to find the means of winning that war).

14. The 1950s and 1960s saw various breakthroughs in the design and construction of prostheses which may have seemed "magical" to the disabled veterans who received these highly sophisticated devices (Serlin, 2006, p. 51), and these technological advancements have only increased over time. The recently published *Wounded Warrior Handbook*, 2d ed., describes the "ambitious Revolutionizing Prosthetics programs that will enable a user to control the prosthesis through thought. The limb, as envisioned, would enable users to move as they normally do, without having to think about the actual process to make it happen" (Hill, Lawhorne, and Philpott, 2012, p. 31).

15. Following the completion of the series, Rowling clarified that the linking of Voldemort and his forces to a Nazi ideology is not as simple as it might seem given that the issues of oppression and prejudice—as stemming from concepts of blood purity—were part of the Ministry of Magic beforehand: "I think you can see in the Ministry even before it's taken over, there are parallels to regimes we all know and love" ("J.K. Rowling at Carnegie Hall").

16. Bartemius Crouch, Sr., the Ministry official in charge of the first war against Voldemort's forces, adopts the dark wizard's own brutal tactics while prosecuting that war: "The Aurors were given new powers – powers to kill rather than capture, for instance…. Crouch fought violence with violence, and authorized the use of the Unforgivable Curses against suspects. I would say he became as ruthless and cruel as many on the Dark Side" (Rowling, 2000, p. 527).

17. Scott Krawczyk (2012) cites the memorable and controversial picture of President George W. Bush jogging with amputee Sgt. Mike McNaughton: "At issue is not McNaughton's indisputable courage but rather the visual rhetoric engendered by

this kind of image, which can be read as leaguing the war cause ... with the triumphalism of technological advancement" (p. 91).

18. Though not focusing exclusively on the subject of government issued prostheses, Krawczyk (2012) has analyzed how "the intervention of the state eventually transformed the body of the broken soldier into a form of public property" (p. 102) through the narratives of sacrifice and service that the government constructed around these bodies.

19. Notably, both characters are victims of media smear campaigns by the Ministry-operated press in *Goblet of Fire* and *Order of the Phoenix*

20. Rowling has also proven herself an incredibly generous supporter of veterans' charities; she arranged for the worldwide publishing royalties of *The Cuckoo's Calling* (2013) to be given to ABF The Soldiers' Charity ("Statement Issued on Behalf of J.K. Rowling," ABF: The Soldiers Charity—Corporate Partners).

21. Rowling ultimately gives a stronger voice to disabled veterans in *The Cuckoo's Calling* through her protagonist, Cormoran Strike, who lost his leg while fighting in Afghanistan. The grittiness and earthiness of *The Cuckoo's Calling*, in contrast to the fantasy and spirituality of the *Harry Potter* series, facilitates a deeper and more complex exploration of the disabled veteran's struggle.

REFERENCES

Ainspan, N.D., & Penk, W.E. (2008). *Returning Wars' Wounded, Injured, and Ill.* Westport, CT: Praeger Security International.

Bousquet, M. (2009). "Harry Potter, the war against evil, and the melodramatization of public culture." In E.E. Heilman (ed.), *Critical Perspectives on Harry Potter*, 2d ed. (177–195). New York: Routledge.

Browne, D. (2009). "Harry Potter is their Peter Pan." 22 July 2009. *NYTimes.* 12 Jan. 2015. http://www.nytimes.com/2009/07/23/fashion/23nostalgia.html.

Demers, A. (2011). "When veterans return: The role of community in reintegration." *Journal of Loss and Trauma: International Perspectives on Stress & Coping, 16(2),* 160–179.

Eig, J. (2003, Nov. 12) "Why you've heard of Jessica Lynch, not Zan Hornbuckle; As sentiment about war evolves, victims grab attention, not fighters." *Wall Street Journal*, A1.

Geiling, J., Rosen, J.M., & Edwards, R.D. (2012). "Medical costs of war in 2035: Long-term care challenges for veterans of Iraq and Afghanistan." *Military Medicine, 177*, 1235–1244.

Gerber, D.A. (2012). "Heroes and misfits: The troubled social reintegration of disabled veterans in *The Best Years of Our Lives*." In D.A. Gerber (ed.), *Disabled Veterans in History* (70–95). Ann Arbor: University of Michigan Press.

_____. (2012). "Introduction." In D.A. Gerber (ed.), *Disabled Veterans in History* (1–51). Ann Arbor: University of Michigan Press.

_____. (2012). "Preface." In D.A. Gerber (ed.), *Disabled Veterans in History* (ix–xxiii). Ann Arbor University of Michigan Press.

Gupta, S. (2003). *Re-Reading Harry Potter*. New York: Palgrave Macmillan.

Hill, J., Lawhorne, C., & Philpott, D. (2012). *The Wounded Warrior Handbook*, 2d ed. Lanham: Scarecrow Press.

Jenette, A. (2013). "Defining the Harry Potter Generation." 29 Sep 2013. *Mugglenet*. 31 Dec 2014. http://blog.mugglenet.com/2013/09/defining-the-harry-potter-gen eration/.

"J.K. Rowling at Carnegie Hall reveals Dumbledore is gay; Neville marries Hannah Abbott, and much more." 20 Oct. 2007. *TheLeakyCauldron.org*. 30 Dec. 2014. http://www.the-leaky-cauldron.org/2007/10/20/j-k-rowling-at-carnegie-hall-reveals-dumbledore-is-gay-neville-marries-hannah-abbott-and-scores-more/.

Krawczyk, S. (2012). "Broken Soldiers: Serving as Public Bodies." *Keats-Shelley Journal, LXI*, 90–102.

Manlove, C. (2003). *From Alice to Harry Potter: Children's Fantasy in England*. Christchurch: Cybereditions.

Mitchell, D.T., & Snyder, S.L. (2000). *Narrative Prosthesis: Disability and the Dependencies of Discourse*. Ann Arbor: University of Michigan Press.

Panek, H. (2014). "The Harry Potter Generation." 4 May. *Millennial Manifesto*. 30 Dec. 2014. http://www.millennialmanifesto.literallydarling.com/harry-potter-gen eration//

Quayson, A. (2007). *Aesthetic Nervousness*. New York: Columbia University Press.

Reagin, N.R. (2011). "Was Voldemort a Nazi? Death eater ideology and national socialism." In N.R. Reagin (ed.), *Harry Potter and History* (127–152). Hoboken, NJ: John Wiley & Sons.

Rowling, J.K. (2000). *Harry Potter and the Goblet of Fire*. New York: Scholastic. Trade Paperback.

_____. (2003). *Harry Potter and the Order of the Phoenix*. New York: Scholastic.

_____. (2005). *Harry Potter and the Half-Blood Prince*. New York: Scholastic.

_____. (2007). *Harry Potter and the Deathly Hallows*. New York: Scholastic.

Serlin, D. (2006). "The other arms race." In L.J. Davis (ed.), *The Disability Studies Reader* (49–66). New York: Routledge.

"Statement issued on behalf of J.K. Rowling." ABF The Soldiers' Charity, Corporate Partners. *SoldiersCharity.org*. http://www.soldierscharity.org/get-involved/cor porate-partnership-item/statement-issued-on-behalf-of-j.k.-rowling.

Thomson, R.G. (1997). *Extraordinary Bodies*. New York: Columbia University Press.

_____. (2002). "The politics of staring: Visual rhetorics of disability in popular pho tography." In S.L. Snyder, B.J. Brueggemann & R.G. Thomson (eds.), *Disability Studies: Enabling the Humanities* (56–75). New York: Modern Language Asso ciation.

Winters, S.F. (2010). "From Satan to Hitler: Theological and Historical Evil in C.S. Lewis, Philip Pullman, and J.K. Rowling." In S. Buttsworth & M. Abbenhuis (eds.), *Monsters in the Mirror: Representations of Nazism in Post-War Popular Culture* (53–74). Santa Barbara: Praeger.

Deconstructing Disability: The Dragons and Girls in Ursula K. Le Guin's Earthsea and Merrie Haskell's Handbook for Dragonslayers

ERIN WYBLE NEWCOMB

Both Ursula K. Le Guin's Earthsea series (1990, 2001) and Merrie Haskell's *Handbook for Dragonslayers* (2013) feature female protagonists who are presumed physically-disabled by their respective communities; both main characters (Le Guin's Therru/Tehanu from *Tehanu* and *The Other Wind* and Haskell's Tilda) suffer mistreatment as a result of their perceived disabilities, yet by the conclusions of the novels, the girls discover their ability to turn into dragons. Their magical shape-shifting alters their own and their societies' interpretations of their bodies, not as physically disabled but as dangerously potent; the characters' transformations illustrate a central paradox of disability, where ability and disability exist along a spectrum that is culturally-determined and can be unstable throughout the lives of individuals. Neither ability nor disability is necessarily constant, philosophically or personally, and the girls' movement from disenfranchisement and abuse to privilege and domination suggests the instability of bodies as well as the categories we use to define them. By examining the false binaries of ability and disability within two fantasy realms, I hope to illuminate the ways that power and (dis)ability reflect and challenge the real world of readers.

At the same time, I argue that the gendering of disability in these young adult novels questions the nature of power as well as the meanings of bodies as sites where fictional characters as well as readers shape-shift in ways both magical and mundane. Using feminist theories of embodiment, I analyze the gendering of disability where Therru/Tehanu and Tilda, through their coming-of-age narratives, deconstruct their cultures' visions of power and able-bodiedness. Further, by embodying adolescent girls (already a subject position marked by transformations) in both human and dragon form, the novels demonstrate the ways that all bodies—even those privileged—are limited by the materiality of bodies themselves; bodies and power mutually constitute each other, while the meaning of neither is fixed or absolute. The fantasy contexts of these novels emphasize extreme forms of bodies and shape-shifting, highlighting the changeability of bodies in the textual and material worlds.

My analysis serves to deconstruct the categories of disability assumed within Le Guin's Earthsea and Haskell's *Handbook for Dragonslayers* so that readers can reimagine the meanings of bodies and embodied categories in the material, non-magical world. Dragon-transformations are specifically significant within fantasy literature because, as Byrne (2011) points out, "the dragon is one of the most enduring, resilient and shape-shifting creations of the human imagination, the prevalence and popularity of dragons in fiction for adolescents bodes well for these readers' ability to appreciate their transformative power" (p. 164). Referring to Le Guin's work, Byrne see the dragon as especially empowering as female "because of her capacity to cross boundaries of gender, species and value … as a valued member of fantasy's vanguard of heroes" (p. 163). Indeed, both Le Guin and Haskell emphasize female bodies and dragons in ways that illustrate the power and instability of those bodies as well as all bodily categories. In each section, I lay out the theoretical issues first and then apply the concepts to the primary texts, so that readers can compare the two novels side-by-side with full awareness of the theory in play. I begin by looking at the limitations imposed on Therru/Tehanu and Tilda; then, I discuss the kinds of attention their bodies—and all bodies—require, which moves my argument into discussion of the instability of bodies and embodied categories like (dis)ability. Finally, I consider the concept of transcendence of human bodies, and the extent to which these characters (and perhaps their readers) can imagine themselves as both embodied and more than bodies.

Able and Allowed

Abrams (2011) distinguishes "[w]hat a body is able to do" (p. 477) from the question "[w]hat is the body permitted to do?" (p. 481). She highlights here a key point that Barnes (1998) establishes as the definition for "the social model of disability" where impairment "refers to biological characteristics of the body and the mind" and disability reflects "society's failure to address the needs of disabled people" (p. 78). Hunt's landmark essay (1998, originally published in 1966) "A Critical Condition" illustrates the way perceptions of disability influence stereotypes of people with disabilities. He points out

> that we are often useless, unable to contribute to the economic good of the community. As such, again we cannot help posing questions about values, about what a person is, what he is for, about whether work in the everyday sense of the word is the most important or the only contribution anyone can make to society [p. 10].

Hunt challenges the image of people with disabilities as "different, abnormal" and "useless" by asking, "What kind of goal is this elusive normality?" (p. 11). These writers expose tension between the concepts of impairment and disability, where the former gets defined by the physical body and the latter gets defined by social interpretation of that body. As Hunt indicates, social assumptions about bodies and their limitations (either real or imagined) point out cultural values about human bodies and human lives. Hunt also challenges the belief that "work in the everyday sense of the word" should be the determining factor of human value, a particularly salient point when one considers how that criterion excludes children and the elderly as well (p. 10); Hunt's challenge indicates the ways that bodies are normalized by their ability to contribute to capitalism, showing that ability/disability is as much about economics as it is about physical capabilities. This point can be particularly pertinent for young adult audiences, many of whom are still only considered potential workers, their value stored in their future ability to earn as opposed to their current economic opportunities.

Who works, and under what conditions, says as much about what bodies are allowed to do as about what they can do. Moving from bodies' abilities to bodies' permissions likewise shows that while bodies never lose their materiality (like the ability to feel pain), all bodies are subject to the strictures of their communities. Schriempf (2001) makes a similar claim in her efforts to bridge feminist theories and disability studies, stating, "Bodies are not presocial nor are social practices divorced from materiality" (p. 68). The relationship between what bodies *can* do and what bodies are *permitted* to do becomes particularly significant as disability and gender intersect. Morris (2001), discussing the reality of "[l]iving in a sexist and heterosexist society as we all do," says, "Disabled women are either attractive in spite of their impairment or unattractive because of their impairment" (p. 10). Butler and Taylor (2009) connect (dis)ability and gender through their conversation about being "culturally ingrained early on to move in certain ways, to walk in certain ways, to gesture in certain ways," and Butler wonders "what it means to be born in a body that can't physically move in the culturally accepted ways" (p. 186). Bodies signal gender identity—or at least the assumption is that they *ought* to— and when physical movement fails to comply with social expectations, either through gender or (dis)ability or the meeting of the two, there are material and social consequences. For instance, Castelnuovo and Guthrie (1998) assert "the bodies of women with disabilities may provide even more radically transgressive challenges to the patriarchal construction of the female body than those of sporting women" (p. 131). Garland Thomson (1997) goes further, seeing "the discursive equation of femaleness with disability" because "the female and the disabled body are cast as deviant and inferior" (p. 19). These intersections of gender and disability—as well as the conflation of femaleness with disability—illustrate the social capitol accorded to bodies and the expectations imposed on embodied subjects. Just as economics plays a role in legitimating some bodies over other, so too do perceptions about gendered identity, and disability contests the value-laden assumptions about work and gender that prize some bodies over others.

Both Le Guin and Haskell grapple with these discourses of the body in their fictional worlds, and though the worlds incorporate fantasy elements, the treatment of the protagonists' bodies mirrors the real world. The worlds Le Guin and Haskell create might be filled with magic and mythical creations like dragons, but these authors' characters still struggle to find meaningful work and social legitimation because of their disabilities. Therru/Tehanu first appears in Le Guin's (1990) novel *Tehanu*; the first chapter and the one that introduces Therru (who does not use the name Tehanu until the book's conclusion) is called "A Bad Thing," and it is unclear whether that title refers to the character or the violence done to her (pp. 1–2). Readers later learn that Therru is raped, beaten, and pushed, unconscious, into a fire (p. 164). Her adopted mother, Tenar, worries about Therru's future based on the permanent injuries (partial blindness, scarring over half her face, and a hand that cannot grip). Here, she imagines Therru's life:

> The averted faces, the signs against evil, the horror and curiosity, the sickly pity and the prying threat, for harm draws harm to it.... And never a man's

arms. Never anyone to hold her. Never anyone but Tenar. Oh, he was right, the child should have died, should be dead [pp. 91–92].

This thought process begins with the way others treat Therru, where she is feared, shunned, and physically-endangered because of the way her society perceives her body. Tenar then moves into the gendered expectations that a female requires male affirmation (making the mother's arms insignificant by comparison), but doubts Therru will ever find a romantic partner, another likely result of the child's disability. Tenar extends her anxiety to a denial of the value of Therru's life itself, whereby the values that legitimate women (and women's bodies) exclude Therru. These cruel reflections come from the caregiver who loves Therru and who continually finds ways to instruct and include the child in everyday tasks; yet, even as they build a life together, Tenar can see no alternative to death, revealing how the cruelty that causes Therru's impairment in the first place continues to devalue and dismiss her life. Tenar considers apprenticing Therru to a local weaver as a way of giving her a place (however peripheral) in society:

> It would be a decent living. The bulk of the work was dull, always the same over, but weaving was an honorable trade and in some hands a noble art. And people expected weavers to be a bit shy, often to be unmarried, shut away at their work as they were; yet they were respected. And working indoors at a loom, Therru would not have to show her face. But the claw hand? Could that hand throw the shuttle, warp the loom? And was she to hide all her life? [pp. 129–130].

As much as Tenar wants to provide a stable economic life for Therru, she is unable to envision that life outside of a context that devalues her daughter because of her physical appearance. This job prospect is as much about concealing Therru from the world as it is about stabilizing her economic future; likewise, Tenar still imagines Therru as physically limited in spite of the child's work around the farm, and socially and sexually isolated. Although Therru's injuries require her to adapt new methods of work, Tenar's vision is restricted by Earthsea's assumptions about Therru than about Therru's physical or social capacities. Even a local witch refuses to apprentice Therru, though witchcraft would provide another solitary (and probably celibate) profession. The witch calls Therru "[a]n ill-used child!" and fears her power, thus dismissing Therru from yet another economic prospect because of what others have done to her. Throughout the novel, Therru's opportunities seem to close around her not because of who she is or what she can do, but because of how those around her interpret her body.

Haskell's character Princess Tilda is similarly defined (at least in the story's beginning) by her community's interpretation of her body. Tilda abdicates her kingdom to her scheming cousin Ivo so that she can escape from the responsibility of ruling people who fear her and her twisted foot. She hides her reasoning from the friends (Judith and Parz) who accompany her, and the three set off hunting dragons; their journey challenges Tilda's physical strength as well as her resolve to leave behind her home and position of power, in spite of her subjects' superstitions. In the beginning of the tale, Tilda notes a servant who "made the sign against the evil eye" upon seeing her, and marked a child imitating her, "a tree branch shoved in his armpit, and he was pretending to limp as he chased the other shrieking children" (p. 14, 16). These events follow Tilda overhearing a conversation between her advisors about a betrothal that fails, in part, because of the princess's foot; the remark "[n]ot *just* the foot" (p. 11) emphasizes the context—probably economic and social—that affect Tilda's future along with her physical disability. It's known that her estate is independent but financially strained, so any marriage to Tilda would bring some freedom along with a lot of careful budgeting, that is, of course, if her foot were not a primary deterrent. Near the novel's end, Tilda realizes her advantages: "a princess, trained from my earliest life in duty and how to care for Alder Brook. Ivo's two good feet were no substitute for that training in how to rule, or how—or when—to curb his own ambition" (p. 191). Even this mature reflection exists within a context where she will be mocked, feared, and devalued because of her disability; she may muster her own strength and capacity as a leader, but her leadership is always influenced by others' readings of her body.

Her body also influences perceptions of her role in the marriage market, no small factor for a royal marriage that must serve as a social and political alliance as well as a means of producing heirs and securing future stability. Her cousin Ivo bluntly informs her,

> They say your mother walked over a grave when she carried you. They say you bring bad luck and death. They say your father died because of you, or because of some sin in his past, the same sin that caused your gravefoot. They say that even if some desperate knight could be convinced to marry you, he'd die before the first year was out, because there's a devil's mark on you. *Everyone* knows you're cursed, Tilda.

While Ivo, who is trying to steal Tilda's kingdom, bears a vested interest in disparaging her, these harsh statements echo the princess's own fears. Ivo's brutal language summarizes the superstition of their community and the limited opportunities it presents for Tilda's future. Later in the story, a subtler enemy preys on those same fears, not by goading them but by showing Tilda that the limitations are not insurmountable. Tilda is shocked by Sir Egin's invitation to dance, admitting, "I hadn't even been trying to hide my foot or crutch or anything. It had to be fairly obvious that I wasn't capable of dancing" (p. 125). Sir Egin literally sweeps her off her feet, lifting her in his arms and spinning around. Yet while Egin's kindness conceals (for a time) that he is a predator, his creativity reveals that tension between impairment and disability, between what bodies can do and what they are allowed to do. Ultimately, Egin doesn't care about Tilda's body at all, because in a Bluebeard-esque turn, he wants to marry her and make her a human sacrifice like he did with his previous seven wives (p. 207). Egin disregards her disability, but he also disregards her life. Meanwhile, when her friend Parz teaches her how to ride, Tilda feels real delight: "I wasn't a sack of turnips. I was *riding*" (p. 132). Based on their friendship and their need for speedier travel, Parz contrives a way to accommodate Tilda's foot so that she can ride, though earlier she'd adamantly refused to go on horseback for fear of further injury (p. 57). It's unclear if Parz harbors romantic feelings for Tilda, though his friendship is evident. While her two potential suitors treat her as an obstacle or an instrument of their own ambitions, Parz regards Tilda as a person with her own feelings and needs. Perhaps because he does not contemplate marriage with Tilda, Parz is able to address the unique needs of her body outside of the context of ruling and reproducing.

The hopelessness Tenar expresses contrasts with the resourcefulness of Tilda and her friends, but both texts, by attending to the bodies of disabled females, foreground the assumptions about gender and disability that readers might bring to the texts as well. Both Therru and Tilda exists in context that assumes femaleness itself as a kind of disability; they each face the assumptions of their cultures that physical impairment somehow removes one from the marriage and maternal markets, further devaluing their perceived worth. And speculations about that worth are always already tied to bodily representations of ability and gender, to say nothing of other attributes.

Attending to Bodies

In the previous section, I discuss the ways that social expectations about female bodies degrade and limit Therru and Tilda. I move next to the way that Le Guin and Haskell both emphasize attention to the body, which illustrates the specific needs of Therru and Tilda but also reminds characters and readers alike that all bodies require care. Wendell (1999) asserts that "attempting to transcend or disengage oneself from the body by ignoring or discounting its needs and sensations is generally a luxury of the healthy and able-bodied. For people who are ill or disabled, a fairly high degree of attention to the body is necessary for survival" (p. 328). Neither of these fictional worlds ignores the body, and that can call on readers to recount the ways that bodily care exists on a spectrum where no one can ignore hunger or thirst or fatigue indefinitely. Clare (1999) extends the appeal to pay attention to bodies to a social level as well as a physical one; he writes, "We cannot ignore the body itself: the sensory, mostly non-verbal experience of our hearts and lungs, muscles and tendons, telling us and the world who we are" (p. 150). In this quote, Clare connects the physical and social understandings of bodies, where bodies are both our vehicles for moving through the world and significant markers for understanding our place in that world. For Clare, "[d]isability snarls into gender. Class wraps around race. Sexuality strains against abuse" because, as he succinctly states "my body has never been singular" (p. 159). He underscores the complexity of bodies, their biological functions as well as the ways those get interpreted within discursive networks. We can read—and misread—bodies, but they demand our attention either way. In the previous section, I showed how Therru and Tilda both work and form meaningful relationships despite their societies' narrow visions of their value and potential; their lives illustrate how embodiment always affects subjectivity, but they also expose the risk of reducing people's whole lives to their bodies. By demonstrating that all bodies require attention, and that disability studies highlights that reality, I demonstrate that bodies matter but cannot dictate the worth of human life.

Butler and Taylor (2009) emphasize that all bodies need attention, but that societies are set up only to legitimize certain sorts of bodies and bodily movements. In their conversation, Taylor shares:

> It's a political protest for me to go in and order a coffee and demand help simply because, in my opinion, help is something we all need. And it's something that is looked down upon and not really taken care of in this society when we *all* need help, when we're all interdependent in all sorts of ways [p. 196].

Here Taylor debunks the myth that distinguishes able-bodied from disabled, independent from dependent. No one survives alone. That concept of interdependence fits within a feminist framework of understanding care and care work, and it illustrates the role of gender in any discussion of embodiment. Says Healey (1993), "Being 'too' needy is based on a standard of 'need' which has no objective measure, but has been set by the patriarchy in which boys and men have had, for the most part, their every need catered to" (p. 72). She relates the concepts of need and care specifically to gender socialization and a hierarchy of feminine caregivers and males who, because of feminine care work, can receive care without attending much to their own bodies (p. 72). That, however, does not make their bodies independent; it has more to do with the invisibility and devaluation of care work and care workers. The gendered distinction between giving and receiving care emphasizes an assumed split between mind and body. Garland Thomson (2002) sees the way that disability and femininity are often conflated, both as negative terms: "[w]omen and the disabled are portrayed as helpless, dependent, weak, vulnerable, and incapable bodies" (p. 8). Yet Hughes and Paterson (1997) remind that "the (impaired) body is not just experienced: It is also the very basic of experience" (p. 335). The world may impose readings onto the body, but the body also allows subjects to interpret the world; we are always-already embodied subjects.

In an essay on *Tehanu* (2014), Wyble Newcomb argues that "Le Guin's decision to authenticate care work through story asks the reader to respect the considerable contributions of care workers like Tenar" (p. 98). Indeed, the novel focuses on Tenar's daily chores like doing the wash, preparing food, making and mending clothes, tending the garden. She and a group of female companions (who also engage in care work) take care of older males who are sick or dying as well as the child Therru. One scene from *Tehanu* poignantly describes the world Tenar and Therru share,

> Therru was fast asleep at last. Tenar slipped her from her lap to the bed and waited a moment to be sure she slept on. Then, after a glance round to be sure she was alone, with an almost guilty quickness, yet with the ceremony of enjoyment, of great pleasure, she laid her narrow, light-skinned hand along the side of the child's face where eye and cheek had been eaten away by fire, leaving a slab bed, bald scar. Under her touch all that was gone. The flesh was whole, a child's round, soft, sleeping face. It was as if her touch restored the truth. Lightly, reluctantly, she lifted her palm, and saw the irremediable loss, the healing that would never be whole. She bent down and kissed the scar [p. 83].

This affectionate scene epitomizes motherhood, where the maternal figure puts the child to bed and indulges in a caress that would have been impossible during the child's active day. The scene shows how Tenar and Therru are just like any mother-daughter pair, a loving touch for a slumbering child who feels safe and secure. But the scene also accentuates the atypical aspect of their relationship—the violence done to Therru that has permanently marked her body; thus the pair are both ordinary and extraordinary, a mother who gives love to a child in need of care and a woman who rescues an abused child from horrific violence condoned (if not enacted) by her biological family. They begin as strangers and become family by the simple, repetitive acts of paying attention to Therru's bodily needs. By kissing Therru's scar, Tenar demonstrates her recognition that Therru's body (not to mention her spirit) needs special attention but also the attention that every child, and every body, requires. By focusing on the mother-child relationship in *Tehanu*, Le Guin reminds readers that all bodies need attention and care in order to survive, and especially to thrive; no human makes it to adulthood—or those elusive and questionable values of financial and sexual autonomy—independently.

As in Earthsea, attention to the body in Haskell's work often displays relationships filled with mutual love and care. Tilda describes her friend and servant Judith and the massages that the latter gives to help them along their quest: "She dug her thumbs into the tight tendons of my foot. I sucked my breath in to keep from crying out.... I tried not to blush. I probably wouldn't be able to sleep for cramping if Judith didn't help me" (p. 74). Tilda's impaired foot often sets the pace of their early journey and dictates points of rest and mode of travel, yet Haskell's protagonist sees her relationship with Judith as even more essential than her healthy foot. When she contemplates her separation from Judith, Tilda thinks: "[I]t would feel like chopping off my foot. And not my crooked foot—the good one. The one I never paid attention to because it wasn't always aching and holding me back, even though it was the foot I really couldn't do without" (p. 149). The bodily imagery that Tilda uses to describe her relationship with Judith draws attention to her physical needs (the care work Judith provides) but also the closeness of their friendship, as if their bodies are shared. In recognizing how much she loves and needs Judith beyond caring for her injured foot, Tilda simultaneously illustrates her embodiment and transcendence of embodiment. Later in the novel, Tilda also realizes that her own social position as princess allows her to care for Judith, too; the princess concludes "there was no reason that when I came of age, I could not carve out some small section of Alder Brook and give her a proper benefice to rule, plus a title to go with the duties and the land." Tilda imagines Judith serving as her steward, and realizes that the only restriction is conventional gender norms (p. 321). Certainly Judith is competent for the tasks, and Tilda's reasoning shows the intersections between economics, gender, and disability, where her own class position enables her to smooth Judith's future just as Judith eases Tilda's own. The care work is mutual, benefiting both their bodies, however indirectly, as well as establishing alternative work and relational practices to enhance their community.

Both the scene from *Tehanu* and this passage from *Handbook for Dragon Slayers* exemplify the interdependence of bodies; all bodies need care and all bodies exist within relationships. Their specific injuries highlight the bodies of Therru and Tilda as exceptional because they look different and require extra care, but the contexts in which they live out their embodied experiences can prompt readers to think about how all bodies, to some extent, require attention, not to mention love. All bodies minimally require food, water, and rest—in addition to some kind of loving connection to others. Le Guin's series and Haskell's novel show these relationships too, with characters with disabilities who live in and contribute to communities. Therru's relationship with Tenar and Tilda's with Judith showcase the strength of feminine friendship and mutual care, an interdependence that highlights all bodies as needy and relational.

Mutable Bodies

Between Therru and Tenar, between Tilda and Judith, love remains constant and grows as the characters care for each other. Yet the relationships, though they are rooted in one character's particular need for care, ultimately illustrate the instability of all bodies and the universality of need. Shildrick and J. Price (1999) say, "Able-bodied carries with it the trace of the other—a trace which must be continually suppressed if able-bodied is to carry a delimited meaning" (p. 439). These theorists suggest that to maintain the discrete category of "able-bodied," the term must be defined in against another kind of body, making some bodies not "able-bodied." Such definitions exist within the cultural context of what abilities are valued, and therefore what ableness means. One category of meaning constitutes the other—so that able-bodied and disabled as ontological groupings can only exist mutually; as Shildrick and Price poignantly imagine, "it is the empty wheelchair that generates dis-ease in the fully mobile" (p. 439). Wendell (1989) makes this image more personal, writing, "If the able-bodied saw the disabled as potentially themselves or as their future selves, they would be more inclined to feel that society should be organized to provide the resources that would make disabled people fully integrated and contributing members" (p. 110). What all of these scholars suggest is that able-bodied and disabled are not in opposition to each other, but rather exist along a spectrum where disability is always possible.

Several writers take up this issue with regard to age. Garland-Thomson (2002) asserts, "Disability is an identity category that anyone can enter at any time, and we will all join it if we live long enough. As such, disability reveals the essential dynamism of identity" (p. 20). Elsewhere, Garland-Thomson (1997) argues that the instability of bodily categories "makes disability more fluid, and perhaps more threatening, to those who identify themselves as normates than such seemingly more stable marginal identities as femaleness, blackness, or nondominant ethnic identities" (p. 14). Unlike many identity markers, (dis)ability offers the possibility of moving into or out of the category, and longer lives raise the likelihood of identifying as disabled. Nussbaum (2006) agrees, stating, "As the life span increases, the relative independence that many people sometimes enjoy looks more and more like a temporary condition" and reminds that "[e]ven in our prime, many of us encounter shorter or longer periods of extreme dependency on others" (p. 101). Nussbaum qualifies bodily categories as contexts that can fluctuate throughout one's life, and she demonstrates that even the "prime" bookended by the dependency of infancy and (potentially in) old age is inconsistent. The inconsistency of bodies is likely to be familiar territory for young adult audiences, for whom puberty is familiar territory and whose age positions them on the cusp of childhood and adulthood; uncontrollable bodies and social limitations will ring true for many adolescents, whether they identify as disabled or able-bodied, because their age denotes their bodies as not yet fully enfranchised.

It is impossible for people to mature from infancy to any other developmental age or stage without bodily fluctuations. Even the standards of ability applied to an infant vary dramatically from the standards applied to a toddler or a teenager, making ability always a contextual construct. Shildrick (1997) describes "one strategy recently advocated in disablement politics is to push the 'healthy' majority to a recognition that they are merely temporarily able bodies" (p. 60). Using the powerful idea of "leaky bodies" for her title, Shildrick destabilizes the boundaries that mark bodies as able or disabled. This concept can extend to individual bodies as well, where the individual body exists within a community of care (or lack thereof) always already interdependent. In Butler and Taylor's (2009) conversation about "Interdependence," the two conclude that regulating bodies and bodily movements leads to "really restrictive ideas about what the human is" (p. 213) because "it's a threat to our most basic categories that we've built our systems of power on" (p. 206). Bodies themselves are unstable, and so are the categories that are meant to separate bodies from each other as well as to designate power. Adolescence as a category intends to distinguish childhood from adulthood, but it is inherently a transitional stage, as illustrated by the concerns about what Therru and Tilda will do in their futures. Both Therru and Tilda face the restrictions of their cultures, and their cultures' ideals about work and marriage, yet these characters also threaten the power structures that bind them. By making meaningful work and meaningful relationships, by adapting to their changing bodies, they challenge the binaries between childhood and adulthood, between impaired and healthy. Their pubescent bodies are unstable, as are their prospects for work and marriage and the very communities that seek to inscribe them.

That kind of social instability forms much of the conflict in Le Guin's *Tehanu* (1990) and *The Other Wind* (2001). The former wizard Ged (whose own powers have left him in the midst of a physical and psychological crisis) disparages Tenar's decision to adopt Therru:

> I don't know ... why you took her, knowing that she cannot be healed. Knowing what her life must be. I suppose it's a part of this time we have lived—a dark time, an age of ruin, an ending time. You took her, I suppose, as I went to meet my enemy, because it was all you could do. And so we must live on into the new age with the spoils of our victory over evil. You with your burned child, and I with nothing at all [Le Guin, 1990, p. 89].

Ged cites his own losses here along with the context of turmoil in Earthsea. His position depicts the intolerance of their community, which conflates embodiment with social value. The same attitude surfaces among their neighbors, whom, Tenar notes, mostly "believed that you are what happens to you. The rich and strong must have virtue; one to whom evil has been done must be bad, and may rightly be punished" (Le Guin, 1990, p. 200). Tenar and readers alike challenge these assumptions and can envision a life for Therru in which, healed or not, she is valued for herself. Indeed, I could argue that in *Tehanu* Le Guin reorients the entire Earthsea series around disability; both Ged and Tenar feature prominently in earlier works in the series as heroes, lauded by their society and imbued with the powers of youth and influence. Those powers are gone by the beginning of *Tehanu*, and neither Ged nor Tenar can physically or socially exert the same influence, as evidenced by the conclusion where Therru rescues them from the evil wizard, Aspen. The shift in the series sees one generation's power diminish as another's rises. As unlikely a heroine as she might seem because of her disability, Therru represents a new era in Earthsea where the nature and wielders of power are changing. In their time and their stories, Tenar and Ged looked the part of epic heroes, but Therru represents a different context and a different kind of power—both underrated like her body.

As it turns out, Therru's birth serves as a sign of bodily instability long before her injuries occur. Therru saves Ged and Tenar at the conclusion of *Tehanu* by calling upon the dragons in "[h]er mother tongue" (p. 278), a phrase that shows the relationship between Therru/Tehanu's power and her body. The child's revealed relationship to dragons prompts her adopted father to further investigate her body's meaning. Ged says, "I saw a child summon the dragon Kalessin, the Eldest: and Kalessin came to her, calling her daughter, as I do. What does that mean?" (Le Guin, 2001, p. 35). Readers learn that Therru, now named Tehanu, can shapeshift as both human and dragon as part of a sign that the two species were at one time singular. The woman/dragon Irian explains:

> Once we were one people. And in sign of that, in every generation of men, one or two are born who are dragons also. And in every generation of our people, longer than the quick lives of men, one of us is born who is also human. Of these one is now living in the Inner Isles. And there is one of them living there now who is a dragon. These two are the messengers, the bringers of choice. There will be no more such born to us or to them. For the balance changes [Le Guin, 2001, pp. 128–129].

Bodies and interpretations of bodies can change over time, not just the temporality of a single life but also over the course of history and within specific communities. The extreme example of dragon/human relationships and a girl who can select her species alignment demonstrates that bodies—as well as the ways we read them—are unstable. Irian, the messenger, embodies this change as she moves easily from dragon to human form and back again; her body, like Tehanu's acts as a medium between the two cultures that share a history and a tumultuous present. When Irian asserts "the balance changes," she refers to the relationships between humans and dragons, the relationships between Tehanu and her communities, and the power within all of those contexts. Though Tehanu has not yet assumed her dragon form, she too is a messenger, a medium who destabilizes the boundaries between human and dragon bodies and communities as well as the power structure that seeks to compartmentalize and discipline bodies. These messengers embody physical and social instability.

Tilda and her friends face the same physical and social uncertainty; while their societies assume that Tehanu and Tilda meet insecure futures because of their physical impairments, in fact their physical impairments underscore the instability of all bodies and all futures. Even healthy and youthful bodies do not necessarily remain so. In one scene from Haskell's novel, Tilda tells readers,

> Judith couldn't assist me any more than I could assist her, between her shoulder and my crutch. My foot was tender and unpleasant to walk on, but I was in many respects in better shape than Judith. For one thing, I was used to my pain, and she was far from accustomed to hers. She could walk all right, but every step was jarring [p. 110].

The perils of their quest, which, like Le Guin's stories takes place in a time of upheaval, leads to numerous injuries for Tilda and her companions. Judith is supposed to serve Tilda but requires just as much physical help in this passage as Tilda does, and the rapid repositioning of Judith's body from able to disabled leaves her unprepared for the experience. Judith suffers another injury (p. 167), and, later, their fellow traveler Parz requires a stretcher (p. 172). In each of these instances, the characters must grapple with challenges to their usual methods of mobility and their typical assumptions about their bodies' capacities. Their journey leads to numerous physical injuries, yet the catalyst for the trip is political unrest and social immobility: the capture of Tilda and her mother and the coup by Ivo displace the female friends, and Parz is a willing participant because he has failed as a squire and faces an unsure economic future himself (p. 60). It is not that the social circumstances cause these friends' injuries, but that able-bodiedness is neither a constant state nor a guarantee of economic or social security. As each injury occurs, Judith and Parz must adjust to limited physical abilities and bodily pain that feels unfamiliar; Tilda's advantage is in her comfort with discomfort, where she, unlike her friends, does not expect her body to cooperate with her.

Although—or perhaps because—Tilda, Judith, and Parz are young, they assume that hunting dragons will be easy, yet their travels illustrate again and again that they are physically endangered and unprepared. As a result, much of Haskell's text is devoted to describing injuries and travel plans that need to accommodate a range of bodily positions and movements. The group eventually winds up convalescing in a cloister where Sister Hildegard "began an extensive regimen" with Tilda's foot (p. 173).

Tilda asks, "Am I—is my foot going to be normal?" to which the Sister responds, "You will be able to walk a little better by the time your friends are healed from their injuries" (p. 174). Here Tilda demonstrates the slippage between her self and her injury as well as the social perceptions of bodily norms. She has to consciously separate what her body can do, how well she can walk without a crutch, from her sense of self; her normalcy is defined in terms of her impairment, even as she resists letting her foot subsume her entire identity. Still, even a lifelong injury like Tilda's can change with time and treatment, and her friends may be healed from these particular injuries only to incur others later. The roles of caretaker and cared for shift throughout their trip, illustrating interdependence and reminding readers that youthful bodies are subject to change as well. Just as Therru/Tehanu moves from receiving Tenar's care to caring for her adopted mother, as well as all of Earthsea, Tilda cares and is cared for by her community.

Seeking "Wholeness"

Both Tehanu and Tilda discover their abilities to change into dragons, bodily forms that leave behind the injuries attending their human figures. These characters shape-shift while retaining at least some of their consciousness, so that they are aware of their changing bodies and the new social positions they inhabit because of those physical transformations. As such, the movement from girl to dragon highlights the relationship between power and the body, where certain kinds of bodies can wield certain kinds of power. Because bodies are always inscribed within cultural contexts, the kinds of power available to them as female humans or as dragons influence the choices each one ultimately adopts for her final form. In this section, I relate the movement from girl to dragon to a concept Wendell (1996) calls "transcendence," which she defines as follows:

> By defending some notion of transcendence of the body I do not mean to suggest that strategies of disembodying the self should be adopted by people without disabilities. Instead, I want to demonstrate how important it is to consider the experiences of people with disabilities when theorizing about the relationship of consciousness to the body. One thing is clear: We cannot speak only of reducing our alienation from our bodies, becoming more aware of them, and celebrating their strengths and pleasures; we must also talk about how to live with the suffering body, with that which cannot be noticed without pain, and that which cannot be celebrated without ambivalence. We

may find that there is a place in our discussion of the body for some concept of transcendence [p. 179].

Here Wendell strives to strike a balance between reducing people, especially people with disabilities, to their bodies and ignoring the body and its needs. It is a call to recognize embodied subjectivity that validates the body without locating personhood solely within one's body. Tehanu and Tilda, like their readers, are embodied, but they are never just bodies. Transcendence can be temporary, or it can be one tool for reimagining bodily possibilities and personhood beyond bodies.

Fiction, and maybe fantasy more than many genres, can offer readers a kind of transcendence, a new lens for imagining and understanding the real worlds audiences inhabit. Applying a disability studies approach to these texts can help readers see bodies within and beyond the texts as never just bodies. Silvers (2000) explores a similar concept in representations of disability in art. She writes, "Art can make impairment powerful. This idea occasionally surfaces in disability studies, but it is treated as an exceptional manifestation rather than as a familiar achievement of art" (pp. 215–216). Silvers asserts, "It is the impoverished political understanding of beauty that prevails in disability studies," but "aestheticizing disability elevates otherness to originality, thereby defeating the hegemony imposed by 'normal' socio-political relations" (p. 218). Byrne (2011) connects a similar point to Earthsea, asserting that "Le Guin's revisioning of the dragon tradition produces literary portraits of women as disturbing the traditional patriarchal order of society through their freedom to cross boundaries and unsettle fixed categories of ontology" (p. 155). As the agents in their own stories, Tehanu and Tilda resist narratives that disempower them as females with disabilities. I think, to an extent, the dragon transformations serve as a metaphor for puberty, where these young girls come into the full power of their sexualized bodies and, in so doing, threaten the societies that mark them as undesirable and undesiring. Instead, Le Guin and Haskell emphasize female, disabled bodies as central—potent and potentially threatening. I do not read either writer as suggesting that women with disabilities are somehow other or lesser because of these dragon transformations, but rather, that their bodies are powerful because they draw attention to bodies—in all their needy, unstable forms. The transcendence and the beauty that Le Guin and Haskell offer with these stories is the beauty of bodies that always exist within cultural contexts but can also change and challenge the injustices of those very worlds.

Tehanu ultimately chooses to live as a dragon among dragons, sacrificing her human life and family. Le Guin foreshadows this decision in *Tehanu* in the exchange between Tenar and Kalessin, Tehanu's human and dragon mothers, respectively. Kalessin tells the child, "I will come back for thee" and alerts Tenar and Ged, "I give you my child, as you will give me yours." Tenar replies, "In time" (p. 278), acknowledging that both the human and dragon communities can claim the child and that Tehanu's life and body will change dramatically based on her cultural context. At the conclusion of *The Other Wind*, one of the wizards informs Tenar, "My lady, I saw Tehanu. She flies golden on the other wind" (p. 207). Le Guin tells us that "Tenar glanced up at him. His face was white and worn, but there was a shadow of glory in his eyes. She struggled and then said, speaking roughly and almost inaudibly, 'Whole?' He nodded" (p. 207). It is a loaded exchange, because while Tehanu may be physically whole as a dragon in a way that she could not be as a human, she has given up a mother whom she dearly loves. There is a cost to Tehanu's "wholeness" that can provoke readers to question what "wholeness" really means, returning full circle to Hunt's (1998) earlier inquiries about "what *kind* of goal is this elusive normality" (p. 11). Readers can likewise ask about the kind and quality of Tehanu's elusive "wholeness." Tehanu transcends the limitations of her human form, but her transcendence is only partial, accompanied by loss of human relationships and simply embodying her in a new way that is also always-already context-laden. The contrast between physical "wholeness" and Tenar's weeping show the cost of transcendence, and the limitedness of even the most powerful bodies. Tenar's understanding of wholeness is limited by her cultural context, and the same is, no doubt, true of audiences as well; though Tehanu may be physically whole in a way that was impossible in her human form, neither she nor Tenar is "whole" given the breach in their relationship. Transcendence is a critical concept because it can remind readers that even the most powerful bodies are not universally perfect, and they cannot remain so for long in a particular culture either. Transcendence takes these characters out of their human bodies to remind them, and their readers, that the self is always more than the evaluation of its physical form.

Tilda also notes the freedom and the cost of transcendence when she transforms into a dragon at the start of Chapter 28, and her first thought is "I am strong" (Haskell, p. 273). Like Tehanu, Tilda glories in the physical power available to her as a dragon, but both characters also lose (at least temporarily) their emotional connections in the human world. Although readers do not get to access a first-person perspective from Tehanu, Tilda-as-dragon reveals a kind of split consciousness that both is and is not

Tilda, and likely applies to both characters; says the dragon version of Tilda, "Tilda-girl and I agree on something else, though. She hated that foot, the twisted foot that made people think and say and do things that they would not do to any straight-foots. I hate that foot, too" (p. 282). Her dragon form alters her perspective, allowing her to see herself differently, without her injured foot but also without many of the human attributes that define her life. Again, there is always a cost. She senses Judith's thoughts and emotions more acutely, recognizing, "She never pitied me for my foot the way she pities me for my dragon's body, the way she pitied me when I tore the page from my beloved book just now with my clumsy paws" (p. 290). A true love's kiss between Tilda and Judith returns the princess to her human body, and Tilda concludes, "No healing miracles there. Just a simple transformation from maiden to dragon and back to maiden. And—and I was happy for it. Mostly" (p. 293). There is, of course, nothing simple about Tilda's transformation; it leaves her with a kind of double-consciousness and an ambiguity about her choice, reminding readers that all bodies face limits and Tilda must still deal with the physical and social discomforts her human impairment brings. Unlike Tehanu, Tilda chooses her human community over her powerful body, implying a different kind of wholeness that transcends the physical. Tilda sacrifices the physical prowess of her dragon form in favor of her human relationships, but her choice is informed by the opportunities available to her as a princess; neither wholeness nor transcendence can fully exist outside of the material world, where money and power and bodies and gender intersect. The idea and act of choosing is a privilege, and Tilda reasons, "[a]s a dragon, I'd been powerful and fast and sleek and strong, but I couldn't think right. I'd rather be splayfooted Tilda than Mathilda the Fiery" (p. 293). Her body reverts to its original state, but Tilda's consciousness is permanently changed by her stint as a dragon. She admits, "Wyrm's Tongue flowed through my mind as though I'd never transformed back to human, and I lay very still, frightened that I might not be able to hold on to human form" (p. 306). Tilda's anxiety can encourage readers to examine why humanness is so slippery, why it is something to choose or hold onto in the first place, and what that elusive wholeness signifies. The back-and-forth between human and dragon, even after she chooses her human community, suggests how little control Tilda feels over her own body; and if humanness is defined so strongly by classification of bodies that resist categorization, then what does it mean to be a human? If being and embodiment are intertwined, then both must be open to dynamic definitions that account for changing materiality and shifting contexts—not static permanence. Perhaps it is that transcendence, after all, however temporary, that defines humans as always embodied and always more-than-bodies.

Conclusion

For Tehanu, Tilda, and their readers, being both embodied and transcending embodiedness means paying attention to bodies while recognizing the instability of all bodies and bodily categories; it means accepting that wholeness and transcendence, like all bodily categories, can be powerful even though they are temporary. The experience of bodies, as presented in these works of fiction, asks readers to reflect on the body—what it means to transform and what it means to pay attention to the mundane physical requirements all humans face. Says Stemp (2004), "The true use of fantasy, it seems to me as a writer, is to allow the author to focus on certain truths and constants while happily bending most of the generally accepted bounds of society." It is unlikely that Le Guin's and Haskell's audiences will transform into dragons, but still, readers can take away the truths of living in unstable bodies and unstable worlds without feeling like those bodies, and those worlds, are unchangeable.

Throughout this essay, I have moved from the limitations imposed on Tehanu and Tilda because of their bodies, to the care and attention that all bodies require to function, to the concept of transcendence that addresses characters and readers as both embodied and more than bodies. In both texts, the figure of the dragon serves as a powerful body that, rather than simply overcoming limitations, points out additional limitations that debunk the myth of the fixed, able body. The transitions that Tehanu and Tilda make between human and dragon bodies further emphasize the fluidity of ability and the changeability of bodies within and throughout life's stages—a point likely to resonate with young adult readers themselves in the throes of physical transformations that can seem as daunting as dragons. By applying Disability Studies to these works of adolescent fantasy literature, I hope to show the simultaneous significance of thinking about the body and thinking beyond it.

References

Abrams, K. (2011). "Performing interdependence: Judith Butler and Sunaura Taylor in *The Examined Life*." *Columbia Journal of Gender and Law, 21(2),* 474–91. Retrieved from http://scholarship.law.berkeley.edu/facpubs/464.

Barnes, C. (1998). The social model of disability: A sociological phenomenon ignored by sociologists? In T. Shakespeare (ed.), *The disability reader: Social science perspectives* (65–78). New York: Continuum.

Butler, J., & Taylor, S. (2009). Interdependence. In A. Taylor (ed.), *Examined Life: Excursions with Contemporary Thinkers* (185–213). New York: The New Press.

Byrne, D. (2011). Woman ←→ dragon: Ursula K. Le Guin's transformations in *Tehanu, The Other Wind,* and *Tales from Earthsea. Mousaion, 29(3),* 154–165.

Castelnuovo, S., & Guthrie, S.R. (1998). *Feminism and the Female Body: Liberating the Amazon Within.* Boulder: Lynne Rienner.

Clare, E. (1999). *Exile and Pride: Disability, Queerness and Liberation.* Cambridge, MA: South End Press.

Garland Thomson, R. (1997). *Extraordinary Bodies: Figuring Physical Disability in American Culture and Literature.* New York: Columbia University Press.

_____. (2002). Integrating disability, transforming feminist theory. *NWSA Journal, 14(3),* 1–32. http://www.jstor.org/.

Haskell, M. (2013). *Handbook for Dragon Slayers.* New York: Harper.

Healey, S. (1993). The common agenda between old women, women with disabilities, and all women. In M.E. Willmuth & L. Holcomb (eds.), *Women with Sisabilities: Found Voices* (65–77). New York: The Haworth Press.

Hughes, B., & Paterson, K. (1997). The social model of disability and the disappearing body: Towards a sociology of impairment. *Disability & Society, 12(3),* 325–40.

Hunt, P. (1998). A critical condition. In T. Shakespeare (ed.), *The Disability Reader: Social Science Perspectives* (7–19). New York: Continuum.

Le Guin, U. (1990). *Tehanu.* New York: Aladdin Paperbacks.

_____. (2001). *The Other Wind.* New York, NY: Ace Books.

Morris, J. (2001). Impairment and disability: Constructing an ethics of care that promotes human rights. *Hypatia, 16(4),* 1–16.

Nussbaum, M.C. (2006). *Frontiers of Justice: Disability, Nationality, Species Membership.* Cambridge: Belknap Press of Harvard University Press.

Schriempf, A. (2001). (Re)fusing the amputated body: An interactionist bridge for feminism and disability. *Hypatia, 16(4),* 53–79.

Shildrick, M. (1997). *Leaky Bodies and Boundaries: Feminism, Postmodernism and (Bio)Ethics.* New York: Routledge.

Shildrick, M., & Price, J. (1999). Breaking the boundaries of the broken body. In J. Price & M. Shildrick (eds.), *Feminist Theory and the Body: A Reader* (432–444). New York: Routledge.

Stemp, J. (2004). Devices and desire: Science fiction, fantasy, and disability in literature for young people. *Disability Studies Quarterly, 24(1).*

Wendell, S. (1999). Feminism, disability, and the transcendence of the body. In J. Price & M. Shildrick (eds.), *Feminist Theory and the Body: A Reader* (324–333). New York: Routledge.

Wyble Newcomb, E. (2014). "Weak as woman's magic": Empowering care work in Ursula Le Guin's *Tehanu.* In L.M. Campbell (ed.), *A Quest of Her Own: Essays on the Female Hero in Modern Fantasy* (95–110). Jefferson, NC: McFarland.

"Without a word or sign": Enmeshing Deaf and Gay Identity in Young Adult Literature

Angel Daniel Matos

> What would you hear
> if my words could   make
>
>   sounds?
>   And if   they
>   did,
>   what   music   would I
>
>   write for you?
> [Smith, 2011, p. 3]

I have always found these opening lines of Andrew Smith's *Stick* (2011) both strange and compelling. The verse form employed in the novel's introduction differs from the conventional prose form that follows it. This opening breaks questions into separate lines, and it portrays various blank spaces between words in the same verse. The form of these verses demands that I read these words more slowly and carefully. The novel's opening has two very important effects. First, it uses the processes of hearing and sound to frame the novel, indicating that these practices will play an important role in the text's narrative. This opening queries the effectiveness of hearing and sound as a method of transmitting and receiving information, and it demonstrates that words do not necessarily need sound in order to be "heard." Secondly, the opening takes a linguistic construction—in this case, questions—and makes it odd, eccentric, and perplexing. The passage seizes a rhetorical practice that I use in my everyday life, and makes it strange.

Both queer and disability studies thrive in making the normal strange, odd, and unfamiliar. By exemplifying the strangeness that exists in every-day ideologies and practices, these theoretical fields seek to dismantle the power and privilege that people associate with normativity in all of its expressions. Using queer and disability studies as a lens to deconstruct texts that represent both deaf and gay characters illustrates the potentiality of both fields of study, which makes Brian Sloan's *A Really Nice Prom Mess* (2005) and Smith's *Stick* ideal novels for this discussion. Both of these works have combined issues of queerness and deafness in thought-provoking ways. Two of *Prom Mess*'s secondary characters are simultane-ously gay and deaf. *Stick*, on the other hand, focuses on two siblings grow-ing up in an abusive household in the Pacific Northwest. One of these siblings has a congenital condition known as anotia, in which the person is born without an ear; the other sibling is gay. I will elucidate how both of these novels construct gayness and deafness, focusing on how content and/or form pushes one to approach deaf and gay identity in unprece-dented ways. I argue that the concurrent literary exploration of deafness and queerness allows these works to seek alternative models of kinship that are not reliant on privileged and normative practices. By representing events in which (spoken) language and heternormativity are made strange, these young adult novels depict imagined worlds that can be read as anti-hierarchical, non-neutral, and queer. By assisting readers in considering the strangeness of normativity, these novels provide a venue where com-fort and optimism triumph in moments of anguish, and where solutions are provided to counteract the pressures of normativity. This essay, ulti-mately, is intended to serve as a model for how poststructuralist readings can aid readers and scholars in performing reparative critiques of young adult novels with disabled and/or queer characters.

Although this is not obvious at first, queer studies and Deaf/disability studies share a solid theoretical and historical foundation. Healy (2007), for instance, points out that queer and Deaf communities are subjugated via traits that are not transmitted through the family. She also points out that both communities "have struggled to define themselves to the larger culture as celebrants of identity, rather than victims of pathology, and both are making more strides now than ever before as they petition for societal acceptance and equal rights under the law" (p. 5). In academia, many have explored the theoretical and practical linkage between queer-ness and disability. Garland-Thomson, for instance, has been a pioneer in framing the parallels that exist between disability and feminist theories. In tandem, McRuer (2006) has not only highlighted relations between queerness and disability, but also between heterosexuality and able-bodied identity. McRuer (2006) emphasizes that these latter two forms of identity depend on similar networks of power, hierarchy, and privilege—other identities are viewed as derivative of heterosexuality and able-bodied identity, thus affirming their so-called inferiority. He argues that heterosexuality and able-bodiedness "are incomprehensible in that each is an identity that is simultaneously the ground on which all identities supposedly rest and an impressive achievement that is always deferred and thus never really guaranteed" (p. 9). By "impressive achievement," McRuer maintains that ability can only be guaranteed if one avoids undergoing any harm that could potentially affect one's ability or bodily neutrality.

Despite the overlap that exists between queer and disability studies, potential problems may arise when conducting a literary analysis on deafness through these lenses. Categorizing deafness as a disability evokes a series of debates and issues. Davis (1995a) points out that many people who are part of Deaf communities resist approaching deafness as disability, because they approach deafness as a socio-cultural or linguistic affiliation, no different from any other community of language speakers. To complicate matters even more, Davis establishes a difference between the Deaf (with a capital D), who are a "community of deaf people who share language, cultural values, history, and social life," and the deaf (lower-case D), who "are simply those who do not hear" (p. 882). This differentiation bears strong resonances with queer sexualities, in that dissimilarities surface between men who simply sleep with other men, and men who are gay and subsequently share cultural values, a history, and social life. Following the guidance of Padden (2005) in her cultural analysis on deafness and disability, my readings are based on the premise that the incorporation of deaf studies into disability studies can lead one to a better understanding of the literary representation of non-normative communities, and the struggles of power that intertwine with this representation.

Further complicating the stakes of my readings, the young adult novels that I will scrutinize depict deafness as a spectrum; these novels portray characters that blur the lines between the deaf and the hearing. *Stick* and *Prom Mess* depict characters that cannot hear through one of their ears due to either a birth defect or accident. One can situate these characters on the fringes of the constructed abled/disabled binary, thus challenging the legitimacy and usefulness of this dichotomy in the first place. These partially deaf characters will allow me to explore the contours of subjugated identities, allowing me to develop an understanding of how hierarchy and power play a role in the imagined lives of teens that are not-quite-abled, and concurrently not-quite-disabled. I trust that the very liminality of these characters, both in terms of their sexuality and their categorization as disabled, will contribute significant richness to conversations on disability and its representation in young adult literature. With this in mind, I will not only discuss how these young adult novels represent the enmeshment of queerness and disability, but also how, through these representations, one can think differently about the everyday, the normal, and the not-quite-normal.

Untangling (Prom) Messes

Portraying a series of seemingly insurmountable obstacles in a fashion that would put a soap opera to shame, Sloan's stock of recognizable characters and impeccable comedic timing ultimately make *Prom Mess*, as *Publishers Weekly* (2005) puts it, "easy to swallow." In spite of the novel's downright bizarre plot (the novel can be approached as a comedy of errors), Sloan's work sets itself apart as one of the few teen novels that portrays gay characters who also happen to be deaf: a partially deaf and gay ex-football player and a Deaf, gay stripper. The presence of these two characters serves as a platform that allows me to simultaneously assess and critique cultural assumptions of deafness and queerness. However, both of these characters exemplify what Rubin and Strauss Watson (1987) would approach as atmospheric characters with disabilities, mostly because they are "peripheral to the main action" (p. 61) of the novel, and they are ostensibly present simply to add more ideological complexity to the work. Although these characters are indeed secondary when it comes to the novel's main plot, their embodiment of both queerness and varying degrees of deafness resonates significantly with the main character's growth, and with discussions regarding identity and resistance towards oppression.

"Disability" and queerness mark Shane, the boyfriend of protagonist Cameron Hayes in *Prom Mess*. During the early stages of the novel, Cameron discloses Shane's partial deafness—meaning that he has completely lost the ability to hear through his right ear. Cameron describes Shane as a tall, good-looking, and masculine figure, and since he plays football in high school, he exhibits attitudes and behaviors that are typically associated with jock culture. Cameron's approach to Shane nearly verges on idolatry. When first introducing Shane and describing his qualities, however, Cameron points out that Shane lacks perfection, and that he possesses certain "flaws" (Sloan, 2005, p. 42) that disrupt his sense of faultlessness. He shares that Shane used to be a star athlete in his high school's football team for three years. Shane lacks enthusiasm for the sport, but he still plays it as a way of pleasing his father. Shane quits playing football during his junior year, however, because he "suffered a freakishly rough tackle at the homecoming game and lost most of the hearing in his right ear. That was the end of his sports career and, believe it or not, Shane was somewhat relieved for that, though the circumstances were pretty much a drag" (Sloan, 2005, pp. 42–43). These circumstances, in addition to ending Shane's sports career, also affect how Cameron approaches Shane's sense of perfection and masculinity.

Shane's partial deafness becomes a prominent element throughout the rest of *Prom Mess*, and it serves as a way of facilitating the discussions on bodily perfection that saturate the novel. The passage above illustrates an issue of deaf representation—Cameron's use of the word "drag" to describe the outcome of the beastly tackle imbues Shane's partial deafness with a sense of tragedy and negativity. The proximity between the discussion of Shane's "flaws" and the discussion of how Shane lost his hearing tethers the association between deafness and imperfection. I would go as far as to argue that Cameron views Shane's partial deafness as no different from other, more readable, forms of disability—"drag," as a slang word, invokes connotations such as lack, absence, or disappointment. Cameron's approach to Shane's partial deafness as a lack becomes even more salient when recalling that deafness comes up shortly after a discussion of Shane's physical perfection. Cameron's description of Shane emphasizes how his boyfriend's outer body complies with expectations of normalcy, neutrality, and beauty prevalent in their society. Cameron approaches Shane's partial deafness as the chink in his knight's shining armor, a notion made overt when he approaches the lack of hearing as his (super) man's limitation: "I'd always found something sad and noble about it, like it was his secret weakness that no one can see. Like Clark and Kryptonite, you know?" (Sloan, 2005, p. 43). Shane, however, also views his partial deafness as an imperfection. He does not want other people to know about his inability to hear through one of his ears, for he does not want to be known as "that hot semideaf guy" (Sloan, 2005, p. 43). Through this impulse to conceal, both Cameron and Shane uphold the binaries between the public and the private, and the abled and the disabled.

Cameron's views of Shane's deafness center on problematic issues regarding the normative expectations of the human body. In Cameron's eyes, Shane's disability not only blemishes his bodily flawlessness, but it also serves as a leveling agent: "I didn't want to be known as that totally skinny gay guy. I always thought that these mutual secrets gave us something in common" (Sloan, 2005, p. 43). Cameron's intense focus on Shane's deafness problematically becomes a way of destabilizing the hierarchical differences that he implements when approaching their relationship. To further complicate matters, just as Cameron cannot grasp the constructed nature of his hierarchical views, he also cannot recognize the constructed nature of Shane's deafness. This notion echoes the views of Garland-Thomson (2002), who approaches disability as a fiction, or as she puts it, "a culturally fabricated narrative of the body" (p. 5) similar to other constructs such as race and gender. Cameron buys into the implementation of a disability/ability system in order to read Shane's body as marked, thus engaging him in the practice of the "unequal distribution" (Garland Thomson, 2002, p. 5) of power that disability and queer studies seeks to challenge. Cameron's abled-oriented reading of his boyfriend not only restricts the story that Shane's body tells, but it also perpetuates the dominant cultural expectation for a "neutral" and abled human body.

Both Cameron and his boyfriend, however, preserve the myths of the human body that enforce a disabled reading of Shane. Shane's partial deafness gives him a sense of self-loathing; his sense of self-shame achieves transparency though the many closets that he inhabits. Shane remains secretive about his inability to hear through his right ear, just as he remains secretive in terms of his sexuality. This sense of secrecy mobilizes the narrative, particularly since Shane's closetedness frames the novel's main plot and developments. Shane convinces Cameron that they both should go to the prom with fake dates in order to conceal their homosexuality—and their relationship—from other classmates and peers. While at the prom, Cameron grows increasingly upset because Shane does not spend any time with him. Cameron's jealousy prompts him to smoke marijuana and to later become involved in a fist-fight with Shane. Because of this fight, Cameron decides to escape the prom with a drug dealer hiding in the men's restroom—the same dealer who sold Cameron the pot that he smoked. Here, the novel presents closetedness as the impetus of the novel's central issues and tensions—and interestingly, issues of closetedness are paramount in both queer and disability studies.

Deceit and concealment are problematic aspects of this novel; however, the various closets in this narrative are important critical spaces that facilitate a queer reading of identity and disability. The most pervasive and often explored tie between queer and disability studies has been the notion of the closet and, in conjunction, the notions of disclosure or the intent to "pass" as either abled or heterosexual. Sedgwick (1999) approaches the "closet" as a speech act of silence that "accrues particularity by fits and starts, in relation to the discourse that surrounds and differentially constitutes it" (p. 322). Sedgwick thus characterizes the coming out process as a linguistic and discursive act that produces a continually surfacing hurdle that highlights the tension between concealment and disclosure. In Shane's case, his hidden identities are easily concealable and not easily interpreted through his body. Shane does not use a hearing aid, nor does he use sign language—making it difficult for his deafness to be "read" by other people. Shane's deafness and his sexuality are unmarked, meaning that even though he embodies deaf and queer traits, these traits are not overtly discernible or visible. Shane's attempts to pass as heterosexual and abled are quite challenging, and harmful, for his personal development, for he actively tries to inhabit normative domains through the concealment of so-called inferior facets of being. Shane's attempts at passing enable one to scrutinize the constructed nature of deafness, because, as Walker (2001) argues, passing "destabilizes identities predicated on the visible to reveal how they are constructed" (p. 10). Understanding Shane's attempts to pass enables a more nuanced understanding of how subjugated identities—regardless of their visibility—are culturally fabricated narratives that uphold hegemonic values.

Shane's decision to keep his sexuality and his disability closeted, I argue, boils down to the presence of many heteronormative and patriarchal practices in his life. For instance, Shane plays football, a sport commonly perceived as a heteronormative practice saturated with hegemonic masculine attitudes.[1] Cameron asserts that Shane does not play football due to interest in the sport, but rather, he plays it as a way of pleasing his father—increasing the view of this practice as a patriarchal enterprise. The hearing loss that Shane develops in consequence of his accident gives him the means to escape these heteronormative and chauvinistic restrictions. Through this interpretation, deafness gives Shane the means to escape a patriarchal pressure, although this escape only becomes possible by unwillingly marking his body through disability. In other words, Shane escapes the construction and the demands of normative gender by embracing another construction that would portray him as unfit to engage in a heteronormative framework. This escape, nonetheless, loses its emancipatory potential through Shane's choice to conceal his disability *and* sexuality after the accident. By tethering his deafness and his sexuality to the realm of the private, Shane, as McRuer (2006) would argue, not only privileges a heterosexual and able-bodied identity no longer available to him, but he goes on to reinforce the very forms of binary thinking that mark his body and his performance as anomalous in the first place.

Shane's partial deafness complicates not only his positioning within the abled/disabled spectrum, but also the notions of concealment associated with closetedness. Compared to other forms of bodily disability, Shane can hide his deafness with relative ease, especially since his partial deafness demands less readability when compared to entirely deaf persons. Deafness attains exposure through performative or discursive means— either through the subject's use of sign language, or through interactions with non-deaf people. Gender and sexuality are parallel in that they are not marked on the body itself, as Butler (1990) has argued, but through performance.[2] As seen through Shane's actions, the act of passing implements the major difference between the concealment of his sexuality and of his deafness. Although he can successfully pass as heterosexual, he cannot always successfully pass as abled when he communicates with other people. Although the unmarked nature of his disability makes it easier for Shane to avoid being read as deaf—enabling his facility to project himself as neutral and normative to his peers—his everyday performance betrays his attempts to conceal his so-called flaw. Shane's partial deafness involuntarily expresses itself in instances in which he does not react or respond to people who speak at his deaf ear, as evidenced in the following passage:

> "Shane," I said in a whisper. "Why do I love you?"
> But he didn't hear me. Right ear. That is, the wrong ear.
> "What?" he said.
> Then in his hearing ear I repeated my confused sentiment. Sorta.
> "I love you, Shane" [Sloan, 2005, p. 53].

This moment highlights the ways in which Shane's deafness actually affects his ability to hear other people. Shane actually has difficulties hearing other people at times; therefore, this characterization proves that he is not partially deaf in name only.

Regrettably, Shane's inability to hear through his right ear becomes a narrative prosthesis used to reflect the problems of the protagonist rather than Shane's issues with his disability and sexuality. By alluding to narrative prosthesis, I refer to Mitchell and Snyder's (2000) assertion of a discursive dependency in which "disability pervades literary narrative, first, as a stock feature of characterization and, second, as an opportunistic metaphorical device" (p. 47). This discursive dependency permeates the rest of the novel, particularly in the instance in which Cameron jokingly refers to a street known as Q Street as "Queer Street." Shane does find humor in this statement, prompting Cameron to offensively state that the joke landed "on deaf ears. (That is, Shane's right ear)" (Sloan, 2005, p. 257). Here, the novel invokes disability to add more nuances to Cameron's characterization and perspectives. Nevertheless, is *Prom Mess* genuinely interested in exploring the challenges of partial deafness, or is Shane's partial deafness simply a narrative device that reifies the problems that exist in his relationship with Cameron?

The notion of narrative prosthesis permeates the novel, in that Shane's partial deafness narratively aids in the construction of Cameron's character much more than it aids in the constructions of the deaf character himself. Much attention in the novel centers on how Cameron perceives the world in a binary fashion: he approaches Shane as the more dominant person in the relationship, whereas he approaches himself as the weak counterpart to Shane's presence. Cameron's heavy reliance on binary approaches to the world controls not only his thinking, but also his discourse—which demands a close reading and deconstruction of the aforementioned inter-action, in which Cameron utters the truth to Shane's deaf ear, yet utters a distortion of the truth to the ear capable of hearing. Note that by posing the question "Why do I love you?" Shane would have to come face-to-face with the dominance and power that he possesses over Cameron. By uttering "I love you," however, Cameron cements his glorification, and perhaps even fetishization, of his relationship with Shane. He does not tell Shane what he feels, but rather, he tells Shane what he expects to hear—leading Cameron to comply with his self-imposed inferior positioning.

I use the term fetishization because Cameron makes it overtly clear that Shane's deafness becomes an object of fixation and attraction. Earlier, I mentioned how Cameron approaches Shane's partial deafness as "noble." In another instance, Cameron remarks that Shane's inability to hear "was cute and gave him character and almost made me feel bad for him, even though he had everything else in life going for him" (Sloan, 2005, p. 123). This confession reveals a great deal about Cameron's self-perception. Cameron constantly alludes to his self-perceived femininity, and he relent-lessly makes remarks about the imperfections that exist in his own body, such as the pointiness of his nose, or his skinniness. Shane's deafness becomes an object of fixation, and ultimately, scorn, because Cameron approaches it as the only "mark" that tattoos a sense of imperfection on Shane's body. Cameron's self-perceived deviation from norms of mas-culinity and perfection coerce his self-positioning as a flawed being. Since Shane does not deviate from traditional masculine norms, with the excep-tion of his very private sexuality, Cameron fetishizes Shane's deafness in order to seemingly justify their relationship and in order to convince him-self of the "fact" that they are both non-normative teenagers.

Cameron's transcendent moment occurs when he learns how to look *beyond* Shane's markedness, and when he realizes that Shane has other "flaws" besides the inability to hear. Cameron admits that his boyfriend's "semideafness" does not actually bother him. Cameron determines that his annoyance stems from the fact that Shane, in his quest for dominance and power, never actually listens to him. After this realization, Cameron approaches deafness not as a literal or bodily problem, but rather, as a metaphorical one:

> there was also this symbolic thing that bothered me about his lack of hearing: Sometimes Shane just didn't seem to *hear* me. Seriously. He often ignored things I said, brushed my repeated concerns about our relationship aside, and was constantly telling me to stop worrying. But standing there in the bathroom, I realized that the real problem with our relationship was not that Shane couldn't hear me, it was more, that I couldn't hear the nuance of what Shane was saying. Or in his case, not saying. He never, ever, not even once, said that he loved me [Sloan, 2005, p. 123].

Here, Cameron comes to grips with the interpersonal limitations of his love for Shane, while also admitting to how he approaches Shane's deafness as a narrative prosthesis for their relationship.

Through a reading focused on construction, non-normativity, and the negative effects of dichotomous thinking, one can potentially realize the extent to which the constructed nature of disability blinds Cameron from coming to grips with the problems and issues in his relationship. Cameron's focus on Shane's inability becomes a symbolic extension, to the point in which he blames the relationship's dysfunction on Shane's deafness. Rather than focusing his attention on his own wrongdoings, Cameron uses Shane's literal and metaphorical deafness as a scapegoat for the tensions he experiences. Cameron's admittance of his own culpability in not hearing the nuances of Shane's (lack of) words leads him to achieve a moment of individual learning about himself and his relationship. I approach Cameron's recognition of the symbolic nature of Shane's deafness, and his consequential moment of growth, as moments that facilitate the comprehension of the fictions that Cameron accepts in order to justify his uneasy relationship with Shane.

The novel's Deaf[3] character, nevertheless, offers readers alternatives to problematic constructions of deafness and sexual identity by challenging the power and effectivity of practices such as oral communication and passing. This other character is a brazen gay stripper who goes by the name of Buck. Cameron meets Buck while visiting a gay bar shortly after escaping the prom with the drug dealer. Although Buck's deafness also reflects the woes of the protagonist, this character enables the potential for disability and queer critiques to flourish. When Cameron first encounters Buck at a gay bar, he does not realize that Buck cannot hear him. While at first Cameron thinks that the bar's loud music creates this auditory obstruction, he notices Buck signing to a patron. Using the bartender as an interpreter, Buck asks for Cameron's name, which prompts Cameron to contemplate the potential benefits of deafness:

> Feeling an overwhelming surge of honesty and, I admit it, curious attraction to this deaf stripper, I offered my real name. The bartender passed on a signed translation of Cameron, which seemed to please Buck and, I have to say, looked kinda pretty from a nonsigner's perspective, like he was mimicking a bouquet of flowers.... He signed and Buck signed back as the music blasted away, and I was struck by this thought: Being deaf is a major advantage in a nightclub, because you never have a problem hearing what your friends are saying [Sloan, 2005, pp. 145–146].

Cameron's approach to Buck's deafness seems affirmative, especially when compared to how he approaches Shane's partial deafness. However, Cameron still fetishizes deafness to some extent. Rather than feeling estranged by Buck's deafness, he goes as far as to be mesmerized by the "flowery" gestures of sign language. Regardless of this issue, the passage above exemplifies how deafness provides an alternative form of being, and an alternative form of communication, in a particular space that deviates from normative expectations or practices. Cameron does not view deafness as a restriction within the context of a gay bar. Conversely, deafness provides Buck with a means to exceed the communicative issues and limitations that surface when loud music and cacophonous chatter disrupt the ability to hear. From a Deaf perspective, the nightclub becomes an egalitarian and anti-hierarchical space in which patrons must resort to means beyond speech to effectively communicate. Although Buck deviates from norms of gender, social acceptability, and ability, the nightclub provides a venue in which the non-neutral and non-heterosexual body can thrive, and ultimately disrupt, expectations of normativity.

Unlike Shane, Buck has no qualms with his identification as gay and Deaf. Buck does not conceal his deafness in any way, for he constantly performs it in *Prom Mess*. Not only does Buck sign, but he can also read lips if he pays close attention to a speaker. Cameron describes Buck as having an "uncertain, lip-reading voice" (Sloan, 2005, p. 149), and towards the end of the novel, he describes the process of using a teletypewriter to communicate with Buck using a telephone. Buck's use of this communicative device not only concretizes his affiliation with the Deaf community, but it also illustrates how Buck, unlike Shane, does not attempt to pass as abled even though his disability can be concealed. Buck's queerness also thrives with no misgivings, since he consistently expresses his attraction towards Cameron. Deafness and queer identity are viewed as non-issues by Buck because he has fully accepted and embodied his non-normative traits, while at the same time situating himself in a space that allows his queer and Deaf identities to flourish.

Buck's act of embodying queerness meshes effectively with Susan Bordo's perspectives on the body as a site of heteronormative resistance. Similarly to Garland-Thomson, Bordo (1993) approaches all bodies as texts that can be read, interpreted, and deliberated; these "texts" facilitate the circulation and perpetuation of cultural norms—but they also present the possibility to *resist* these norms. In Bordo's discussion of the representation of femininity through the body, she posits that the body—drawing from the theories of Pierre Bourdieu and Michel Foucault—through everyday practices, becomes a method of fixing and regulating power: "The body is ... a *practical*, direct locus of social control. Banally, through table manners and toilet habits, through seemingly trivial routines, rules, and practices, culture is "*made* body," as Bourdieu puts it—converted into automatic, habitual activity" (p. 165). Thus, in addition to the body itself, the activities and practices that the body performs also define normativity's rejection or embrace by the performer.

Based on the ability of the body to produce meaning, Bordo (1993) argues that it should be approached as a "site of struggle" (p. 184), in which humans must actively strive to align daily practices to the resistance of gender domination and not towards a neutral or normative aim. She also remarks on the difficulty of this work, stating that it depends not only on being cynical towards "routes of seeming liberation" offered by cultural institutions, but also on an awareness of the contradictions that exist "between image and practice, between rhetoric and reality" (Bordo, 1993, p. 184). Along these lines, I maintain that disability can and *should* be challenged through everyday practices and through an active questioning of the differences between a construction and reality—enabling readers and scholars, as Wilkerson (2002) puts it, to contest the "illusory ideal mind and body at the expense of bodies of all shapes and sizes" (p. 36). In *Prom Mess*, Buck epitomizes radical sentiments precisely because he aligns his body and his practices against the norm. Even when outside the liberating cultural institution of the gay bar, Buck continues to sign, and he does not hesitate to express his gayness, as seen through his open attraction to Cameron and his nonchalance when venturing around the streets of Washington, D.C., clad in his gold-colored undergarments. The difference between Shane and Buck becomes clear here, in that Shane struggles with his deafness and sexuality whereas Buck's everyday practices are aligned in resistance to heteronormativity and abled-identity.

Buck pushes Cameron to appreciate the liberating effects of positioning the body in resistance to norms. While Cameron lingers at the gay bar with Buck, police suddenly raid the place—a serious problem because Cameron is an underage teen in an establishment that sells alcohol. Unbeknownst to Cameron, it turns out that the police are in search of Dimitri, the drug dealer that Cameron met at the prom, because they believe Cameron was kidnapped by him. Cameron escapes from the bar with Buck's help, and they both end up in Dimitri's car, thus commencing a wild and outlandish police chase through the streets of the city. In this chase, Cameron sits on Buck's lap since the car has no back seat. After this chase subsides, one of the most meaningful exchanges in *Prom Mess* takes place:

> Exhausted by the tension of our chase, all my muscles finally able to relax, I collapsed back into Buck, my human bucket seat. *Without a word or a sign or anything*, Buck wrapped his arms around my waist and sensing my fatigue, held me tight. It was a simple gesture really, nothing terribly sexy or insanely romantic. But it was done without prompting and without prescience. And that was ... something unique. Feeling Buck's casual hold as we raced through the city, going God knows where at God knows what illegal speed, it struck me that this was something that Shane had never done. He'd never touched me at all out in the world, the only shared intimacies occurring in dark bedrooms or locked closets [Sloan, 2005, p. 161, emphasis mine].

This passage reveals much in terms of the enmeshment of queerness and deafness in *Prom Mess*. This excerpt focuses on the power of the human touch as a liberating practice, precisely because it takes place within an open public space. Cameron and Shane only share any sense of intimacy within confined or restricted spaces. They even share their first kiss within a dark closet, a not-so-subtle symbol of the status of their relationship. Buck, contrarily, uses his body to express tenderness towards Cameron in a public space, careless of who sees them or who they might encounter.

With Buck's public embrace, both he and Cameron shatter the concealed nature of gayness without having to reflect upon their marked status in society. Their embrace implodes the restrictive confines of the closet— queer intimacy and deafness are no longer represented as things that must be kept in dark, confined spaces. When it comes to this embrace, *neither* *language nor sound*s convey intent and meaning.[4] This moment alludes to what Davis (1995a) would refer to as a "deafened moment," which he describes as a critical instance where dialectical exchange does not involve the process of speaking or hearing (p. 883). I approach this embrace as a full-fledged expression of "the language of the deaf," precisely because it portrays a meaningful and semantically rich exchange that "mediates between speech and silence" (Davis, 1995a, p. 893). This meaningful exchange between Buck and Cameron destabilizes the hierarchical priv-ileging of speech, sight, and sound as the primary forms of exchanging meaning—thus challenging the categorization of deafness as a disability in the first place. Queerness and disability channel the language of the deaf to express that which cannot be transmitted through the spoken work, or through the restrictive signifiers of heteronormativity.

Sloan's novel, on the surface level, may seem obtuse in terms of its representation of deafness and Deaf cultures. However, *Prom Mess* pro-vides a platform for an effective critical reading to take place. The novel's representative shortcomings are destabilized when taking into account that its content facilitates an analysis that disengages disability and queer-ness from the binds of hierarchy and construction. The novel presents gayness and deafness as identities that should not only be celebrated, but that are capable of exceeding the expressive dimensions of normativity. A public, albeit silent touch teaches Cameron more about identity and resist-ance in a way that words simply could not. *Prom Mess* provides the reader with small but significant sites of struggle that allow one to reassess the constructed nature of identity and deafness in a culture bound to issues such as normativity and neutrality. Sloan's novel portrays a convoluted series of unfortunate circumstances imbued with clichéd narratives and problematic representations. However, the novel's disabled and queer characters provide a platform for readers to perform powerful critiques. Characters that simultaneously embody Deaf and gay identity, such as Buck, exemplify how one can resort to means beyond words—such as touch and emotion—to contest sites of normativity. This contestation not only prioritizes the expressive abilities of pathos over spoken language, but it also demonstrates how emotion and touch are forms of communi-cation that are not reliant on hierarchical or normative pressures.

Fraternal Filiations

Stick, as a novel, also represents deafness through its content *and* through its narrative form and sentence structure. By channeling issues of queerness and disability through its content and its form, *Stick* offers readers moments in which heteronormativity and homophobia are subverted through deafened moments. This novel focuses on thirteen year-old Stark (known as Stick because of his weight and height) and his older brother Bosten, who live in an abusive and violent household. The two siblings view each other as the only sources of love and affection in their lives as they try to cope with the ludicrous rules, and the even more extreme punishments, that their parents uphold. The novel resembles a literary work—a diary of sorts—that Stick crafts in order to discuss how he and his brother escaped the clutches of their physically abusive parents. Furthermore, Stick shares the precarious journey that he had to go through in his search for Bosten—who runs away from home after their father learns about Bosten's homosexuality.

Unlike Shane and Buck from *Prom Mess,* both physical means and performance mark Stick's disability, thus complicating Stick's relationship to notions of concealment. Stick has a medical condition known as anotia: he was "born without an ear" (Smith , 2011, p. 250). Stick describes his lack of a right ear quite vividly: "I have what looks like the outline of a normal boy's ear, but it's pressed down into the flesh, squashed like potter's clay. No hole—a canal, they call it" (Smith, 2011, p. 6). Because of his lack of a right ear canal, Stick affirms his partial deafness, for "nothing gets into [his] head that way" (p. 6). Adding to the fact that Stick's father does not let him grow his hair long (ostensibly because long hair contravenes masculinity according the father), Stick cannot pass as abled even if he wanted to. Either people notice his lack of a right ear, or they notice his inability to grasp words when uttered to a particular side of his head. When it comes to Stick's deafness, there is simply no closet that he can possibly inhabit.

Deafness permeates *Stick* not only in terms of content, but especially in terms of form. The narrative mode and inventive structure implemented in *Stick* differentiates its deaf representation significantly from the representation found in *Prom Mess.* Through the employment of a first-person narrative mode, Stick is in control of his own representation as a deaf character. Unlike the depiction of Shane and Buck, the perspective of an abled individual does not control Stick's narrative. Thus, the literary invocation of deafness manifests for means beyond the implementation of atmosphere. Stick's self-conscious implementation of verse form, blank space, and line breaks further add to the centrality of deafness in this novel because it represents and replicates his own hearing process. In other words, Stick deliberately uses textual form as a way of inviting the reader to inhabit a disabled positionality:

I can't easily hide it because my dad won't let me grow my
hair long. He yells at me if I wear a hat indoors. He says there's
nothing   wrong with   me.
                                                  But I'm ugly.
You see what I'm doing, don't you? I   am   making
                                                  you hear me.
        The way   I   hear the   world.
But I won't do it too much, I   promise
                                                  [Smith, 2001, p. 6].[5]

Through the use of this narrative innovation, Stick attempts to imitate
how he perceives language. He points out that he recognizes the effects
of missing an ear: he "know[s] what it can do to you to not have that hole
there" (Smith, 2011, p. 7). Stick's structuring of his words, as I discussed
in the introduction of this discussion, have an estranging effect on the
reader. Stick intends for readers to feel discomfort with his words not only
by disrupting the linearity that one might expect from prose novels, but
also by inserting deliberate gaps between the words he invokes. Even in
the sections that are not written in verse form, Stick inserts blank spaces
that disrupt the reading process—challenging the efficacy of language to
convey meaning: "I turned on the water and rinsed our plates so I couldn't
hear. But some sounds don't get killed easily" (Smith, 2011, p. 15). The
striking gaps between words create a sense of absence and interruption,
in which sentences, when approached through Stick's perspective, are
viewed as puzzles with missing pieces. Through this form of narrativization, the reader gathers a sense of what deafness "can do to you." This narrative innovation allows the novel to escape the discourse of narrative
prosthesis, for it prevents deafness from being read symbolically or alle-
gorically. Stick's unique form of narrativization takes advantage of the
written word to approximate the sense of isolation and confusion that
spoken language can sometimes impart on the deaf.

I approach the structure of *Stick* as a brilliant moment of subversion,
for Stick seizes the power of the abled gaze and directs it towards the
reader—pushing one to inhabit the discomfort of not being able to fully
grasp or master language. Stick emphasizes how his anotia creates a sense
of distance between him and other people, thus creating an artificial binary
between those with neutral bodies and those with marked ones. He
stresses, in particular, how he constantly feels alienated through the gazes
of strangers, in that others approach him as an object of fascination and/or
horror, which fuels Stick's sense of self-deprecation: "Most people don't

notice it right away, but once they do, I see their faces; I watch how they'll move around toward that side—the one with the missing part—so they can see what's wrong with me" (Smith, 2011, p. 6). The notion of Stick's definition as a disabled person through the gazes of other people stresses what Davis (1995b) calls the "specular" temperament of disability, in which gazes "control, limit, and patrol" the disabled person, and are typically accompanied by a repertoire "of powerful emotional responses" (p. 12). Through innovations in narrative structure, Stick controls a reader's gaze towards the text—his use of form goes as far as to control and limit how one perceives the language being employed. The horrified acknowledgement and fascination of abled characters cements Stick's categorization as an Other, but this Otherness is also emphasized through the lack of acknowledgement as well. Stick admits that while he often feels displaced and pathologized by gazes, the failure to acknowledge his lack of an ear creates an equally marginalizing effect: "My mother never talks about my ear. She hardly ever talks to me at all. I believe she is sad, horrified. I think she blames herself. Mostly, I think she wishes I was never born" (Smith, 2011, p. 7). Both the gaze and the lack of gazing emphasize Stick's categorization as a subjugated individual.

Deaf identity, as I pointed out previously, is not the only subjugated identity present in *Stick*. Given that Smith's novel focuses primarily on the relationship between two siblings, it unavoidably creates the foundation for associations between Stick's deaf identity and Bosten's gay identity. The narrative frames Bosten's homosexuality using the same techniques that frame Stick's disability—particularly through the use of gazes that invoke strong and visceral emotional responses. During a chapter where Stick looks for Bosten and his friend Paul in the woods, he encounters his older brother and his friend *in flagrante delicto*. The language that Stick uses to describe his reaction to this this encounter reveals much about his initial feelings towards his brother's queerness: "I was scared and ashamed at the same time. It was like watching my house catch fire, but I couldn't look away, because how many times do you ever get to see a house burn down?" (Smith, 2011, p. 76). Stick gets over this initial shock and fear rather quickly—stating that more than anything, he was simply surprised to have discovered his brother's gayness in the way that he did. Stick's initial reaction, however, significantly aids one in understanding the overlaps between deafness and queerness. Ironically, even though Stick complains about how other people are fascinated, horrified, and/or repulsed by his lack of an ear, he reacts to the discovery of his brother's homosexuality in a visceral and emotionally charged fashion imbued with awe and revulsion. Here, the ties between gay identity and deaf identity become concretized in the novel, for both forms of being are subjected to, and constructed by, normalizing gazes and tendencies. Gay and deaf identity are not only viewed as complementary to one another, but they are also depicted as identities that belong to the same "fraternal" strain.

In Smith's novel, queer and deaf fraternity highlight the potential of deafened moments to represent instances of intense affection and kinship that are not reliant on the hierarchy or privilege of language and normativity. The instance that best reflects this critical moment occurs shortly after Stick encounters Bosten having sex with his boyfriend. This discovery, as mentioned above, greatly surprises Stick, but he quickly reveals to his brother that "it doesn't matter" (Smith, 2011, p. 83). Rather than expressing the fear and shock that he felt when he encountered Bosten in the forest with Paul, and rather than asking expected questions about gayness, Stick inquires to know what being in love with someone feels like. After Bosten shares how wonderful being in love with Paul feels, the two siblings contemplate on how their abusive parents would react if they found out about Bosten's homosexuality, leading Stick to warn his older brother to be careful because he "doesn't want nothing bad to happen" (Smith, 2011, p. 84). Rather than addressing Stick's concerns with words, Bosten addresses these concerns with a moving gesture: "Bosten put his hand out, and I held it. We didn't need to say anything after that. It's just how things were. Everything else could change and go crazy. But not that" (Smith, 2011, p. 84). Although sparse in terms of words, this passage is anything but sparse in terms of affection or meaning.

Parallel to the scene in *Prom Mess*, where Buck embraces Cameron in the car chase, the moment in which Stick and Bosten hold hands arbitrates the semantic space between speech and silence. Although language and speech are not used, the act of hand holding expresses things that are difficult to articulate in words. This one gesture signifies the bond between the two brothers, it signifies how Stick will love and support Bosten even when others refuse to do so, it signifies comfort in a moment of fear and despair, and it signifies a moment of affective filiation between two people who are non-normative—either through their deviation from heteronormativity or from ability. Although this particular deafened moment does not challenge notions of closetedness, I insist that this moment exudes queerness because, as Halberstam (2011) would argue, it portrays two teens, who are queered through their practices and abilities, uniting "hand in hand to open up new and different ways of being in relation to time, truth, being, living, and dying" (55). Stick and Bosten are tethered to each other not only by blood, but also by how they are read by other people and how they read each other. Stick views his relationship as the only reliable and constant factor in his life. Everything else in Stick's life might "go crazy," but his non-normative attachment with his queer sibling provides an escape from this craziness. This queer union becomes the only reliable and bolstering element in their otherwise strange and chaotic world. Stick and Bosten's non-normative unity achieves its ultimate expression not though words, but through a deafened moment—a pathos-infused instance reliant on methods of communication that are not oppressive to the deaf or the queer.

This union between two brothers, deaf and queer, develops into the narrative strain that unites all of the events present in the novel. When Bosten runs away to Los Angeles as a way of escaping the violence of their household, Stick steals his father's car and heads to California in search of him. After a series of intense and precarious events, Stick eventually locates Bosten at a decrepit youth shelter. Track marks pepper Bosten's arm—indicating that he has pumped his body full of drugs that he obtains by selling his body to other men. The two brothers then move into their aunt's house in California. Bosten's arm improves, and he begins to attend continuation school in order to finish his high school studies, but Stick believes that his brother has not "learned how to continue very well" (Smith, 2011, p. 292). Stick eventually embraces and accepts his anotia when finding out that there are other people with this condition, but the novel concludes with the suggestion that both siblings have been broken in different ways.

The abuse that both siblings endure, not only at their parents' household, but also from other people and institutions due to their non-normative embodiment, leaves both brothers with a pain and emptiness that nobody "could give a name to" (Smith, 2011, 292). How do they cope with this emptiness and pain, especially when it cannot be articulated through words? They do so by resorting to means other than language. They push these speechless feelings aside, and they attempt to find comfort in deafened moments. Stick concludes his narrative by stating that he and Bosten "sleep in the same bed at [their aunt's] house" (Smith, 2011, p. 292), basking in a sense of togetherness that inevitably conveys a hint of optimism. These boys have been broken by their family, and by normative, patriarchal, and violent cultural institutions, but one cannot help but anticipate that together, they will find a way to repair each other. Readers cannot but hope, and expect, that affection will assist Stick and Bosten in challenging the normative strictures that oppress them, even after escaping the clutches of their abusive parents.

Breaking (Sound) Barriers

I have illustrated how the juncture between deaf and gay identity has been constructed and represented in two young adult novels. The confluence of these two identities is not very common in the genre, but I hope that this analysis has illustrated how young adult novels, either consciously or unconsciously, seek alternatives to the demands of both normativity and hierarchy through the concurrent representation of these identities. Through the inclusion of partially deaf characters, Deaf characters, and queer characters in their narratives, these novels have the potential to be read in ways that assist one in recognizing and challenging the very signifiers that categorize people as disabled and/or queer in the first place. Sloan's novel, for instance, exemplifies how notions of closetedness and concealment haunt both deaf and queer people. Through the incorporation of a Deaf gay stripper in its narrative, *Prom Mess* emphasizes the importance of aligning everyday practices and ideologies in resistance to normativity in all of its forms. By refusing to restrict gayness and deafness to the realm of the private—as Shane clearly does—Buck potentially directs the reader to new routes of liberation that simultaneously celebrate non-normativity while making the normal strange.

Andrew Smith's *Stick*, on the other hand, illustrates how form and structure can aid an author in delivering a narrative that attempts to situate readers in the place of the disabled—thus offering opportunities for empathy, embodiment, and understanding. His novel not only illustrates how both disability and gayness are constructed through similar processes of gazing, but it also shows how deafened moments—instances that mediate between speech and silence—offer possibilities for emancipation that are not reliant on restrictive and normative practices. These deafened moments are also present in Brian Sloan's *A Really Nice Prom Mess*, in which two characters communicate emotion-driven information without resorting to the restrictive binds of language. Touch, in both novels, serves as a method of communication that both the deaf and the queer can engage in, enabling the expression of non-normative (and potentially revolutionary) kinship and filiation.

This discussion has approached both disability and queerness beyond matters of representation. As Davis (1995a) has argued, although focusing on the representation and treatment of disabled characters in literary works has indeed been an emancipatory and innovative move, it has also become obstructive as a critical literary approach: "there is a limit to what can be said—that disabled characters are usually villains or outcasts, but when they are not they are glorified and held up as testaments to the human spirit" (p. 898). While I have paid significant attention to how deafness and gayness are represented and constructed in *A Really Nice Prom Mess* and *Stick*, I have also endeavored to determine how these representations enable "[a] consideration of deafness (or any disability) in literature [that] can amount to more than a compilation of the ways deaf characters are treated in literary works" (Davis, 1995, p. 898). My analysis illustrates how representations of deafness and gayness can be deconstructed in order to highlight how young adult literature can assist one in challenging normative and condescending categorizations.

Ultimately, this discussion may serve as a model on how poststructuralist critical theories may aid readers in performing effective and reparative critiques on any young adult text with queer and/or disabled characters. The populism and university that these works invoke through their very categorization as young adult novels, in my opinion, makes these novels worthy of critical attention. These works not only teach, inspire, and entertain, but they offer solace and optimism in moments of desolation and despair. Even within the murky depths of normativity, these novels manage to find a way out. Brian Sloan's *A Really Nice Prom Mess* and Andrew Smith's *Stick* provide readers with a platform from which to execute nuanced and insightful readings of the cultural messes in our society. They assist its readers in approaching the everyday and the normal, and making them strange.[6]

NOTES

1. In their discussion on sports and the cultural shift away from homohysteria, Bullingham, Magrath, and Anderson (2014) point out how most, if not all, organized sports regulate gendered practices and beliefs. They argue that organized sports have "maintained the purpose of turning young boys towards a hegemonic perspective of male heterosexuality; one distanced from femininity and homosexuality" (p. 275). Conversations on the association between homophobia, heteronormativity, and American football in national media reached their peak in 2014, when Michael Sam was announced as the first openly gay player to be drafted by the National Football League.

2. Here, I am referring to Butler's (1990) now famous statement, in which she approaches gender as "the repeated stylization of the body, a set of repeated acts within a highly rigid regulatory frame that congeal over time to produce the appearance of substance, of a natural sort of being" (p. 33).

3. I approach Buck as Deaf (with an uppercase D) because the novel portrays him as a character that identifies with this community. For instance, unlike the other characters that I analyze in this discussion, Buck knows sign language and he uses a teletypewriter.

4. In addition to being a deafened moment, this moment is groundbreaking because the divide between public and private is disjointed through the creation of a small gay community between Cameron, Buck, and Dimitri the drug dealer. For more on gay world-making through the use of public spaces, refer to Chauncey (1994).

5. Attempting to replicate the form of Smith's novel is difficult due to the erratic and unpredictable formatting of the text. I tried to replicate the structure and spacing of Smith's words as accurately as possible, but there might be some errors in term of exact spacing and formatting.

6. I would like to thank the participants of Notre Dame's Gender Studies Research Workshop for their insightful and constructive feedback on this project.

References

Bordo, S. (1993). The body and the reproduction of femininity. *Unbearable Weight: Feminism, Western Culture, and the Body* (165–184). Berkeley: University of California Press.

Bullingham, R., Magrath, R. & Anderson, E. (2014). "Changing the game: Sport and a cultural shift away from homohysteria." In J. Hargreaves & E. Anderson (eds.), *Routledge Handbook of Sport, Gender, and Sexuality.* New York: Routledge.

Butler, J. (1990). *Gender Trouble: Feminism and the Subversion of Identity.* New York: Routledge.

Chauncey, G. (1994). "Privacy could only be had in public": Forging a gay world in the streets. *Gay New York: Gender, Urban Culture, and the Making of the Gay Male World, 1890–1940.* New York: BasicBooks.

Davis, L.J. (1995a). Deafness and insight: The deafened moment as critical modality. *College English, 57(8),* 881–900.

_____. (1995b). Introduction: Disability, the missing term in the race, class, gender triad. *Enforcing Normalcy: Disability, Deafness, and the Body* (1–22). New York: Verso.

Garland-Thomson, R. (2002). Integrating disability, transforming feminist theory. *NWSA Journal, 14(3),* 1–32.

Halberstam, J. (2011). *The Queer Art of Failure.* Durham: Duke University Press.

Healy, C. (2007). Living on the edge: Parallels between the deaf and gay communities in the United States. *Swarthmore College.* Retrieved from http://www.swarthmore.edu/sites/default/files/assets/documents/linguistics/2007_healy_catherine.pdf/

McRuer, R. (2006). Introduction: Compulsory able-bodiedness and queer/disabled existence. *Crip Theory: Cultural Signs of Queerness and Disability* (1–32). New York: New York University Press.

Mitchell, D.T., & Snyder, S.L. (2000). Narrative prosthesis and the materiality of metaphor. *Narrative Prosthesis: Disability and the Dependencies of Discourse* (47–64). Ann Arbor: University of Michigan Press.

Padden, C.A. (2005). Talking culture: Deaf people and disability studies. *PMLA, 120(2),* 508–513.

Publishers Weekly. (2005). A really nice prom mess. *Publisher's Weekly.* Retrieved from http://www.publishersweekly.com/978-0-689-87438-3.

Rubin, E., & Strauss Watson, E. (1987). Disability bias in children's literature. *The Lion and the Unicorn, 11(1),* 60–67.

Sedgwick, E.K. (1999). Axiomatic. *The Cultural Studies Reader* (320–336). New York: Routledge.

Sloan, B. (2005). *A Really Nice Prom Mess.* New York: Simon Pulse.

Smith, A. (2011). *Stick.* New York: Feiwel and Friends.

Walker, L. (2001). *Looking Like What You Are: Sexual Style, Race, and Lesbian Identity.* New York: New York University Press.

Wilkerson, A. (2002). Disability, sex radicalism, and political agency. *NWSA Journal, 14(3),* 33–57.

About the Contributors

Lesley **Craig-Unkefer** is an associate professor in the College of Education at Middle Tennessee State University where he teaches courses in assistive technology, characteristics of Autism Spectrum Disorders and introduction to special education. His research interests include the promotion of social communication skill for children at-risk and with developmental delays and the employment of individuals with intellectual disabilities.

A former high school English teacher, Janine J. **Darragh** is an assistant professor of literacy and ENL (English as a New Language) at University of Idaho where she teaches courses in secondary English methods, young adult literature, content area literacy and ENL. Her research interests are sociocultural issues in teaching and learning, YA literature and teacher preparation.

Jeanne **Dutton** is an assistant professor of English and director of developmental writing at Hiram College. She is the author of two novels for young adults under the pen name J.T. Dutton, *Freaked* (HarperTeen 2009) and *Stranded* (HarperTeen 2010).

Jeanne Gilliam **Fain** is an associate professor in the College of Education at Lipscomb University, where she teaches research in classroom practice, literacy courses and English language learning courses. Her primary research and teaching interests are classroom-based research, literacy and linguistically and culturally diverse learners and family literature discussion.

Anne **Katz** is an assistant professor of reading in the College of Education at Armstrong State University. She teaches undergraduate and graduate coursework in language development, literacy assessment, reading theory and diagnosis and remediation of reading difficulties.

Angel Daniel **Matos** is a PhD candidate in English at the University of Notre Dame. His research interests include LGBTQ fiction, young adult literature, queer theory and narratology. His dissertation explores the ways in which queerness provides young adult literature with the optimism and utopianism typically embodied by novels written for younger audiences.

Abbye **Meyer** received a PhD in English with concentrations in children's and young adult literature and disability studies from the University of Connecticut. She has been published in *The Children's Literature Association Quarterly* and *The Huffington Post*, and she has been working and teaching with non-profit education organizations and schools in the Boston area for much of the past decade.

Jennifer **Miller** is a professor of education at Hiram College. She is a National Board Certified teacher in early adolescence/English language arts. Her research interests include adolescent literacy, adolescent literature and middle childhood teacher preparation.

Darcy **Mullen** is a PhD student at University at Albany, focusing on rhetoric and social movement studies (specifically the rhetoric of local food systems). Her dissertation interrogates the role of space and place in contemporary food protest writing. Other research interests include pedagogical methodology, variations in discourse communities, and the rhetoric of humor.

Marc **Napolitano** received a PhD in English from the University of North Carolina at Chapel Hill. His primary areas of expertise are the Victorian novel and the works of Charles Dickens. He has also published on children's fiction in *The Journal of Children's Literature Studies* and in the collection *Roald Dahl and Philosophy*.

Erin Wyble **Newcomb** teaches English at SUNY New Paltz. Her research interests focus on feminist theory and young adult literature. Her essays have appeared in the collections *The Gothic Fairytale in Young Adult Literature, A Quest of Her Own* and *Contemporary Dystopian Fiction for Young Adults*.

Jacob **Stratman** is an associate professor of English and chair of the Humanities and Social Sciences Division at John Brown University. His articles on young adult literature have been published in *SIGNAL* and *English Journal*.

A former middle and high school teacher, Emily **Wender** is an assistant professor of English at Indiana University of Pennsylvania where she specializes in English education. Her work focuses on the intersections between emotion and reading. She has published in *Teaching English in the Two Year College, English Journal* and *The ALAN Review*.

Index

www.ingramcontent.com/pod-product-compliance
Lightning Source LLC
Chambersburg PA
CBHW031125270326
41929CB00011B/1505